DEAR LEADER TALES

EDITED BY:
E. E. KING *AND* DAN M. KALIN

FERAL CAT PUBLISHERS
Melbourne, FL USA
2020

Dear Leader Tales is a work of fiction. Names, places, and incidents either are a product of the author's imagination or are used fictitiously.

Copyright © 2020 by Feral Cat Publishers

Individual story copyrights appear in the final section.

Feral Cat
PUBLISHERS

Published by Feral Cat Publishers, Melbourne, FL

www.feralcatpublishers.com

All rights reserved. No part of this publication may be reproduced, or stored in a retrieval system, or transmitted in any form or by any means, electronic, mechanical, photocopying, recording, or otherwise, without the prior express written permission of the publisher, except as provided by USA copyright law.

Version 1.0, September 2020

KDP Print ISBN: 978-1970-087147

IngramSpark Print ISBN: 978-1970-087130

ebook ISBN: 978-1970-087123

Contents

FOREWORD
  by E.E. King..i

ROGUE SCHOLARS
  By Eric Avedissian.......................................1

CATMANDER-IN-CHIEF
  by Richard Lau...23

THE CURIOUS CAT OF CULPEPPER COUNTY
  by Margaret S. E. Smith..............................29

FLORENCE
  by Jane Blanchard......................................37

THE Z WORD
  by Jeff Seeman...39

CONRAD'S MOUSTACHE
  by John H. Kalin..49

AN HONEST POLITICIAN
  by Jim Robb...67

DEAR JOYCE
  by Langley Hyde..77

THE MUG LIED
  by Sarah M. Kalin......................................87

NEIGHBORHOOD WATCH
  by Lauren Stoker.......................................89

BABA YAGA'S APPRENTICE
  by Louis Evans..97

CHARISMA
  by Dan M. Kalin......................................103

SUPERLATIVE
by Robert Morgan Fisher 123

A GREAT GOAT
by Peter Ntephe 129

AN OFFICE PARTY
by Nicole M. Pyles 135

TEAM BUILDING AND OTHER HORRORS
by Jill Hand 137

THE ELVES' REBELLION
by N.E. Griffin 149

REVOLT OF THE TUBAS
by Mark Nutter 155

THE DICTATOR'S DREAM ABOUT PAINTING
by Katrina Dybzynska 161

THE FAITHLESS ANGEL
by E. E. King 163

A NIGHT OF RAPTURE
by Margaret S. E. Smith 169

A FEAST TALE
by Cathy Adams 173

IDEA DOLLY BOSS
by Warren Brown 181

CORVID-19: THE CROWS! THE CROWS!
by Andrew Jensen 183

MINUTES
by Buzz Dixon 193

A MORALITY TAIL
   by E.E. King..213
DAMAGE CONTROL
   by Will Isenberg...219
FEMALE GOD
   by Mike Ekunno 233
HEREDITY
   by Paul L. Bates...235
THE SCOURGE
   by Derek Des Anges 241
SIX VIEWS OF THE WALL
   by Daniel Ausema 251
FREEDOM OVER GOOD
   by Devo Cutler...257
HINDSIGHT 2020: THE DEVOLUTION
AND HISTORY OF THE NEW BREED
   by Kate Maxwell..261
A FRIEND OF THE WORKING MAN
   by J.J.J. Kearns 273
THE GREATEST SHOW ON EARTH
   by Lena Ng...295
A HISTORY LESSON
   by Ben Boegehold...303
DEAR MR. PRESIDENT
   by Jim Courter 305
THE ELECTION-YEAR GENIE
   by Richard Lau...311

THE MASQUE OF THE 19
  by E. E. King..319
HOSTAGE AT THE HILTON
  by Teresa Milbrodt...327
THE WENDIGO
  by Andrea Goyan..333
COPYRIGHT AND AUTHOR INFORMATION................ 343

FOREWORD
by E.E. King

A few months ago, I was trading story ideas with my friend; writer, and head of Feral Cat Publishing, Dan Kalin.

"I bet there are a lot of funny stories about rotten leaders out there," one of us said. "We could probably put together a great collection of tales." And so, the anthology was conceived.

Dan neatly dealt with all the nasty stuff and I got to read fabulous stories. I was amazed and delighted that we received tales from India, Africa, the corners of Europe and the edges of the Americas, the Middle East, the far East, and the Mid-West. It appears that death and taxes are not the only things that are ubications.

We'd asked for humorous or satirical fictions and poetry to help us weather this election year and we got many. I only wish we could have published more. There were so very many wonderful stories. They ranged from tales of incompetence and mustachios in World War I, to conniving cats, carnivorous deer and murderous vegetables. I found it heartening to read the words of writers from all around the world and to see our similar needs, desires and longings made manifest through imagination.

This is a timeless collect that will help you laugh your way through this and every season. We've always had bad leaders and we always will. But this is also a hopeful collection. A promise that we will continue to joke, and poke fun at our humorless, narcissistic oppressors and that with our words we shall overcome, or at least we'll have a good laugh trying.

I thank all of the great writers who entrusted us with their words, I am sorry we could not publish you all. I am more than grateful to Dan Kalin, Sarah Kalin, and all the Feral Kittens. And I also thank you, gentle reader, for perusing these pages and allowing all of us, however briefly, to enter your mind and share our world with you.

August 23, 2020

ROGUE SCHOLARS

By Eric Avedissian

The student death squad led the dissidents deep into the jungle, marching them through thick underbrush and rugged terrain until they arrived at a natural clearing.

Tropical bird calls echoed from the forest canopy and verdant vegetation festooned near a crystalline waterfall. If it weren't for the emaciated prisoners shuffling to their doom, this would've resembled a holiday resort.

The procession's leader, a man in a drab olive-green uniform, consulted his clipboard and motioned to a spot in the clearing. Silently following orders, the students positioned the dissidents in a line.

"Excellent work, cadets," the leader said. "Now what do we do? You've tortured your rebels and starved them in violation of international law, seized their assets and homes, and marched them to a remote area without a trial. What's the next step?"

A girl of about eighteen raised her hand. "Order their execution?"

"Obviously. This isn't a picnic. How are dissidents to be disposed?" the leader asked.

"Violently and swiftly?" a freckle-faced boy offered.

"Good, but I'm looking for a method," the leader said. "Anyone know?"

"It depends," a girl with auburn hair said. "If you're setting an example or want a confession, you slowly torture them either by breaking their bones or making several cuts in the skin. If you're sending a message to the other agitators, you execute one slowly in front of the others and frighten them."

The leader nodded. "Very good, Penelope. How shall we proceed?"

"Shoot them?" the boy offered.

"Yes, Renaldo. Firing squads are traditional. What happens if a firing squad is not available?"

Penelope raised her hand. "Use your personal sidearm and walk down the line. Headshot. One bullet each."

"That's right," the leader said. "A simple headshot will dispose of your dissidents and make less noise than a firing squad. Now demonstrate."

Penelope drew a pistol from her holster and approached the first agitator. Perspiration slicked the man's face and drenched his shirt. Penelope raised her handgun to the prisoner's head. He was two feet taller than her, a discrepancy Penelope compensated for by ordering the man to kneel. When the dissident refused, she kicked him sharply in his calves until he tumbled to the ground.

Penelope's lips curled into a sinister smile. Without hesitation she aimed the pistol at the man's temple and fired.

***

Dear Penelope Valdez,

Congratulations! Your application was accepted and payment successfully wired to our overseas account. As President let me welcome you to Ironfist

University for Authoritarian Studies. This four-year school offers students a wide range of subjects and fields, from hardline political leadership, to degrees in the torture sciences and advanced munitions deployment, to our coveted Internship with Dictators Program.

Here at Ironfist we believe stalwart leaders are made, not born. Tomorrow's tyrants must be well-trained to handle any crisis such as uprisings, media intrusion, and nosy international inspectors. From suppressing the hoi polloi and bending them to your will, to competently enacting a military coup, Ironfist has the skills you need in this unpredictable, ideologically fragile world.

I wish you success in your studies and hope you'll take heart in our motto: "Tyrannide In Sempiternum" – "Tyranny Forever"!

May your time at Ironfist be both productive and sadistic.

Go Weasels!
Dr. Odin Suarez
University President and Former Dictator of the People's Republic of Costa Lamante

***

Penelope was late for Modern Torture Techniques.

She had attended Ironfist for a month and a half, but the orientation never said the volcanic island had a network of steam tunnels snaking beneath the campus. The older students used the tunnels as shortcuts, but the subterranean maze proved confusing and Penelope had become hopelessly lost. An exit for the Medical Experimentation Pavilion actually led to the Disinformation Center. Flustered, she doubled back, and that's when she lost her Antisocial Studies book in the dimly-lit passageways.

Penelope apologized to her professor, took her twenty lashes, and pledged in front of the class that she'd never be tardy again.

Thin, with long auburn hair and dark brown eyes, Penelope kept both herself and her school uniform immaculate. A legion of nannies and tutors taught her refinement, while her father's ministers schooled her in the world's brutal realities. Despite these skills, Penelope still had trouble adjusting to campus life. Her schedule was a bold choice even for an overachiever: Modern Torture Techniques, Intro to Surveillance, History of Propaganda, Juntas 101, Authoritarian Politics, and Manipulative Psychology. Next year's classes looked especially daunting: Creative Financing, Juntas 201, Government Restructuring, Advanced Blackmail, and Intro to Political Subversion.

After a particularly satisfying blood-splattered class, Penelope sat in the quad and flipped through her notebook. She was memorizing anatomical pressure points when a short-haired girl from her Juntas 101 class appeared. The girl sported a charm bracelet with tiny automatic rifles and skulls.

"Penelope, is it?" the girl asked. "I'm Angelica. Nice work in the jungle yesterday. You've got an affinity for executing dissidents."

Penelope grinned. "My grandfather showed me back home. A family that slays together stays together."

Angelica laughed, a tiny lilting sound Penelope found infectious.

"My dad runs San Flamongo, so I know what you mean," Angelica said.

Penelope heard of San Flamongo, a brutal island nation ringed by barbed wire fences and lava moats and home to the world's only fascist theme-park, DystopiaLand.

"My parents think I'm a megalomaniac and perfect candidate for replacing them," Angelica said.

"Same with my parents," Penelope bragged. "I'm the heir apparent to Santo Monstruo."

"Your father runs Santo Monstruo?" Angelica asked. "That's the country so bad it made the United Nation's watchlist for human rights abuses for twenty consecutive years. You must be so proud!"

Penelope blushed. "Thanks. I have some pretty big jackboots to fill."

Angelica smiled a mouthful of perfect teeth. She was so deliciously pretty that Penelope wanted to eat her face.

A tall boy with blue eyes and blonde hair caught Penelope's gaze. He carried a backpack on his broad shoulders and looked dashing in his school uniform.

"Who's that?" Penelope asked, practically salivating.

"Friedrich Mogul," Angelica said.

"What's his story?"

"Friedrich is the son of an industrialist and poised to seize control of his native Slayenkia."

Penelope whipped out her smartphone and learned Slayenkia was a tiny country tucked amid the snowcapped peaks in Eastern Europe. Slayenkia's main exports were wheat, manganese, and fierce authoritarianism.

"I'm going to introduce myself," Penelope said.

Angelica winced. "Uh, why?"

"Because I think he's cute. Don't you?"

"Yeah. He's a hottie. I already talked to him. Not much of a conversationalist."

"I don't want to debate him," Penelope said. "I want to date him."

Penelope walked over to Friedrich like a lioness stalking her prey. She chuckled, flashed her eyes, and bit her lip.

"Friedrich, is it?" She slowly extended her hand. "I'm Penelope Vasquez. I understand you're from Slayenkia. Maybe we can go for coffee and you can tell me all about your country's vicious nationalism that keeps the intelligentsia awake at night."

Friedrich smiled and opened his mouth to speak, but Angelica swooped in.

"Oh, Friedrich! What's up?" Angelica hugged her books close to her chest. "Don't forget about our study date tonight."

"Angelica! I haven't forgotten," Friedrich said. "Looking forward to going over chapter seven in Despotic Political Theory with you. It sounds so dry and boring, right?"

Angelica flipped a shock of her brunette hair behind her ears. "So boring, but necessary, right? Midterms are coming up and Professor Nikos isn't going to be gentle."

Friedrich's pale blue eyes practically twinkled at Angelica. "Don't I know it. I heard last semester he punished his students by making them enact the Night of Bloody Faces." Though Penelope found Friedrich amusing when he pronounced "faces" like "feces," she resented Angelica.

"Friedrich and I were going out for coffee," Penelope said.

"Sorry, but I can't. Maybe some other time?" he apologized. "I must study with Angelica. Nice meeting you, Penelope."

"Well, maybe I can come along," Penelope said, each word bursting from her mouth.

"Why? You're not even in Despotic Political Theory," Angelica said. "You two can get together another day, okay? Toodles!"

Angelica and Friedrich briskly walked through the quad arm-in-arm. Penelope watched them leave, each one growing smaller until the redbrick buildings swallowed them.

***

Dear Mumsy,

University isn't what I expected. Los Mortos Island may be secluded and impenetrable, and the dormant volcano intimidating, but a girl can get bored here. Not that I'm ungrateful or anything. I know you and Dadums worked hard and repressed a peasant revolt to send me here. Is it true Dadums is an Ironfist alumnus? Maybe he can put in a good word with my Authoritarian Politics professor, Mr. Felix. He's relentless, especially when he gives us pop quizzes and essays. I loathe and detest writing. I'd rather be out in the jungles raising hell.

My Modern Torture Techniques professor, Mr. Amir, is pretty nice. He let us dissect a few bodies. Sometimes they're still alive, which is an added bonus!

Then there's my History of Propaganda professor, Mr. Richter. He enjoys yelling, cursing and slapping the students when we get the answers wrong. I hope he doesn't go too easy on us for the rest of the semester. You know how I like challenges.

Thanks for the care package of cookies, tea, and a solid gold knuckleduster. You never know when it might come in handy for settling disputes and basic protection. There's literally no security on this campus, only mounted machineguns at the entrance.

Mumsy, I met a boy! His name is Friedrich and he's an absolute dream. He's so cute and nice. There is a catch. Angelica. She's this girl who Friedrich likes. It's so unfair! Did you ever become sad because some boy doesn't even know you're alive and he automatically dismisses you? Of course not. You were head of Dadum's security forces. He totally noticed you. Successfully coordinating the bombing of an opposition newspaper will get you noticed. Dadums must've fallen in love with you right then and there.

Sorry for complaining. It's not what our family does, I know.

Until next time, Mumsy.
Your little muffin monster,
P.

***

"What are the four reasons for societal collapse?" the professor asked. He was in his forties and sported salt and pepper hair, a black suit, and a jagged scar across his neck.

Penelope raised her hand.

The professor straightened his thick tortoiseshell glasses. "Miss Valdez?"

"Societal collapse is caused by depopulation, natural cataclysm, disease or war," Penelope replied.

"Excellent. Now who can tell me how one sows discontent among the populace?" the professor asked.

Penelope's hand shot up again.

The professor grinned. "You're on a roll, Miss Valdez."

"Play to the people's outrage and prejudices by scapegoating or convincing them that they're way of life is under attack," Penelope said. "This can be achieved through propaganda, gaslighting or brutal force."

"And what if outside agitators question your conclusions, and label you a fear-monger or agent provocateur?" The professor folded his arms and waited expectantly for her answer.

Penelope thought for a moment. "I guess you accuse them of treason for questioning your sound judgment and patriotism and turn the mob against them."

"And how does one retain power once they've achieved it?"

"Voter suppression, appointing family members to government offices, martial law, and widespread surveillance."

"Correct," the professor said. "I see you've read your assignment, Miss Valdez."

"That's why I'm here, Mr. Felix."

Penelope turned towards Angelica and Friedrich, who sat behind her. Both lovebirds stared at each other with an intensity Penelope had never known. They were lost in each other, in the moment. Penelope's heart palpitated and her palms felt sweaty. She didn't participate in the rest of the lecture and focused on her textbook.

After class, Penelope gathered her things and made a beeline towards Friedrich.

"Friedrich! Do you want to get that coffee later and chat?" Penelope asked.

Friedrich scratched his forehead. "So sorry, uh…"

"Penelope."

"Penelope! Of course. No, I can't. I will be studying with Angelica," he said, just as Angelica hovered nearby.

"We're going to the Eugenics is Fun exhibit at the Unnatural History Museum. You're free to tag along," Angelica offered.

"That's okay," Penelope said. "I'm probably going to watch a movie anyway. There's a propaganda film festival at the student center."

"Sounds tasty, but Friedrich and I are busy." Angelica wrapped her arm around Friedrich's waist.

"Perhaps some other time," Friedrich said.

The sight of Friedrich with Angelica crushed Penelope. She regretted ever reaching out to him, ever allowing herself to develop feelings for a boy. Her whole body tensed and her throat went dry. Penelope wanted to fly over the school's fortifications and vanish into the jungles forever.

"You were exceptional in class today, Miss Valdez," Mr. Felix said. He approached Penelope after Angelica and Friedrich left, briefcase in hand.

"Thanks, sir."

"Remember that the world is changing, and we must prevent that. Your feelings are unnecessary. They're hindrances. Only cold logic and expediency shall govern us."

"Yes, sir."

"Dismissed."

Penelope sprinted back to her dorm room and cried into her pillow. Bothered by her tantrum, her roommate muttered something about "cohabitating with a drama queen" and headed to the weekly book burning in the quad.

***

Dear Mumsy,

I'm devastated! It is awful not being popular! Friedrich and Angelica kissed in public the other day. It destroyed me inside! I tried talking to Friedrich. He's oblivious to my feelings. Every time I get close, he pulls away. I know this sounds like pointless high school drivel, but ever since Dadums burned down my high school because they taught evolution, I guess I'm having high school flashbacks.

Classes are progressing well. I got an A on my Juntas 101 report, and Mr. Amir complemented my handling of blunt instruments in the Modern Torture Techniques midterm. The only sore spot was Mr. Richter humiliating the girl sitting next to me. He heaped abuse on her and called her a dirty proletariat whore, but not me! Why can't I suffer the same indignities? I'll try harder next time.

Mr. Felix gave me an especially challenging assignment: write a paper on why democracy is a flawed ideology. I'm hitting the library as soon as I finish this letter. I have a good feeling about this one!

How's Dadums? Are the U.N. inspectors done searching the weapons facility? Those internationalists can be so nosey! I'm sure there are a few rats in the ranks that need exterminating. Dadums will undoubtedly root them out and execute them on live television like he did before with the ringleaders of the Freedom Seven. That was must-watch TV!

Well, Mumsy, I've got to go. Give Dadums, General Bloodyhands, and War Minister Longknives my love.
As always, your little muffin monster,
P.

***

The football game between the Ironfist Weasels and Hardline Polytechnic's Vultures was held in a massive brutalist stadium with sweeping colonnades and uncomfortable seating. Ironfist's mascot, Whiplash Weasel, danced onto the field with the cheerleaders. Behind them, Ironfist's team entered the arena in their black and gray uniforms and spiked helmets.

Penelope sat in the stands with Angelica and Friedrich. She felt like a third wheel, redundant and unnecessary, but heeded Mr. Felix's advice and suppressed her emotions. She didn't mind that Angelica and Friedrich held hands. It didn't tear her up inside that they smooched. Penelope kept her attention focused on the field and the bloodiest football game she ever witnessed, where bloodshed was the norm and concealed melee weapons permitted.

At halftime, Ironfist students sang their school fight song, belting out the lyrics in full-throated harmony:

> *Fight, Weasels! All day and night!*
> *Fight until our enemies expire*
> *Break their will and crush their bones*
> *And strangle them with barbed wire*
>
> *If the forces of freedom undermine our quest*
> *We'll defeat them soundly with ruthlessness*

Fight, Weasels! Fight tooth and claw!
Fight until your foes are no more
May their blood embolden your legacy
And their corpses litter the floor

Through the night you shine like a house aflame
Burn them down so they won't forget your name

Hail, Hail our Ironfist!
Emblem of absolute rule
Onward to battle our nemesis
Three cheers for our fascist school!

During the third quarter when it looked like Ironfist would shank the Vulture's quarterback in the ribs again, Penelope tapped Angelica in the shoulder.

"Look, I'm sorry about everything. I was jealous," Penelope said.

"Jealous? Of what?" Angelica said, her fingers grasping Friedrich's hand.

"Of you two. This budding romance…"

"Budding romance?" Angelica giggled. "It's nothing. We're good friends. Friedrich and I aren't going steady."

Penelope blinked. "It sure looks that way to me."

"Oh, Penelope! You're reading too much into this. We're just flirty friends," Angelica said.

Friedrich turned to me. "More than just flirty friends. More like friends with bennies."

"Bennies? Who's Benny?" Penelope asked.

"Benefits. Friends with benefits," Angelica said. "You know."

Penelope nodded, but she didn't know. Sex was something not discussed around the banquet table in her father's palace. One simply didn't mention such things publicly, and anyone caught doing so was lashed to an oxcart and driven out of town, bayoneted in the killing fields and left for dead. And that was the minimum penalty.

"I want a college romance, a chance for love between the studying and yelling at plebs," Penelope said.

"Romance is for the weak. Lust is where it's at." Angelica and Friedrich kissed. It wasn't a sloppy lip-smacker with tongues and gooey saliva but a firm, quick peck.

"There's still so much I could learn from you. Maybe we can have coffee sometime Angelica. Just us girls," Penelope said. "I'd like to hear more about this benefits thing."

Angelica agreed and they watched Ironfist slaughter Hardline's wide receiver with a dagger to the spleen.

***

Mumsy,

What do you do when nobody respects your feelings? There's so much I like about this school and so much I don't. I hate being this way.

What do you suggest? I know you're not one for dispensing advice, but any assistance would be appreciated, that is if you're not too busy attending galas and taking lovers. How's Dadums? Is he done with his Glorious Three-Year Plan for the People? Remember his last plan where everybody starved and he turned the peasants against the intelligentsia? I hope his latest scheme goes just as swimmingly.

Angelica is super smart and pretty and I envy her. I know she's going to graduate and take over her family's nation and rule it with absolute cruelty and unquestionable authority. She can literally manipulate anyone.

Is everything a charade, Mumsy? Are we all strangers faking our personalities, laughing when we cry and sleeping when we're awake? I might be your gullible girl, but I know there's a sickening feeling in my tummy all the time I'm near Friedrich. Is that what love is, or am I just lying to myself?

Mr. Felix thinks I'm a model student. He praised my endeavors in front of the class. This might be the only bright spot in an otherwise gloomy semester. I hear things might improve next term when we're allowed to make our own propaganda dioramas.

Well, Mumsy, I must go. Another class awaits. Wish I could end on a positive note, but I guess I'm homesick for my native country. I miss gunfire in the night and the screams of the oppressed. I hope Uncle Blackmask has the torture equipment all oiled and ready. I'd like to play with a few peasants during spring break.

P.

***

Penelope invited Angelica for coffee at the student annex, one of the least populated areas of campus. She ordered two coffees from the cafeteria, poured them into paper cups, added the cream and sugar and snagged two ginger biscuits. The day faded into late afternoon and the tropical sun cast long shadows over the courtyard.

Penelope carefully brought the coffee over to Angelica, who reclined on a bench beneath the Monument to Khaos, a statue of the Greek primordial goddess, whose outstretch arms both welcomed and terrified.

Angelica smiled pleasantly and held her cup.

"Thanks for this. I'm so busy with my studying that I never take breaks," she said.

"Friedrich probably keeps you busy, though," Penelope held her cup up to her lips and blew.

"Friedrich? We're just friends," Angelica said.

"With benefits. I looked it up. You went all the way."

"We're two consenting adults with rampant libidos. Why do you care about him so much? Do you like him?"

Penelope sighed. "Sorry. I shouldn't have been so aggressive. I know he's your boy toy."

"He's hardly that. Friedrich doesn't know what to make of you, Penelope. He hopes you're not weirded out because him and I have been intimate." Angelica tasted her coffee.

Penelope smirked. "It's fine. I'm not weirded out. Besides, I have no time for romantic entanglements."

"That's not what you told me."

"People change, don't they?" Penelope asked.

"Not around here. This place isn't one of those indoctrinating colleges where free thought flows," Angelica sipped her coffee.

"I'm focusing on my studies now. I've got a country to terrorize." Penelope took another sip. "Last thing I want is to get between a woman and her man. Besties?"

"Besties. I appreciate your honesty. Thank you, Penelope."

Angelica put the cup to her lips and imbibed. The coffee went down easily but the taste seemed a little off. She took another hearty swig.

"What's the matter? Too much creamer?" Penelope asked.

Angelica's eyes widened. Her stomach rumbled. She clutched her neck. Her throat constricted shut. She couldn't breathe.

"What…did…you…do?" Angelica rasped.

"Me? You did this to yourself. You got your talons in poor Friedrich. Turned that boy all soft and gooey with your hand-holding and kisses," Penelope said. "You knew I was interested. You wanted him all to yourself."

"Penelope. I…didn't…know."

"You knew. People like you always overextend themselves. Too confident and greedy. Pretty girls batting their eyelashes and padding their bras. Well guess what? You can't have him now."

Angelica's face filled with panic. She clawed her throat like a feral beast and her eyeballs rolled back. When she fell to the floor, Angelica's muscles tensed and cramped. She arched her back and violently convulsed with disturbing spasms. Bubbling froth formed in the corners of her mouth. Penelope silently watched as Angelica's arms went limp and her chest stopped heaving. Angelica's body sprawled on the floor, head cocked to the side, legs bent horribly askew, mouth a ghastly rictus. Penelope thought about the best way to dispose of the corpse when she heard someone behind her.

"You took another student's life, Miss Valdez. Why?" Mr. Felix leaned against a wall.

Penelope pushed her auburn tresses from her eyes and exhaled.

"I'm waiting," he demanded.

"It was over a boy," Penelope admitted. "Angelica dated this boy we both liked. She got in my way."

"And how was the deed done?"

"Poison," Penelope said flatly.

"What type of poison?"

"Strychnine. I put strychnine in her coffee."

"Where did you get the strychnine?"

"Care package from my Mumsy," Penelope said, realizing she'd used her childish sobriquet and quickly corrected herself. "My mother."

"Cyanide would've been faster."

"I didn't want fast."

Mr. Felix walked towards Penelope and stared down at Angelica's lifeless body. He pushed his glasses closer to the bridge of his nose.

"Commendable work," Mr. Felix said. "Admirable. So ruthless and calculating."

"Am I in trouble?"

"Trouble? Normally murdering another student is grounds for expulsion and a firing squad, but these aren't normal circumstances," Mr. Felix said. "Truth is, I've had my eye on you."

Penelope winced. "Ew."

"Not that way, Miss Valdez," Mr. Felix clarified. "Every so often I get a pupil whose passion eclipses their academic prowess. You have applied yourself here using the skills only a heartless power-mad dictator would."

"But I killed her out of jealousy."

Mr. Felix exhaled. "Back when I was a supreme ruler, my intelligence officer learned my wife planned to take my young son and flee the country. She made a deal with the Americans to reveal all my military secrets. I had several choices. I chose the only logical one. I had her and my son killed. He was seven years old."

Penelope felt nauseous. "That's horrible."

"Horrible? I extinguished everything I loved for nationalism. For my legacy and comfort." Professor Felix cracked his knuckles. "Fascism devours your soul, but if you can live with yourself, if you can look at your reflection in the mirror and not flinch, you're truly more powerful than the scum you lead."

Penelope shivered at the implications. "But that's so heartless."

"Heartless or necessary? We live in ridiculous times. Ridiculous times call for ridiculous leaders. Oversized suits and drooping long neckties. Military uniforms cluttered with phony medals. Pomposity and cruelty. We become parodies, walking caricatures, symbols of humanity's worst impulses."

"Why? Why choose power for its own sake? Why not hold free elections and give the people what they want?"

"Because power shouldn't be shared. And as for the people, have you met any? Truly spent time with the great unwashed masses? They believe wrestling is real. They drink non-alcoholic beer and troll people on their cellphones. They fritter the best years of their lives on entertainment and petty diversions," Professor Felix said. "People are a waste. Empires were built on cruelty and keeping the people in line."

Penelope thought about her family's history. Slavery, suppression of free thought, might makes right. Every authoritarian's wet dream manifest into decisive, brutal action.

"But won't people eventually rise up and stop the dictator waiting in the wings?" she asked.

Professor Felix acknowledged her query with a curt nod. "Perhaps, but mostly they won't. Do you know how the Dear Leader rises to power? He does so with the clueless rabble's consent. Sometimes they unwittingly participate in the ascension of their worst nightmares."

"Why, though? Why do people advocate for things that aren't in their best interest?"

"Because when the crowd falls silent after the tightrope walker plummets and everything in the circus grinds to a terrible halt, you need a distraction. You send for the clowns. The clowns do funny dances and sing nostalgic songs and smoosh pies in their faces. When the audience is distracted from the carnage, that's when you stealthily shackle them to their seats. That's when they become part of the act and you release the lions. Then the real show begins," Professor Felix said.

Penelope dug her fingernails into her forearms. "What happens to me now?"

"First, you find that boy. You tell him this girl didn't want to see him and left Ironfist. I'll handle the rest," Mr. Felix said.

"You'll handle the rest?"

"I can make cadavers vanish completely. Like magic."

Penelope couldn't believe what she had done. A tinge of sadistic power flowed through her. Was the world better without Angelica? Penelope begrudgingly thought so.

"Thank you, Mr. Felix." Penelope gazed longingly at Angelica's lifeless body, fascinated by her gruesome handiwork.

"This was vicious and efficient, Miss Valdez. You had the will to do what others merely dreamed. Such actions don't go unrewarded."

He handed Penelope an envelope.

"Here's my recommendation for your inclusion in the Internship with Dictators Program. Only a select few students are chosen. One day the world will tremble before you, young lady," Mr. Felix said.

"Yes, sir."

"Dismissed."

Penelope regarded Mr. Felix through narrowed eyes. "Cold logic and expediency. That's what you told me, sir."

She left the courtyard and never looked back.

***

> Mumsy,
>
> Have you heard? My professor was caught loading a dead student onto a speedboat! Turns out University President Suarez received an anonymous letter about Mr. Felix's activities. An inquest proved that Mr. Felix murdered Angelica! Poisoned the poor girl. Mr. Felix denied it and even pinned the blame on yours truly, but the investigation discovered a phial containing strychnine in his office. Shocking, right?
>
> The students were hastily organized into a firing squad and we executed Mr. Felix. Now we need another Authoritarian Politics professor. Before his demise, Mr. Felix recommended me for the Internship with Dictators Program! I hope you and Dadums are proud.

One day I'll return and burn this campus to the ground and make them all pay for making me sad. But for now, I feel lighter than a feather.

Guess what? Friedrich and I have a date tomorrow! He was badly shaken by Angelica's demise. Someone should comfort that poor boy, don't you think? I know with absolute certainty that both Friedrich – and the future – will be mine.

Cuddles and kisses from your little muffin monster.
P.

CATMANDER-IN-CHIEF
by Richard Lau

In the long, strange history of American politics, Charlie was not the first cat to run for President. She was, however, the first cat actually to be elected. And technically, Charlie became the first female President, as well.

Nobody had expected Charlie to win. But there was hope among the millions of disenfranchised voters that electing a cat would send a strong and much-needed message to Washington.

When it came to political opponents and critics, Charlie was no different from any other candidate.

"How do we know you'll do what's right for America and not be overly influenced by Bast?" one reporter asked, echoing the concern some people held about the Catholic John F. Kennedy and the Pope.

Charlie's reply was an unambiguous hiss, to which her campaign manager quickly explained that her candidate had misheard the reporter and thought he had said, "Bath."

An opposing campaign ran a commercial showing a press conference where Charlie again hissed after vets had been mentioned. People who had served in the military became upset, but Charlie's campaign manager explained that this hiss was taken out of context. The manager further explained that Charlie was hissing at the mean medical veterinarians who worked in back-alley animal clinics, not veterans of the military. Still, Charlie was practical and willing to change the title of the Surgeon General to the Veterinarian General just to be more inclusive.

Another rival claimed Charlie's foreign policy wandered all over the place. Charlie, recalling her younger, formulative years as a stray when she, too, wandered all over the place, defined wandering as a "learning experience not to be shunned but embraced and acknowledged."

Charlie had spoken, and the people listened. The people then spoke with their ballots, giving Charlie the popular vote.

Even more astonishingly, the Electoral College went along with the popular count. Though it was noted that a surprising number of the electors had what appeared to be stray strands of cat hair on their clothing.

At her inauguration, Charlie didn't stay on her perch for the entire oath of office. There was quite a titter from the crowd as the Secret Service and the Chief Justice, still reciting the oath, scampered after the newly elected Commander-in-Chief around the plaza.

The result was a rather ignominious rescue, after which the vicious print media ran headlines similar to "Most Powerful Feline in the World Stuck in a Tree."

It was later revealed that there was a Secret Service sniper on a nearby rooftop. The red dot from his rifle's laser scope caught Charlie's attention.

In a panic, the security agent quickly tried to move his aimed rifle barrel away from the incoming President, but as the officer reported later, "The damn cat kept chasing the dot and running into my shot!" The shaken agent received a newly created Toy Mouse of Honor for his valor, skill, and self-control. He was also promoted to a high position at the Pentagon, and all was forgiven.

Charlie's first day in the Oval Office was also marked with controversy. Literally marked.

One of the younger Secret Service agents wrinkled her nose in disgust. "Couldn't she have just clawed the curtains?"

A more senior agent who had served under several other presidencies whispered back, "That's nothing. I was here years ago when the new guy…"

And like most administrations, Charlie's term wasn't without the occasional scandal or minor controversy. It was suspected that the tuna industry lobbied for a larger presence on the USDA's food pyramid. What disturbed most people, though, was the sudden specific inclusion of mice and catnip.

Then there was an infamous 18 seconds of missing recordings from a meeting in the Oval Office. The leaked tape revealed Charlie purring and what sounded like a brief and distinctive "woof."

Responding in a press release, Charlie denied meeting with a canine, attributing the suspected bark to a feline advisor with kennel cough.

By far, the worse scandal was a fecal "present" left on the Speaker of the House's chair.

"My chair is not a litterbox!" thundered the Speaker, and unfortunately, his quote became an Internet meme, with folks chiming in with "My slipper is not a litterbox!" and "My pillow is not a litterbox!" Even some supposed "cats" posted, "My litterbox is not a litterbox!"

When asked by reporters to describe what exactly was left on the chair, the Speaker responded with several words that could not be reported on television or radio without an FCC fine.

"Would I do that?" asked Charlie, as print and video media carried her wide-eyed, kittenishly innocent expression. Cuteness carried the day.

Charlie also took naps during meetings, but a previous occupier of the Oval Office had set that Presidential precedent. Detractors pointed out that Charlie had 1,460 days of vacation during her four years in office. And, complained lobbyists and business leaders, not one of those days was spent on a golf course, so advantageous deals were few and far between. Ethical and watchdog groups hailed this absence as a vast improvement at getting corruption out of government.

Still, Charlie signed no controversial laws, made no offensive speeches, and raised no taxes. She was gracious in meeting foreign dignitaries, especially the ones with dander allergies.

Negotiators found under that soft fur were claws of steel. Or an aloofness, exhibited by a preoccupation with grooming. "I felt myself wanting to lick the back of my hand," complained one emissary.

Since Charlie was largely nocturnal, these meetings were held late at night to her advantage. But afterwards, good will was exhibited by all with a joint singing session by the participants on the White House lawn by a rear fence.

Of course, not everyone sang in English or even the same song. However, the resulting caterwauling made these leaders look all the more human or at least feline. It was both a bonding and humbling experience that led to fond memories and mutually friendly treaties days later.

CATMANDER-IN-CHIEF

When she ran for re-election, Charlie said her job still was not done. There was an illusive mouse in the White House, but she had a plan for its capture.

So, the voters decided to give Charlie "fur" more years.

THE CURIOUS CAT OF CULPEPPER COUNTY

by Margaret S. E. Smith

Tom hated clichés, but unfortunately, he was one. In all honesty, it wasn't his fault but that of his last human, who hadn't had an original idea since 1957, or so he had heard from his mother, the Queen, who heard it passed down through the royal family line (and anyone who had cared to listen to the tale knew exactly how *that* particular misadventure had ended: a call to the fire department, three dead mice, and a pair of women's bloomers waving from atop a slightly singed magnolia tree). Maybe the incident had scared the originality right out of her — why else would she have named him "Tom" simply because he was one. Even her passing six months ago had been despairingly unoriginal; she simply went to sleep and never woke up again. Be that as it may and all things being considered, Tom was exceedingly confident in his standing as Supreme Entity to the various bedraggled denizens of Culpepper County, and as he sashayed along Mary Mavis's very cliché white picket fence on a ridiculously stereotypical bright summer day, he made a point of holding his woefully common orange-tabby head high in a decidedly uncommon fashion to reflect his sovereignty.

by Margaret S. E. Smith

Now, Culpepper County was a smidge of acreage cowering nervously between miles of swampland on the north and east sides, and miles of marshlands on the south and west sides, in an attempt to go unnoticed by the rest of the world. It was a remarkably successful attempt. Culpepper County was not the sort of place the rest of the world was likely to comprehend anyway, and nearly every resident — human, dog, mosquito, and the like — held some fear of invasion by "them outsiders". Tom was of a different mind, but that was only logical considering he was Supreme Entity and above such paranoid nonsense. In fact, it was Tom's curiosity of "them outsiders" and the conquerable world beyond marshlands and swamplands, which had him striding so purposefully past Portman's market without even a tail twitch at the newly caught catfish Benny Portman was hurriedly arranging in the fish bin to try, once again, to coax Tom's patronage.

Everywhere Tom went it was the same; humans vied for his attention in the oddest of ways. Widow Thompson, who seemed to be some sort of leather and chain fetishist, was always attempting to fit him with the latest fashion in bondage gear — and although he appreciated her thoughtful, albeit misplaced, generosity, the strange harness and collar contraptions where simply not his style. Old man Scruggs, who had apparently taken up cobbling, would — in a desperate bid to win Tom's favor of his skill — suddenly toss a sample of his newest creation at him for inspection whenever Tom would go for his midnight serenades past the man's home. And even Portia Patterson, who tended the most exquisite herb and flower garden Tom had ever tasted, was desperate to encourage a royal match between Tom and her animal MouMou, whom she always released from the house whenever Tom chose to visit the lovely garden to help fertilize the biennials. Of course, Tom always politely declined before making a tactful (if somewhat hasty) retreat from his overenthusiastic paramour. Although flattered at the attention, Tom just couldn't envision a successful future for the two, what with MouMou being a pit bull. Besides, Tom had much bigger plans for the future than settling down in an arranged partnership — much bigger plans... and that was why he was letting nothing draw his focus away from his destination: seventh house on the left past the rose trellis scratching post. That was where he would find *her* — the one he had heard gossip about last night as he mingled with his subjects in the courtyard of Rosie's Outdoor Cafe. The one who would enable him to expand his kingdom beyond Culpepper County out into the mystical land beyond. The one they all called, *The Cat Whisperer.*

Apparently, this Cat Whisperer was Rosie's niece — a Doctor of Veterinary Medicine and specialist in interspecies communication. If she proved to be as gifted as the gossip claimed, Tom would offer her a position as court physician and royal liaison. With her help, Tom would be able to easily disseminate his great wisdom and philosophy to educate the masses and provide superlative governance to his people; it was very difficult to rule them effectively when they lacked the most basic communication skills of an eight-week-old kitten.

Hopping down from the fence with the grace and panache befitting his station, Tom trotted quickly over to the white cottage-style home with the periwinkle-blue door — sparing the stone water garden pond with the complimentary goldfish only a passing glance. Now was not a time for delicacies; Tom was here on serious business.

by Margaret S. E. Smith

"You. Human. Hello," he called, tail twitching impatiently when no answer was forthcoming. He had learned early on that humans were rather slow, both in action and in thought, a good majority of the time unless strongly encouraged to be otherwise. "Human. Human. Human. Human. Now. Now. Now. Now," Tom

encouraged, and was rewarded when the door flung open revealing a rather delicate looking female with owlish eyes and a short shock of red curls on her head.

"Good heavens what is this ruckus... oh!" the female eyed Tom with surprise. "Well my goodness! Hello there."

"Hello human. I have come to speak with you on a matter most urgent and to make you a very generous offer."

The human knelt before him, as is only appropriate when in the presence of royalty. "Where on earth did you come from?"

"That is neither here nor there; we have important matters to discuss."

"You look half-starved. Why don't you come in and let me get you something," the female continued as she held the door open for him in invitation. "I was just making myself a seafood salad. I bet you'd like some nice pink salmon wouldn't you."

Tom, always one for good manners, followed her inside. "I haven't really time for... salmon did you say?" Tom continued to follow her through a cozy sitting room into a spacious kitchen where a cast iron brewing pot sat bubbling atop an antique wood-burning stove. A fragrant cinnamon-apple aroma wafted from the pot to fill the room with a comforting ambience.

"Hmm," the human hummed delightedly, "tea is almost ready. But you're not interested in that, are you handsome," she said as she pulled a can down from a shelf and started that magical process that seemed a uniquely human skill: opening it.

Instantly, Tom's senses were flooded with a mouth-watering bouquet from the enticing cuisine, and an undignified mewl escaped him before he could stop it. Obviously, it had been a mistake to bypass the goldfish

The human chuckled as she began scooping the salmon onto a lovely filigree saucer, "I've heard about you, you know. Everyone in town talks about you."

"Of course, they do," Tom responded with a sniff.

"You're quite the mischief maker, aren't you," she continued.

"What are you talking about woman? You obviously have me confused with someone else. Do you not know who I am?" Tom asked indignantly.

"You run this place with an iron paw, don't you handsome."

"Ah! You have heard of me. Good, then we can get down to..." Tom stopped and stared at the saucer of salmon that had been placed before him, then looked up at the woman again, "Really? On the floor, you place it?" He sighed in resignation at the déclassé behavior — obviously, this human would require training in proper etiquette, poor heathen that she was — then he began picking at the offering with appropriate indifference.

The woman folded herself down beside him and proceeded to massage him in that peculiar manner humans had, and Tom had to admit it was quite a pleasant sensation — one he hadn't experienced for ages, and in cat-time, that was a very long time, indeed.

"I heard you lost your human, poor thing, and have been on your own for quite some time."

"True, but unimportant," Tom said between nibbles. "My subjects have provided me sustenance and, I have managed to continue my reign despite the inconvenience."

"I think a regal beauty like you should always have a human to pamper them and cater to their every wish — don't you agree?" Tom did agree but was too polite to speak with his mouth full, so instead, he responded with a deep, rumbling purr of contentment, causing the human to laugh once more. Tom decided he rather liked the sound.

The woman continued, "Tell you what; I'm going to make you an offer. You come stay with me and let me be your new human, and you can have a nice home filled with all the amenities a majestic Felis catus like you deserves. And," she coughed, then continued under her breath, "I'm sure that would please the other residents of Culpepper as well."

Tom, being a cat, heard this last comment and agreed, so he looked up from his aperitif to consider the offer, while tactfully grooming away any remaining evidence of the meal, "It is true my subjects would feel more at ease knowing their Liege was being appropriately attended; still, I hope your intention is not to pamper me into lassitude; I cannot govern nor expand my kingdom if I become indolent."

"I travel a great deal to other towns, even out of state sometimes," the female remarked as she pulled a large paper from a nearby drawer and unfolded it on the floor, "I could take you with me. It would be so nice to have a traveling companion for a change."

"Aha! So, you would be willing to help me in my quest to expand my kingdom.

"Excellent!" Tom said, prancing excitedly around the diagram before him.

The human moved her finger along a path from the bottom right corner of the paper to a spot a short distance above it, "I have a convention to attend in Georgia next week, I'm going to be there for three days — I don't see why you couldn't keep me company."

Tom ogled the scribbles depicting the land of "Georgia", then allowed his eyes to roam hungrily over the paper and the scribbles that seemed to go off in every direction endlessly. Coming to a decision, he climbed upon the paper and sat regally in the center, staring at the woman, "Human, I have decided to accept your offer to serve me and assist in my quest to expand my kingdom beyond Culpepper County. This "Georgia" seems as good a place to start as any. I will travel with you to gather Intel in preparation for eventual conquest. Tell me, does this land of "Georgia" have a sovereign, or are they without rule? Is there an army in place; rival clans splitting territories? Tell me everything you know."

His new human smiled happily at him, "You certainly are a curious cat. I've never met another quite like you. You know, Aunt Rosie didn't seem to know what your last human named you. Hmmm… you look like a "King" to me. How do you like that? Shall I call you King?"

"That," Tom said, spreading himself out to cover as much of the scribbles below him as possible, "would be entirely appropriate."

FLORENCE
by Jane Blanchard

9/11/2018

America faces a serious threat,
So government sources inform.
The danger's as bad as a danger can get
When weather and words become warm.

This hurricane could be the worst ever yet
Since nature departs from the norm.
"It's tremendously big and tremendously wet,"
The President says of the storm.

THE Z WORD
by Jeff Seeman

Nobody wanted to use "the Z word." At best it seemed melodramatic; at worst, just plain silly. So for weeks the government and the news media struggled to find terminology that would convey the global situation with adequate gravitas. Most news sites and cable channels, from the New York Times to CNN, finally settled on "the infected." Some Christian radio stations, in an attempt to emphasize the biblical aspect of the epidemic, preferred "the arisen." And on NPR, Mary Louise Kelly even interviewed an etymologist who explained that "the Z word" was an obvious misnomer, more properly associated with the voodoo rituals of Haiti—and that if one were searching for an appropriate colloquialism, "ghoul" would at least be more accurate.

But users of Twitter, Facebook, and Instagram cared not a whit for such linguistic niceties. When the dead began rising from their graves to feed on the living, people on social networking platforms didn't mince words. They were zombies, pure and simple.

The residents of Harrisfield read the news reports with much the same horror as everyone else around the world. Whenever an attack in a major metropolitan area was reported, they would text their families and friends in New

York or Los Angeles or Houston to make sure they were safe and were sheltering in place as authorities had advised. But sequestered as they were in an isolated area of the state, twenty miles from the nearest major highway, the residents of Harrisfield felt somehow removed from the whole situation. Certainly it was unlikely the plague would ever find its way to the borders of their small town.

All that changed late one Saturday afternoon when one of the "infected" wandered out of a wooded area on the outskirts of town and attacked a homeowner mowing his lawn, tearing open his throat with yellowing teeth and setting forth a geyser of blood from his carotid artery. By dusk, attacks were erupting all over town. At the Pump 'n' Go, a man was torn apart while pumping gas, his steaming entrails ripped from his stomach. At the Food Mart, a woman was devoured while shopping for zucchini, her blood smearing the floor of the produce aisle.

As darkness fell and the attacks spread, the residents of Harrisfield scrambled for safety. Those who were able to make it back to their homes locked their doors, boarded their windows, and huddled together with their families. The less fortunate ones—those who couldn't make it home, those who found their paths blocked by hordes of ravenous zombies—ran to the safest place in town they could think of. They ran to the sheriff's office.

Tom Dooley, former cop from Philly, had taken over as sheriff just six months earlier. Thus far, the town had offered him exactly the kind of semi-retirement he'd hoped for. Aside from local teens committing the occasional acts of vandalism and an odd complaint of public drunkenness now and then, he'd thus far had a pretty easy tenure. He expected this Saturday night to be no different. He was wrong.

THE Z WORD

Dooley looked up from his desk as the terrified group burst into his office—George and Annie Casidos, proprietors of the local dry cleaning store (Annie sobbing, shaking, near hysterical, George with his arm thrown around his wife's shoulders, trying to comfort her), Cheryl Knacker, cashier at the Food Mart (her expression blank, her eyes wide with shock, even her perpetual gum-chewing ceased), Bud Muessler (youngest of the Muessler boys and the only one who hadn't moved away from Harrisfield years ago), and finally old Doc Wilkins (carrying his cane, but mostly leaning on Bud for support). Bud slammed the door shut behind them.

"Told you, you should have left me back there," said Doc Wilkins. "I'm just slowing you down."

"No way we were gonna do that," Bud insisted.

Sheriff Dooley looked at them with curiosity. "What's up?"

They stared back at him.

"What's up?" Doc Wilkins hobbled forward on his cane. "What's up?! Zombies! All over the damn town! Haven't you heard? Hasn't anyone reported them?"

"Oh, that. Yeah, sure they have. I've been hearing this all day. Zombies this, zombies that." Sheriff Dooley snickered. "Hoaxes. Just hoaxes."

"Hoaxes? What do you mean hoaxes? It's happening all over the country! All over the world! Haven't you watched the news for the past two months?"

"Fake news," said the sheriff. "Everyone knows that's fake news. Fake news from fake news organizations. It's disgusting, that's what it is. It shouldn't be allowed, let me tell you."

"They're right outside your office!" insisted the doctor.

"Nonsense."

"Look out the window!"

Sheriff Dooley sighed and strode wearily to the window. Across the street, beneath the glare of a streetlamp, a shambling group of bloody, disheveled zombies had gathered.

"Immigrants," said Sheriff Dooley.

"Immigrants?" said Doc Wilson.

"It's a horrible problem," said the sheriff. "Horrible. The most horrible problem we've ever had. They come to this country looking for a handout. And they're bringing drugs. They're bringing crime. Look at them. They look like they haven't had a bath in weeks."

"Because they're dead," said the doctor. "Look, that one's eating a foot."

"Chicken leg," said the sheriff.

"A chicken leg with toes?"

"How are we going to get out of here?!" Cheryl interjected.

A few more zombies staggered out of the darkness, joining the group across the street.

"I don't think there's anything to worry about," said the sheriff. "I have a very good feeling about this. A very good feeling. I think they're breaking up."

"They're not breaking up!" said the doc. "There's more of them now!"

"No, they're breaking up. This whole thing will probably blow over by tomorrow. It's going to disappear. It's like a miracle, it will disappear."

"How on earth...? Why would you think that?"

"Sunlight," said the sheriff. "As soon as the sun comes up, they'll all die. The whole concept of the light, the way it kills them in one minute, that's pretty powerful."

"Sunlight doesn't kill them," said the doc. "You're thinking of vampires."

"There's no such thing as vampires."

"I didn't say there were!" Doc Wilson shook his head. "Look, do you have a car? Isn't there a patrol car somewhere?"

"Sure," said the sheriff. "Right down the street. In front of the drug store."

"I'll go," said Bud.

"No!" George let go of his wife and turned to face Bud. "We can't let you do that. It's too dangerous."

"Look, someone has to make a break for it," said Bud. "You can't go. Annie needs you. And Doc can't make it with a bum leg. I'm the obvious choice. Single, male, no wife, no children. If someone needs to take one for the team, it should be me. Plus I played football in high school. I have a better chance of making it than anyone else."

There was an awkward silence as everyone quietly, shamefully agreed.

"I'll get the car," said Bud. "Swing it around. Pull it right up here on the sidewalk. Right outside the door. Everyone jumps in and we get the hell out of here."

"Where are the keys?" Doc Wilson asked the sheriff.

"In the car."

"You left the keys in the car?"

"Why not? No one would dare steal my car. Hold on." Sheriff Dooley unlocked a cabinet and produced a shotgun. He loaded it with shells, pumped one into the chamber, and handed it to Bud.

"If they come at you, shoot. Only way to stop them."
"Got it," said Bud.
"And you have to aim for the foot," said the sheriff.
"No, the head!" said the doc.
"I heard it's the foot," said the sheriff. "People are saying it's the foot."
"No one is saying that! No one has ever said that! You need to aim for the head."
Sheriff Dooley glared at him. "You ever seen a zombie shot in the foot?"
Doc Wilson blinked. "Have I ever…? No, of course not."
"Then how do you know?"
"Stop it!" yelled Cheryl. "For God's sake, Doctor, he's the sheriff! He knows what he's doing! Why are you arguing with him?"
Bud gripped the shotgun. "Get the door," he said.
Cheryl put her hand on the doorknob. Bud took a deep breath and nodded to her. She swung the door open for Bud to dash through, then slammed the door behind him.
From the window, the group watched as Bud sprinted down the street towards the patrol car, shotgun clutched to his chest, dodging zombies along the way, a running back with a football weaving through a phalanx of defensive players. All at once, ahead of him and to his right, a zombie burst forth from a side alley. Bud swung the shotgun and blasted the zombie's right foot. Undeterred, the zombie staggered forward and latched onto him. It sank its teeth into Bud's right shoulder and tore off a chunk of bloody red flesh. Bud screamed and went down as a swarm of the living dead closed in and devoured him.

Sheriff Dooley shook his head. "Maybe it's the left foot."

Annie burst into another round of hysterical crying while the rest of the group just stared in horror.

"What the hell did you just do?!" demanded Doc Wilkins.

"What did I do? I didn't do anything. I take no responsibility for what just happened."

"He needed to aim for the head! What you told him just got him killed!"

Sheriff Dooley glared at him. "That's a nasty remark. You're a very nasty doctor, you know that? Very nasty."

"I've done a fantastic job as sheriff," he continued. "A fantastic job. And it hasn't been appreciated, I'll tell you that. I didn't need to take this job, you know. I was doing very well. Very well. I could have just retired. I came here to help you people. And all anyone does is complain. Complain, that's all you do. You should be thanking me. That's what you should be doing."

"But what do we do now?" asked Cheryl.

Sheriff Dooly thought for a moment. "Garlic," he said finally. "I've heard garlic keeps them away."

"No!" said Doc Wilkins. "You're thinking of vampires again!"

"No, zombies. Why do you keep bringing up vampires?"

"You're the one who keeps bringing them up."

"Never mentioned vampires. Never mentioned a word about vampires." He looked at Cheryl and shrugged towards the doctor. "Vampires, he says. Can you believe this guy?"

"Should I go online and try to order some garlic?" asked Cheryl. "Maybe we can get it delivered express."

"Yeah, good idea. And get some wolfsbane, too. The combination of garlic and wolfsbane will work for sure."

The doctor sputtered as Cheryl pulled the cell phone from her back pocket and thumbed her way onto the Internet.

"That's not even—," began the doctor. "There's no evidence that garlic and wolfsbane—."

"I have the evidence," said the sheriff. "I have it right here." He tapped the side of his head. "That's all the evidence I need. Everything's right up here. I have a good instinct for this stuff. I'm not a doctor, but I'm a person who has a good brain. I'm, like, really smart. I'm a very smart guy."

"Amazon's sold out of garlic," said Cheryl. "And I can't find wolfsbane at all."

"Sure," said the sheriff. "People are probably hoarding it. Which just proves that it works."

The conversation was cut short by the sound of breaking glass. Everyone spun around to see that a hideous, undead hand had burst through the window pane. The arm snaked its way through the bars on the window, fingers trying to clutch, grasp whatever it could reach, the skin a ghastly shade of whitish-blue, the fingernails black. The zombies were moving closer.

"I'll go," said George with determination.

"No!" shrieked Annie, the first actual word they'd heard her say since the ordeal began. She gawked at her husband. "You can't leave me!"

George took her by the shoulders and looked into her eyes. "I have to, honey. I'm doing this for you. Do you understand? It's the only chance we've got. If we don't do something, we're all dead. It has to be me."

"No!"

He pulled her closer, kissed her hard, then ripped himself out of her arms and turned to the sheriff.

"Give my your sidearm."

"My sidearm?" said the sheriff.

"Give it to him," the doctor insisted.

Reluctantly, the sheriff removed the revolver from his holster and handed it to George.

"Get the door," said George to the doctor. "On three. One… Two… Three!"

Doc Wilkins swung open the door and George burst through, pointing the gun straight out in front of him as he ran. The zombies swarmed towards him.

"The left foot!" Sheriff Dooley shouted after him through the broken window. "The left foot!"

George took aim. The zombies charged.

CONRAD'S MOUSTACHE
by John H. Kalin

Oskar was growing restless. He'd never been a fan of rail travel, though he wasn't even sure this qualified; they'd been sitting at the station for four hours now. Every time he pulled back the curtain to check the station clock, it hadn't budged. He laughed to himself, imagining some government appointee turning off the clock in a futile effort to pretend the trains were still running on time... Or it was simply broken, either was possible at this rail hub south of Budapest.

Oskar lit another cigarette, doubting he'd brought enough for the trip at this rate. Another quick look out the window robbed him of any desire to buy more: it was really a mess. There had to be ten thousand men spilling off of the platform now, some in uniform but most in well-worn travel clothes. They formed something between a line and a mob, waiting to board the train. Though, mercifully, not Oskar's carriage. As a member of the general staff, he was in a luxury carriage on loan from the Emperor for the campaign. He was grateful for the extra space, and suspected half the men outside would end up on top of the other cars before they got moving.

Looking around his mostly-empty carriage, Oskar didn't see many familiar faces. Some looked old enough to have marched against Napoleon, others looked ready to hit puberty any day now. Most of the command staff had caught the first train three days ago, what remained was an assortment of recalled retirees and generals' sons... and Oskar himself, of course. He wasn't sure why he'd been lumped in with third-tier officers, but chalked it up to just another example of a disorganized mobilization.

Succumbing to desperate boredom, Oskar grabbed an abandoned newspaper from the adjacent table to pass the time. As a general rule, he hated newspapers. As often as not, they were full of lies and seemed intent on escalating every setback into a crisis. A quick glance at the headline was enough to cement this belief, EUROPE MOBILIZES. So dramatic. He smiled at the accompanying picture of Field Marshall Conrad von Hötzendorf, his commanding moustache leaping out at the reader, conveying a sense of power and prestige. Oskar took no small amount of pride in knowing that he himself had shaped and managed that very moustache on the day the picture was taken, some seven years earlier.

In many ways, Oskar owed his charmed career to the Field Marshall. Oskar had been one of the first graduates of the Kriegsschule in Vienna where he majored in Combat Moustachery with a minor in Field Artillery, the latter being added to remedy an early misunderstanding of the military academy's charter. For his final trials, Oskar sculped a twenty-centimeter handlebar moustache that held its shape for thirteen hours in the August heat. Conrad von Hötzendorf, then a tactical instructor, was suitably impressed and assigned Oskar to his staff. There he stayed for the last thirty years, managing the moustache of perhaps the greatest military genius of his time.

"Looks like he's finally got his war, eh?" A genial voice said from behind.

Oskar looked up from the paper to see a young officer he didn't recognize. "Pardon?" Oskar inquired, trying to figure out if he should know the man. He looked to be in his mid-twenties with black hair; his clean-shaven face revealed a somewhat dark complexion and more scars than someone would normally see in a soldier on his first campaign. It was definitely his first campaign, no veteran would bother to get fancied up in his pristine dress uniform for a train ride.

"Conrad," the man said while gesturing to the newspaper in Oskar's hands. "He's wanted Serbia for years, now he's got it."

Oskar bristled slightly at the familiarity, was this young Captain somehow on a first-name basis with the Army Chief of Staff or was he just irreverent about his superiors? There was some truth to what he was saying, of course: Conrad had wanted to annex Serbia for over a decade. He'd lobbied the Emperor to declare war no less than thirty times over the years, sometimes getting pretty close. "Well, they didn't give us much of a choice this time, did they, Captain-?"

"Frederick Von Frank." The man introduced himself, extending his hand. "May I sit?"

Oskar recognized the name, no doubt he was the 5th army commander's son. "Oskar Potiorek." He said, shaking Frederick's hand before gesturing to the empty seat opposite himself. "Is this your first campaign?"

"That obvious, eh?" Frederick said with a laugh. "Fresh back from Kamerun, actually. Been serving as attaché in the German African colonies for the better part of a decade."

by John H. Kalin

This piqued Oskar's interest, as he'd always wanted to study hair care in tropical climates. "Really? Didn't realize the Empire had African ambitions."

"If they do, they never told me. I was initially there to observe the pacification of the Herero rebels, but never got reassigned. I suspect they forgot about me, so I just kind of drifted from one native uprising to the next. That's the beauty of Africa, there's always some angry locals stirring things up somewhere."

"What brings you back now?"

"This, of course." Frederick said while gesturing at the mobilization in progress all around them. "I think this is the big one... and so do the Germans, they were training up local militia and fortifying Duala when I left." He paused a moment before adding, "They'll be fine as long as the Brits keep out of it."

"I can't imagine they would fight over a country of killers and thieves."

"Is that not what we're doing?" Frederick jested.

"Not the same. We're bringing killers to justice. Who in their right mind would go to war to defend them? They had their chance to help investigate the Archduke's murder, and they wasted it." The train whistle sounded in the distance. "Sounds like we're finally getting underway."

"You read our demands?" Frederick asked, ignoring the change of subject. "They were always going to refuse that. It's a land grab, no matter how much we tart it up. Don't get me wrong: it's got to be done. Last thing we need is a Slavic puppet on our flank. I just think we should've invaded weeks ago without the buildup."

The conversation had firmly turned away from African facial hair, and Oskar was losing interest fast. There was something about this young, outspoken captain that he just didn't like. It could be his smooth face, or his blind arrogance. Frederick seemed to think his opinion on the present crisis was more valid just because he was better informed. Oskar hated that kind of intellectual elitism that favored objective provable facts over inner-truths. "I don't think Russia or anyone else will get involved, but if they do I'm glad we have Conrad."

Oskar, like all Austrians, held Conrad von Hötzendorf in very high regard. He was world-renowned as a master strategist. True, he'd seen little combat relative to generals in more bellicose countries, but he'd literally written the book on modern tactics. Several books, in fact. Using nothing more than his own brilliance, and a large body of similar pre-existing literature, he innovated the offense-oriented tactics that would surely define modern conflicts. Thirty years ago, he challenged the old guard to abandon their antiquated views and embrace modern weaponry and command structure, and the army being assembled today was the very definition of 30-year-old innovation.

"I hope you're right," Frederick said, seeming to catch on that the conversation was making Oskar uncomfortable.

The train started moving, and a round of cheers erupted from the throng outside. Both men looked out the window once more, surprised to see that so many men were still out there. They watched as the station disappeared in the distance. "Now that we're underway, if you'll excuse me, I'm going to try to get some sleep." Oskar was grateful for the opportunity to extricate himself from the conversation.

"Of course." Frederick rose to leave, turning back to add, "I'm sure Conrad knows what he's doing." He nodded towards something outside the window and took his leave.

by John H. Kalin

Oskar turned to look out the window and saw whole companies of soldiers that were walking alongside the tracks as the train slowly passed, apparently having given up on the idea of getting a ride to the front. He didn't realize how slow the train was moving until a group of bicycles passed his window, easily outpacing the train. Oskar fell asleep staring out at the bungled mobilization, secure in the knowledge that Conrad would fix it.

***

Frederick was pretty sure they wouldn't have the element of surprise, that much was clear. Two weeks had passed since his snail-paced train ride to the staging area, and troops were still trickling into camp. Most had given up on the train and just walked, which seemed to be faster somehow. Of course, Conrad hailed the 'rapid' mobilization as a huge success. What appeared to be a disorganized mess was really a masterful ruse to keep Serbian spies guessing. It was never clear to Frederick if Conrad really believed the nonsense he said, but everyone else sure seemed to buy what he was selling.

Frederick spent much of the morning walking through the camp, checking with unit commanders to determine their strength. He'd been expecting to get summary reports with information like this during command staff meetings, but today's meeting was the first summons he'd received since arriving. Part of him hoped there had been daily meetings and he just wasn't invited. The alternative was a command staff with no idea of the tactical situation on the eve of an invasion.

CONRAD'S MOUSTACHE

Upon arriving at the requisitioned hotel serving as command headquarters, Frederick was shown into a large conference room. Most of the other officers had arrived already and were milling about, but Frederick's attention was immediately drawn towards a series of maps on display. The largest map depicted their present location just west of Serbia, though Frederick was dismayed to see that Bosnia was still a Turkish province on this map. Exactly how old was the invasion plan he was about to hear?

After an awkward twenty minutes spent making careful small talk with Conrad's sycophants, the man himself arrived and everyone took their seats. Looking around the table, Frederick couldn't help but marvel at the eclectic mix of soldiers. There were a couple people like himself, sons of important officials only added to the group as a courtesy. Frederick knew he owed his presence on the council to nepotism, but he was also pretty sure that his minimal experience in Africa was more than anyone else at the table could boast. Except perhaps for Colonel Betrug, whom everyone simply called 'The Colonel'.

The man looked to be about 70-years-old and acted like he was 90. The Colonel was something of a story-teller, every word out of his mouth was either incomprehensible gibberish or a flat lie. He claimed to have marched against Napoleon despite being at least fifty years too young for that, maybe he meant Napoleon III, which seemed less impressive. Some of his stories were so ridiculous that Frederick wasn't even convinced he was a soldier, he could've just found the uniform somewhere. Plus, Frederick was pretty sure the Colonel's eyepatch used to be on the other eye.

by John H. Kalin

Oskar was present, of course. As was Conrad's personal tailor, Hans. Frederick wasn't thrilled at their inclusion, but their talents were on full display today. Conrad looked like he was attending a ball rather than a strategy meeting, his dress uniform was modified to incorporate the sort of gold braids that were already old-fashioned a hundred years ago. His moustache was clearly dyed black and shaped into a rigid curl that could poke your eye out if you walked too close to him. Maybe that's what happened to the Colonel's eye, he thought with a chuckle.

Finally, there was Captain Schnitzel, arguably the most capable commander in the room. He was by far the youngest officer present, yet he wore more medals on his uniform than Frederick could ever hope to earn. His only fears were bath time and thunderstorms... leave it to Conrad to commission his basset hound. Frederick had just realized with dismay that Captain Schnitzel technically outranked him when Conrad rose to address the group.

"Welcome everybody, I'll jump right in. I'm sure you all know Russia declared war and is mobilizing to invade Galicia as we speak. Now, I did account for this possibility when planning the invasion of Serbia, and we will redeploy the 2nd army to meet them. However, the transportation ministry has informed me that it will be impossible to redeploy the 2nd for another ten days due to railway congestion in Hungary. This presents us with a unique opportunity-"

Not the word I'd choose, Frederick thought to himself.

Conrad continued, "This give us ten days to use the 2nd army before we lose them to the east." He walked over to the big map. "They are currently across the Danube from Belgrade, and have been bombarding its defenses for a week. I have reason to believe it is lightly held, with the bulk of the Serbs massing opposite us here. The 2nd will start crossing tomorrow as a diversion, then our forces here will cut through this gap and envelop the Serbs as they reposition to defend Belgrade," he pointed between two Serbian armies on the map.

For the product of decades of planning, this felt pretty half-assed to Frederick.

"Now, I've planned this very carefully, but I make no claims of perfection." Conrad laughed, as did everyone but Frederick and Captain Schnitzel. "So, we'll go around the room. Don't hold back if you think something needs to be adjusted. You're all here because I value your input, I'm not seeking the approval of a bunch of yes-men." Conrad said to his carefully-selected collection of yes-men. "Oskar? Your thoughts?"

"I think it's another brilliant plan, and I'm just grateful to be a part of it." Oskar paused before adding, "That said, I think we should push back a day. The forecast calls for rain in the afternoon and general high humidity, which is going to make your moustache difficult to secure during combat."

"Agreed. Your battle uniform is quite heavy and doesn't breathe well. Waiting for dry weather would definitely be better," Hans chimed in.

"With respect, I don't think we should make tactical decisions based on-," Frederick started.

"Good point, let's shoot for Wednesday then," Conrad cut off Frederick. "Colonel, your thoughts?"

"It's a good plan. If you grab a tiger's tail, you need to be ready to turn the flank. When I led the Dalmatian suppression, their cavalry got behind us, and we moved to the south hill before sundown. In the night we moved to the adjacent hill before moving back to the original hill the next day."

"… Well said, Colonel."

Nobody had any idea what the Colonel was talking about.

"What about you, Frederick?" Conrad prompted.

"Respectfully, sir, I have some concerns. Reconnaissance confirms they are massing opposite the Drina River. They have already moved behind Belgrade, and will not defend it, so a feint on Belgrade won't divert any troops from the west. I think the 2nd should just hold that approach and take minimum casualties so their units are intact when deployed to Galicia."

"I see what you mean, but the Serbs will not allow their capital to fall without a fight."

"If that were the case, sir, surely they wouldn't have retreated behind it before hostilities commenced. They know it's right on the border and indefensible, I'd expect them to declare it an open city the second our first troops arrive."

"As someone who has studied the Serbs extensively, I can assure you that they will be compelled to defend when pressed, this is exactly how we will trap them." Conrad had clearly become frustrated at having his strategy questioned even a little. "Captain Schnitzel, do you have any thoughts?" Conrad jokingly asked in an attempt to move things along.

Captain Schnitzel was busy aggressively licking himself, which Frederick took to mean he was ceding his time. "I think there are one or two other considerations we should address, sir." Frederick carefully interjected as he walked over to the map. "You've outlined our main thrust as being through this gap between the two Serbian armies, but I'm concerned there is no gap. The space between them is secured by Mount Cer, which we cannot cross quickly enough to perform an envelopment. If they spot us during the crossing, we will be wedged between two armies."

Conrad walked up to the map, closely inspecting it for a moment. Clearly this was the first he had heard about his proposed route being through a mountain. Like any good leader, he was unwilling to back down when confronted with facts that challenged his assumptions. He quickly recovered, "Exactly, Frederick. Only a fool would try to attack over a mountain, and they know I'm no fool. That's exactly why they won't be expecting it, and why we must attack over the mountain."

Frederick had to hand it to him, this was a special kind of stupidity he had not previously encountered. "I'm sorry to press the issue, but I feel I must. Their scouting is as good as ours, and they will discover the movement before we can move the heavy guns."

"How long do you think the crossing will take? Can it be accomplished overnight?"

"We can get infantry over the mountain before daybreak. They will not have artillery or machine gun support for at least another day after that. If that's the route we're taking, I recommend moving the infantry and digging temporary emplacements to fight off counter attacks until our artillery can catch up."

Conrad laughed dismissively. "You just don't get it, son. Heavy equipment, fortifications, these are anchors that will drown an army in modern warfare. The second you tie yourself to a position, you are inviting encirclement and ultimately defeat. This was the lesson of Sedan, and frankly I'm astounded your father never taught you this most basic principle." Conrad had abandoned all pretense of being open-minded, and the room had gone dead quiet except for Captain Schnitzel's persistent slurping.

"The Battle of Sedan was over forty years ago, sir. There weren't machine guns, there weren't aircraft, there wasn't rapid artillery. The Serbs have all three, and they've had practice using them. If you put us in a position that forfeits every strategic advantage, we will be unable to guarantee the issue." Frederick's rage was barely contained.

"Son, I welcome constructive criticism, but won't stand for your defeatism. The attack will begin as planned on Wednesday, moustache-weather permitting. Go brief your respective units. Dismissed."

Conrad left abruptly, with his aides and Captain Schnitzel in tow. Everyone else avoided eye contact with Frederick, and he suspected his outburst would probably damage his career. On the walk back to camp, Frederick found himself wondering if the great Conrad von Hötzendorf had always been so oblivious. He grew angry at the realization that the inevitable victory would undoubtedly add to his legend, even with double or triple predicted casualties. Though, if anyone could snatch defeat out of the jaws of victory this time, it was Conrad.

"Maybe I should have trained as a battle-mime," Frederick said to himself with a laugh. "Then maybe Conrad would take me seriously."

***

CONRAD'S MOUSTACHE

Agreeable mustache weather did not present itself until Thursday, so the operation ended up getting pushed back another day. As far as Oskar was concerned, this was a small price to pay. It was a beautiful day for moustaching, almost perfect but for the persistent thud of artillery fire in the distance. The main thrust over the mountain started last night, with Frederick assigned to coordinate the assault from the front. Oskar suspected the assignment was Conrad's way of getting Frederick out of camp, thereby ending the tedious daily arguments nitpicking a well-planned assault.

The morning began in command headquarters, but the incessant clicking of telegraph traffic from the front drove Conrad to move to a nearby café. Even without the clicking, Conrad seemed irritated. Word was coming in from the Belgrade front suggesting the feint on the capital wasn't working as intended. In fact, it never got off the ground at all. The army had not yet even attempted to cross the river, claiming they were never sent the necessary pontoons. Conrad was understandably upset at this obvious act of sabotage and possible mutiny. It's not as though he would've neglected something as important as how they were going to cross the river.

So much for the diversion! But, as Conrad was quick to point out, the Belgrade front was always a secondary objective. If anything, the level of seeming incompetence on display would lull the Serbs into a false sense of security. The man was a genius, able to outmaneuver battle-hardened foes in his sleep... sometimes literally. If they weren't a gang of criminals, Oskar would have felt bad for the Serbs.

Close to midday, a runner's arrival sent Conrad into an uncharacteristic rage. He started angrily pacing and yelling profanity-laced commands. Oskar had never seen him so angry, and frankly he was worried. If Conrad kept sweating like this, that moustache was never going to hold.

Managing to get a hold of the message that started the outburst, Oskar immediately understood. It was from Frederick, which was probably already enough to piss off Conrad, but its contents were even worse. Frederick had crossed Mount Cer in the night with the advance troops, and their party was immediately discovered by Serbian bicycle scouts at dawn. So Frederick ordered the men to dig in and allow the artillery to catch up before attempting to advance.

Not only had Conrad explicitly rejected this idea several days ago, but it was an idiotic plan. To Conrad, defensive fortifications were like giving a pilot a parachute, completely useless and arguably dangerous. If you give a pilot a parachute, he won't try to land an expensive airplane when it's damaged. Likewise, if you give a man a trench, he'll never be as motivated during an attack, knowing he has a safe place to retreat to at the first sign of trouble. Conrad wasted no time in countermanding the order and relieving Frederick of his command.

As the day wore on, Conrad's mood swung from angry to alarmed. All the heavy equipment was still at least a day away, but the advance units were already fighting off Serb counterattacks from both sides. Within a few hours, Serbian artillery started hitting the exposed units. It was becoming clear the forward position could not be held as it was. Conrad ordered the last reserves over the mountain to get the offensive moving again.

CONRAD'S MOUSTACHE

Conrad approached Oskar, his moustache in a sorry state. "Oskar, I have a mission for you."

"Of course, sir." Oskar instinctively replied. He'd spent his whole life preparing for nightmare moustache scenarios and was more than ready to take on this challenge. He grabbed his bag of grooming tools and his emergency jar of horse semen mixed with cinnamon… for extra firm hold.

Conrad saw what he was doing and cut him off "No, not that. The attack has stalled, but the Serbs are definitely stretched thin and about to break. I'm going to redeploy the 2nd to attack from the rear, but it's a delicate maneuver that I can't trust just anyone with."

Oskar dreaded what he was going to say next.

"Don't worry, I'm not asking you to lead the attack. I have to do it myself. I am going to leave immediately to join the 2nd. I need you to assume command here. All you need to do is hold the current positions and coordinate efforts as reports come in."

Conrad made it sound so simple. Strategists of his caliber came around once every couple hundred years, and war came so naturally to them they couldn't comprehend how difficult it was for everyone else. "Sir, I don't think I'm capable of-"

"Nonsense. I'm leaving the Colonel and Hans with you for counsel. Just keep current plans in progress. I'll send more detailed instructions when I have the 2nd in position. I have complete confidence in you." Without waiting for a reply, Conrad mounted up and rode off.

Oskar suddenly felt very alone, but he was determined not to mess up the plan. He immediately requested status reports from all forward units. It took about half an hour for the first replies to come, and they were not encouraging.

Under artillery fire without entrenchments, many units had been forced to seek shelter in scattered villages. That eased the artillery bombardment, but villages were changing hands over and over again following attacks and counter-attacks.

Recognizing that he was facing unforeseen circumstances that nobody could have possibly predicted, Oskar ordered all units to re-form the line and dig in. A single reply soon came, claiming it was impossible to dig under fire and that it was too late for that, the only option was withdrawal. Oskar supposed he shouldn't be surprised to see that the insubordinate reply was from Frederick. Apparently, he was back in command after several officers' deaths… lucky bastard.

"To avoid the mouse trap you just kill the cat. Press forward out of contact and live off the land until they move from the hill, then circle back and attack from the treetops to clear the lines."

"Not now, Colonel!" Oskar was sure it was good advice, coming from such a seasoned veteran, but couldn't decipher the sophisticated military jargon. Instead, he replied to Frederick, repeating the order to immediately re-form the line and dig trenches.

No reply ever came, but the situation became clear over the next couple hours. The sounds of fighting grew closer and closer, and what started as a trickle of wounded men gave way to a flood of exhausted men running back. Some officers attempted to rally the men, but most had joined them in flight. Unsure what to do, Oskar simply joined them and ran for his life. He had let Conrad down.

Mercifully, the pursuing Serbs stopped at the river and allowed the Austrians to regroup, though there was little point in continuing the offensive. Oskar was horrified when he looked at after-action reports. The Serbs had captured just about every piece of artillery, most machine guns and all of the supply wagons east of the river. Conrad's grand plan had cost at least 50,000 casualties, several hundred of whom died by drowning. Drowning deaths are something of a rarity in mountain battles, but Conrad had always been an innovator. Among the dead were the Colonel and Frederick. The latter apparently died trying to dig a foxhole in an open field during an artillery barrage for some reason Oskar couldn't comprehend.

Oskar dreaded what Conrad would say when he found out, but mercifully communication was down for now. With supplies running low, there was little choice but to completely withdraw the army, which Oskar grudgingly ordered.

After a couple days, with the withdrawal progressing smoothly, Oskar took the next train to Vienna to help explain the defeat to the Emperor. His mind raced as he rode the train, hoping he could help deflect some of the blame Conrad was sure to receive. With hindsight, Oskar could see the plan was flawed. But there was no way any rational person could have foreseen this disaster. The only person who said a word against the plan had been Frederick, and he only did so because he was a contrarian. Grabbing a nearby newspaper to distract himself, Oskar saw the lead story.

by John H. Kalin

Disaster at Mount Cer

Austrian forces withdraw from Serbia following a disastrous battle on the slopes of Mount Cer. Army Chief of Staff, Conrad von Hötzendorf, currently organizing the defense of Galicia against an expected Russian attack, declined to formally comment until the investigations into the defeat have concluded.

"I delegated the details of the Serbia campaign to Major Oskar Potiorek so I could focus on the greater threat from Russia," explained Hötzendorf. "And while it certainly looks like Oskar took several unnecessary risks that doomed the campaign to failure, it would be premature to assign blame until we've had a chance to hear his side of the story."

Others on Hötzendorf's staff have been less diplomatic about Potiorek's failure. Responding to inquiries via telegram, Major Schnitzel described Hötzendorf as being furious behind closed doors-

Oskar stopped reading the article and looked down to the accompanying picture. It was Conrad, regal as ever, with a hint of a smile on his face… his moustache was perfect.

AN HONEST POLITICIAN
by Jim Robb

The dark blue minivan was last in a line of several vehicles waiting for the traffic light to change. It was very ordinary-looking, several years old, and hadn't been through a car wash in quite some time.

Its occupants were somewhat less ordinary.

The driver styled himself the Pink Chameleon. He was a super-villain, although neither well-known publicly nor highly-regarded within his chosen profession. This was only partly because his super-power, the ability to change his appearance and voice to impersonate anyone he wished, was less than formidable by super-villain standards. His lack of standing was also influenced by the fact that he was unremarkable both intellectually and physically. He was in his early thirties, out of shape, and showing signs of premature baldness. He wore a somewhat threadbare blazer over an open-collared shirt, grey trousers, and tan loafers which could have used a shine.

The passenger seat was occupied by his evil sidekick, who was known in super-villain circles as Soporific Lass. She, too, ranked in the lower tier of super-power rankings, having the ability to put people into a state of suspended animation. She was in her late twenties and rather plain-looking, but made the most of her appearance through regular exercise and by cultivating a style she thought of as "second-hand chic".

One measure of the duo's lack of success as super-villains was that the minivan and its contents comprised every possession they had in the world. In fact, the minivan itself was theirs only by virtue of their having stolen it two days and several states ago. They were using it to flee from the scene of their latest unsuccessful evil plan, in which the Pink Chameleon had assumed the identity of a bank president. This impersonation had failed when the other bank employees discovered his utter lack of knowledge of the banking industry, specifically his belief that the term "amortization schedule" referred to the timetable for cleaning the carpeting in his office.

They were listening to the election results, not by choice but because that was what every radio station was broadcasting.

"Looks like Morgan Phelps managed to pull his chestnuts out of the fire," Soporific Lass said.

The Pink Chameleon frowned. "Who the heck is …?"

"Holy crap," Soporific Lass shouted. "Some guy just fell off a fire escape over there! Quick, pull into the alley!" She jumped out of the van while it was still moving and rushed to the crumpled form lying on the pavement beside a dumpster.

"How is he?" the Pink Chameleon asked as he opened his door.

"He's dead. Eww, he smells like a distillery." She pulled a flashlight out of her purse and shone it on the man's face. "Holy crap, do you know who this is?" she asked.

"Should I?"

"This is Morgan Phelps. He just won re-election for state governor."

"Maybe he's got some money, then. Check his wallet."

"Honey," Soporific Lass said, "don't you see the possibilities here? He doesn't have a wife or any living relatives. You could be him. You could be governor!"

"Hey, you're right! Great idea! Help me drag him over in front of the headlights so I can see what he looks like."

Soon a facsimile Morgan Phelps stood where the Pink Chameleon had stood before.

"Here's his wallet, his watch, and ... and his hip flask," Soporific Lass said. "You go in and give your acceptance speech. I'll be back after I lose the body and the van."

"Acceptance speech? I've never given one before. What do I say?"

"Don't worry about it. Someone will have written it for you. And if they haven't, it doesn't matter. Phelps was never known for his speech-making ability."

***

"Sir, there's a call for you on the secure line," said Soporific Lass, now using the name Laura Lister and serving as the governor's executive assistant. Then, in an undertone, she added, "It's the Master Malefactor."

"You deserve to be in on this call as much as I do," Governor Phelps said. "Close the door so we can put it on speaker."

Laura closed the door and sat down in one of the two vast armchairs facing the desk. Governor Phelps looked back and forth between her and the red telephone sitting on the desk between them. Finally catching on, Laura stood up, pressed two buttons on the phone, and sat back down again.

by Jim Robb

"Good afternoon, Your Deviousness," the Pink Chameleon said, reverting to his own voice. "You're on speaker."

The voice on the other end of the line was so clear he could have been standing in the room. "First, let me offer my congratulations. Who would have thought that you, the Pink Chameleon, would be the first super-villain to succeed in taking over a government? You and your henchperson Soporific Lass are the evildoers of the hour. You must offer her my congratulations as well."

"Thank you, Your Deviousness. That is high praise indeed. And Soporific Lass is right here."

"Your success is truly remarkable, truly remarkable indeed, especially considering your comparatively limited super-abilities."

The Pink Chameleon and Soporific Lass exchanged a glance. Their postures were slightly less proud when they returned their attention to the call.

"We should start with an after-action report. How did you pull this off? You didn't kill the real Morgan Phelps, did you? That would be a serious violation of the Comics Code."

"Actually, he managed that all by himself," Soporific Lass said. "He was drunk and fell off a third-floor fire escape. We just happened to be in the right place at the right time."

"Well," the Master Malefactor said, "you won't receive as much credit as you would have for executing a cunning plan, but seizing an opportunity will still improve your super-villain rankings. Anyway, let's get down to business. Do you want to negotiate for exclusivity of super-evildoing in your newly-won territory?"

"Of course," the Pink Chameleon said. "But we want to phase it in over the next few years. That way, it'll look like my tough-on-crime program is the cause."

"That makes sense. And what do you offer in return?"

"How about safe haven for super-villains in this state? As long as they perpetrate their evil elsewhere, they can come here to enjoy their ill-gotten gains. We can even help them launder their money."

"Go on."

The Pink Chameleon looked at Soporific Lass and gestured toward the phone.

"We can bury their ill-gotten gains in the receipts for the state lottery we plan to implement," she said, "and then arrange for them to win a percentage of it back."

"Not bad."

"Also, this state has no limits on campaign contributions. They can make generous cash contributions to Governor Phelps's campaign fund, up to a reasonable amount of course, and then take jobs as political strategists. We'll pay them a salary amounting to 80% of their 'donation' over his remaining time in office — 90% if they're actually willing to work on his next campaign."

Judging from the sounds coming from the speaker, the Master Malefactor was clapping his hands in glee. "I think we have a deal," he said. "I take it you're planning on carrying on your nefarious scheme for some time."

"Well, Your Deviousness," Soporific Lass said, "as you yourself pointed out, our super-abilities aren't exactly high-end. Let's face it, we probably couldn't hope to earn basic arch-enemy status, not even versus a minor superhero. We're never going to achieve total world domination, but we have achieved constitutionally-limited state domination. We'd like to see where it can take us, and for how long. Besides, the money's not bad. It's like a paid vacation from villainy."

***

Laura's voice shook as she spoke over the intercom. "Governor, you have a visitor," she said. "A special visitor," she added in a subdued voice.

"Expletive deleted," the Pink Chameleon muttered. "Which one?"

"Captain California."

"Send him in. I'll keep him occupied as long as I can so you can make your getaway." He rose to his feet and prepared to meet his fate.

The door opened and Captain California strode across the room, stopping in front of the desk. "Hello, Pink," he said. "It's been a while."

"Captain," the Pink Chameleon replied, desperately trying to display a degree of urbanity befitting a super-villain. "Have a seat. Can I offer you something? Coffee? Tea? An energy drink?"

"No, but thanks," Captain Confederation said, sitting down on one of the armchairs. His massive build made the armchair look considerably less vast.

The Pink Chameleon slumped into his own chair. "It's been almost three years now. What gave the show away?"

"I suspected something was going on when Morgan Phelps suddenly gained the ability to speak coherently and intelligently. I had the liquor bills for the governor's mansion audited, and that's when I knew for sure."

A puzzled expression crossed the Pink Chameleon's face. "How long have you known, then?"

AN HONEST POLITICIAN

"Almost three years."

"And you waited this long? Why? To make this hurt that much more?"

"Actually, I was curious to see how well you'd do. And quite frankly, you've done a pretty good job, especially for someone with no previous political experience. How did you manage to handle things so well?"

The Pink Chameleon shrugged his shoulders. "The tough-on-crime initiative was pretty easy for me, given my, ah, background. As for the rest, unlike Professor Irwin Corey I'm not the world's foremost authority, and unlike that guy in Washington I know it. Soporific Lass went out and gathered together a group of people who actually knew the score. We listen to their advice, and except for a couple of special situations I've always acted upon it."

Captain California nodded and sat back in his chair.

"So I imagine the police are waiting in the outer office?" the Pink Chameleon said, rising to his feet.

"Sit down," Captain California ordered. "I'm not through with you yet." He waited for the Pink Chameleon to comply before he continued. "There's a saying attributed to a politician from around the time of the Civil War, but it could well date back to the time of the Greek city-states: 'An honest politician is one who, when he is bought, will stay bought.' Far too many politicians are just super-villains without super-powers. I wondered how it would go if we had a politician who is fully qualified in that respect."

"And now you know. So what?"

"You've been doing a pretty good job as governor. I have to take that into consideration."

by Jim Robb

"But I'm a super-villain, and you've caught me in a nefarious act! As an All-American Superhero, aren't you duty-bound to enforce the law and bring me to justice?"

"The law is only a tool, and like any tool the end it serves, whether justice or injustice, is governed by the hand that wields it."

"You're just full of sayings today. I'm not sure I understood it, but it sounded really smart."

"All right, let's try this one. 'If Satan should ever replace God, he would find it necessary to assume the attributes of Divinity.' Ever heard it?"

"Yes, of course. Robert Heinlein wrote it in 'Double Star'. It was one of my favourite novels growing up. I'm sure you can understand why."

"That's good, because I believe you're living it right now. You've grown into this role, and now you want it enough that you're willing to work your butt off and do the best job you can in order to keep it. That's what I hope, anyway, because I'm proposing to leave you right where you are."

"Let me get this straight. You're actually talking about letting me stay on — as governor?"

"If you prefer, think of it as home confinement at hard labor, except you'll be running the state instead of stamping out its license plates or making small rocks out of big ones. And I'll be watching to keep you on the straight and narrow. Besides, do you have any idea how much it costs to keep a super-villain in prison? Even one whose super-powers are as modest as yours? This will save the state treasury a fortune."

The room was silent for a moment.

"Well? Do we have a deal?" Captain Confederation asked, extending his hand.

Struck dumb, the Pink Chameleon nodded and returned the handshake.

"One more thing," Captain California said. "I *am* going to start apprehending the other super-villains who have taken up residence in your state."

"But this isn't California. You don't have jurisdiction in this state, and our crime rate is so low that the Federal Bureau of Superheroes closed its office here." The Pink Chameleon waved his hand. "Why do you think Soporific Lass pushed so hard for that tough-on-crime initiative, anyway?"

"As long as I can get them before a court in my home state, the judge won't care how they got there."

Captain California stood up, took a couple of steps toward the door, and turned around. "Remember, I'll be watching."

"Oh, crap!" the Pink Chameleon said.

"What's the matter?" Captain California asked as he reached the door.

"Soporific Lass. I've been stalling you while she makes her getaway, and I have no idea where she's fleeing to."

Captain California engaged his x-ray vision. "She's still sitting at her desk in the outer office," he said. "I guess she cares for you enough that she's willing to share your fate."

He lowered his voice. "Since you're willing to take advice, here's some from me. You know as well as I do she's the brains of this outfit. You should consider promoting her to First Lady."

DEAR JOYCE

by Langley Hyde

Dear Joyce,

    Last week a wizard abducted me and my best friend R. The wizard claims I'm the rightful heir to the Alabaster Throne, that my destiny is to kill King Mnabapt, to marry a princess, and to restore Riverell to prosperity, and that King Mnabapt has sent a bloodseeker to kill me.

    At least the bloodseeker part is true—I saw it rip into Farmer J, R's dad. I don't know if R will ever get over that.

    As for the rest?

    I really, really do NOT want to marry a princess.

    Sure, I'm an orphan and I always felt I was destined for greater things, but I thought maybe I'd go to college and become a financial adviser instead of a farmer. Turnips are boring.

    What do you think? Have I found my destiny, or has it found me? What should I do?

    - Can't Have Original Situation Ever Now

***

by Langley Hyde

Dear CHOSEN,

You gloss over this part a little, so I feel the need to place this all in caps: YOU HAVE BEEN ABDUCTED.

Your first responsibility is your and R's safety. Your second is to escape. If you have the opportunity, please do not hesitate to call the authorities.

It sounds also like your abductor is extremely manipulative. He's using his knowledge of your background and your dreams to induce you to stay with him. In the best case scenario—if he's right about your parentage and destiny—it would mean that he intends to expose you, a minor, to extreme danger, force you into an unwanted marriage, and compel you to commit murder.

I highly suggest that you leave this situation immediately. Once safe, you may consider reading A Survivor's Guide: Overcoming Stockholm's, Brainwashing, Gaslighting, and Other Manipulation Techniques Abusers Use to Control You.

- Joyce

***

Dear Joyce,

Huge fan. Great advice. Read your column every morning.

- Maybe Not As Bad As People Think

***

Dear Mnabapt,
Thank you.
- Joyce

DEAR JOYCE

***

Dear Joyce,

Very disturbing experience last week. Some background: I've been in the blood-seeking sector since its advent two centuries ago. I gladly undertook the ensorcelled physical transmutations in order to do my job better. Nothing's too good for King Mnabapt.

But last week, as I ate Farmer J, and his son R cried and cried, I just didn't feel good about my work anymore. Blood doesn't taste like it used to, and while rolling in entrails does give my fur a nice shine, I'm considering switching to conditioner. Plus, no matter how viciously I crack the bones of my victims in my maw, the marrow isn't sweet anymore. What's even worse? When I devour the eyeballs of innocents, all I dream of is ordering a nice pasta Alfredo at a sit-down restaurant. I think I'm ready to move on.

Is it possible for me, at this point in my life, to make a real change?

- Career Has Achievement but No Gratification Ever Really

***

Dear CHANGER,

It's hard to change your career mid-life and harder still to do it when you're older. But the only way you'll be able to find out if you can really change is by trying.

It sounds to me like you're overdue for retirement, so I suggest you consider living on your pension while you think about what you want to do next. Many universities, colleges, and trade schools have special rates for seniors.

Try getting involved in the community and consider writing about your experiences. This may help you figure out what you really want.
- Joyce

***

Dear Joyce,
I think you should butt out of the king's personnel retention and stick to what you're good at: advising farm boys.
- Maybe Not As Bad As People Think

***

Dear Mnabapt,
Your opinion is noted.
- Joyce

***

Dear Joyce,
Thank you for saving my life, as well as my best friend R's, from that "wizard." I look back now and see so many red flags. He must've been very insecure about his masculinity to be so obsessed with his staff, and that beard? Talk about overcompensating.

R and I didn't end up returning to the farm—too many memories—but made a new life in the city together. We have an apartment, I've been accepted into a groundbreaking financial management program for commoners at the university, and R is considering military service to support me while I go to school.

Our only problem? I don't want R to join the military. The military has strict rules regarding men like us, and I'm afraid of what will happen to him if we're caught. I don't want to break up with him, but feel that our relationship puts R in danger. Should I leave him for his own safety?

- Can't Have Open Sexual Engagement Now

***

Dear CHOSEN,

Because my species can't pass as human and we aren't allowed to serve, I have no personal knowledge about the military. But as an advice columnist, it's my job to advise, so here it goes.

The only thing breaking up with him will do is hurt you both.

It strikes me that this is a very adult argument: you're justifiably concerned for his safety, and he's pushing back because it's his career. Congratulations. And the thing about adult arguments is that there are usually no good answers.

Sit down with him. Talk. If he really wants to join up, be prepared to listen to his reasons. Think hard about the strain this will put on your relationship, and decide together if it's worth it to you both.

Good luck.

- Joyce

***

by Langley Hyde

Dear Joyce,
This is the last time you will meddle with my personnel and my internal security. These policies are in place for a reason. You are sabotaging my military structure and I will not have it. Be careful, Joyce. I'm coming for you.
- Maybe Not As Bad As People Think

***

Dear Mnabapt,
Thanks for the warning.
- Joyce

***

Dear Joyce,
Thank you so much for your advice. I ended up writing a tell-all exposé about the blood-seeking sector. Truth Is in Their Blood will be on the shelves this fall.
- Career Has Altered for Now Gainfully Employed Reader

***

CHANGER,
I'll be sure to pick up a copy.
- Joyce

***

Dear Joyce,
I had it all in hand: the boy, his friend, the princess awaiting her prince. DESTINY. But no, you had to go about giving advice. I may still have my beard and my staff, but King Mnabapt is still sitting on the Alabaster Throne

and his bloodseekers are still terrorizing people and his army is still invading Irkenguard and the grandeur of Riverell will never be restored. You must be so proud of yourself. The world is ending, thanks to you.
- Why IZ Advice Readership Dumb

***

Dear WIZARD,
You're welcome.
- Joyce

***

Dear Joyce,
What do you do if you've waited your whole life for something but then it never happens?
From a young age I knew I'd be queen, and everything my governesses and numerous tutors did was to prepare me for governance—a task that was meant to be especially monumental, as my arranged match was to come from a more common background and so he would not have a deep understanding or intuition about court or international politics. I learned and I loved learning about policymaking and laws and I wanted dearly to be able to serve the public and the common good with all my heart. But now I have to face the facts: he's not coming to me. My arranged marriage was a sham. I have nothing left to live for.
My life is stifling. I just want out. Please help.
- Please Respond, I Now Could Ease Self's Suffering

***

Dear PRINCESS,

Your letter was so alarming I felt like it needed an immediate reply: please do not hurt yourself or do anything drastic. The Guild of Therapists and Mental Physicians provides responsive, confidential service. I recommend them highly.

It sounds to me like you attached a great deal of your self-worth to someone you've never met, and as a result you've taken his rejection quite personally. I'd suggest building up your own self-image and self-esteem independently based on who you are and what you can do. Your passion for governance and policymaking and working on behalf of the common good came from within. Why not pursue that?

It's my understanding that several political parties are forming with the idea of promoting a functional democratic system. You may find that you're the perfect compromise candidate: aristocratic enough to appeal to conservative monarchists but young and radical enough to appeal to liberal anti-government forces.

I know it's hard. You'll find that you're stronger and braver than you ever could have imagined.

- Joyce

***

Dear Joyce,
You're very hard to find considering how big you are.
- Maybe Not As Bad As People Think

***

DEAR JOYCE

Dear Mnabapt,
Good.
- Joyce

***

Dear Joyce,
Well, the worst came to pass—they found out about me and R. Just not like I expected they would.

A few weeks ago R refused to kill a dragon. He'd been ordered to steal its hoard for the king. He was court-martialed and sentenced to death for treason. I had to break him out of prison, but needed some help. I talked to his unit. It turns out that many of the men had read Truth Is in Their Blood. They had severe misgivings about the military after all that business about human sacrifice came out, so they were happy to help.

We're now working with this ex-princess to plan an attack on Fort Darkness and I'm the revolution's financial adviser. Any stock tips?

- Change Happens Oddly Sometimes Even Now

***

Dear CHOSEN,
Could you thank R on my behalf? Not every dragon is rolling in gold. Some of us are columnists.

For stock tips I'd try writing to Edward Redtooth. He's highly experienced with sustainable and ethical investing. He writes for Draconian Financials. Disclaimer: I am a regular reader of his columns and also a close friend.

by Langley Hyde

If you need aerial support during your attack on Fort Darkness, do write to let me know. I know several fire-breathers who'd enjoy frying King Mnabapt.

- Joyce

***

Dear Joyce,
Could use your advice about surrendering. Not a joke. Maybe some book recs please?
Thanks,
- Maybe Not As Bad As People Think

THE MUG LIED

by Sarah M. Kalin

Fred was the best boss.
His mug told me so.
In hand or on desk, it proclaimed its small truth:
ceramic virtue with a handle.
A mug has no reason to lie.

Did the mug speak of Fred's courage?
His kindness? His tact?
    It's hard to make much of those three.
Perhaps the mug thought him quite clever and wise
for his eyes ever-bent toward the sky.

There are so many wonders to see up above –
    unfettered from worries below.
And if Fred stumbled o'er those of us here,
    he'd shift us aside with a toe.

How mug-like, Fred's path!
How noble! How grand!
    Staying open to gifts as they come.

And who united these two kindred vessels?
Etched on the bottom:
    "To Freddie – Love, Mum"

NEIGHBORHOOD WATCH
by Lauren Stoker

Gustav Grimbold slumped in his desk chair, kneading his scalp around the base of his horns. Already he regretted his promotion: Executive Vice President of Plagues. He'd been rather hoping for Acquisitions. That was something you could really get your hands into. Or onto. Viruses and bacteria were such uncertain little beasts. They could never seem to make up their minds about whom to target.

The Man Downstairs undoubtedly thought that was the point: impartial evil, wiping out the good along with the bad. But the Man Downstairs didn't have to negotiate with the little bastards, try to aim them at bigger goals, not just felling the low-hanging fruit—the frail and senile. Honestly! Folks in nursing homes or with (he shuddered) pre-existing conditions? Big whoop. Grimbold knew that to get the biggest bang out of your mayhem buck, you had to have a strategy. Take, for instance, the current POTUS. What better way to wreak absolute havoc than take down the leader of a major, first-world country? They'd thought they had a good chance with old Boris and Charlie; it had been close but no corona.

Grimbold gave his neck a tweak and turned up the AC in his office (one of the perks of being an infernal exec.). The COVID-19 pandemic was his own project. His boss had praised him at the onset of the scheme: globally wipe out thousands of humans, striking the fear of God into them (Gustav always chuckled over that irony—the Man *Up*stairs always got the blame for their dirty work), sink the world's economies, stir up suspicion toward all governments but leave people powerless to do anything, cowering at home in lock-down. Genius!

And it would go a long way toward solving the population explosion. Even in Hell, they were running out of room.

Apparently it was too much genius for the devil down the hall. Smitewright was forever sticking his nose in, asking with a sneer how the Great Pandemic (finger quotes) was going and relating the latest human triumphs against it. Grimbold knew Percy Smitewright's nose was out of joint from being passed over for Plagues. And he sure as hell hated being reassigned as Grimbold's undersecretary.

Speaking of the devil... After a perfunctory tippy-tap on the door, Percy walked in and clicked his heels—his snarky jab at Grimbold's heritage.

Grimbold took off his readers and laid them on his desk atop the briefing he'd been reading. "Yes, Percy. What is it?" He massaged the bridge of his nose and blinked his eyes wider open to focus on the little twerp.

Percy always stood like there was a stick up his butt. Probably residual memory of the days when he first arrived, before he'd recanted and warmed to his devilry. Now he stood fire-poker straight, his lips pursed in perpetual distaste. Grimbold longed to reinsert an even longer poker if only to remind Percy what a real pain in the ass he was. Offense bristling from every orifice, Percy tilted his head and looked down his pinched nose. "You did ask for an update on the viruses, did you not?" He clutched a file to his chest.

"Correct. So what have you got now?" Grimbold reached out for the file, but Smitewright snatched it back. "I'm still working on my notes. And in any case, what I've come about isn't the file. It's... *they're* here—in person. Or would you call it 'in organism'?"

Grimbold frowned. "The COVID-19 gang? Here?"

"Well, just their union representatives or whatever. Seems they'd like to air some complaints."

"Complaints! Free travel—*worldwide*, mind you—good retirement plan, and all the cells you can eat? What the heaven do *they* have to complain about?" Grimbold thundered back.

"I'm just the messenger. And they're right outside."

"Fine. Send 'em in." Grimbold ran a hand through his thinning widow's peak and straightened his long, red tie.

Percy minced back to the door and ushered them in.

As a bunch of corpulent guys in Hawaiian shirts shuffled through, Grimbold sighed. The red splotches on white background reminded him of hibiscus. He folded his hands on his desk, striving to maintain patience.

"What may I do for you?" he asked what appeared to be the viral leader. The guy had a name tag on him that said, "Hi! My name is Bob," below which was his rank, sewn to his shirt: "M.P. Union Chief, COVID-19, First Airborne, Post 2020."

Bob took off his cap and elbowed his lads to do the same. Clearing his throat, or what passed for one, he began, "We're here, sir, to make it known that we coronaviruses object to certain current working conditions. Sir!" Here Bob tried a salute, but his virion proteins were all over the place.

"Could you be more specific, perhaps?" Grimbold drummed his fingers.

"It's this chap on Pennsylvania Avenue, sir."

"What about him?"

"Well, I mean, we may all be mercenary, flesh-wasting organisms, but I mean . . ."

"What *do* you mean, Bob?" Grimbold's eyes narrowed to a menace. He checked his watch pointedly.

"Well, sir, what I mean, what *we* mean, is even us debilitators have *some* principles."

Grimbold turned his head to the smirking Percy. "Would you care to expand, Mr. Smitewright?"

"Certainly." Percy's chest swelled as he opened his file, thumbing through it. "Although I did mention my notes aren't as yet complete."

"That's fine. Just give me what you have, please."

Percy consulted his notes. "Ah, here we are. On the 7th March, Year of Our Bad, troops of coronavirus were dispatched at Palm Beach, Florida to a dinner party that the Brazilian president and Target No. 1 were attending. Strategic approach was reported as good, but at deployment several troops balked and refused to go forward with the invasion. They did, however, have some success with the Brazilian president and his press secretary."

Percy licked a finger and flipped a page.

"Then the following day, another attack was launched, but was once again unsuccessful. You might say it was a Schlapp in our face."

"Very droll, Smitewright. Is there anything further?"

Bob and his lads stood, looking down and fidgeting.

"Well, a corpsman in the second deployment (who wishes to remain nameless) has related the dialogue he overheard among several of the troops. The following is a rough transcript, from memory, you understand:

> Sergeant A.P. Clypso: 'Get a move on!'
> Soldier 1: '*You* jump on him!'
> Soldier 2: 'No, *you* jump on him!'
> Sergeant Clypso: 'Come on, lads, we need to do this for the sake of the planet!'
> Where upon Lt. 2nd Class Eugene Splodge—"

Here, Bob interrupted. "'E was one of our best, sir. You shoulda seen him—big bloke, could tear through rhino hide without a break in his stride."

"Impressive. Go on, Percy."

"To continue, Lt. Splodge is reported to have leapt onto Target No. 1, exclaiming, 'For the planet!' whereupon the squadron followed."

"Brave, brave, lads, sir," Bob interjected. "Always stand by their own, 'cuz they know it's the right thing to do."

"Then why didn't they succeed?"

Bob stepped forward. "I can tell you that part, sir. The entire second squadron was wiped out, all except our Tim and Earnest here. It's them that came back and told me about how things went down. Said they'd never seen a site so disgusting in their lives. It just wasn't safe!"

"Oh, come now. Surely there's a way to penetrate, especially a target with a perpetually open mouth *and no bloody mask*. You lot are the worst the planet's seen."

"Maybe, but there are some things too nasty to touch," said Bob.

Just then there was another knock at the door. Dotty, the boss's secretary dithered at the threshold with an apologetic wince.

"Sorry Mr. Grimbold but I've an urgent memo from—" she gestured her horns downwards toward Mr. Big's suite on the Doomsday level (across from the Ninth Circle Club).

Grimbold got up and took the memo from her claw, thanking her. Dotty scampered off, not waiting for his reaction. *So this is going to be one of* those *memos, is it?* They were dubbed HFADs (Hell Fire And Damnations) and brooked no opposition.

> Re: Project COVID-19 - Effective today, all further assaults on Target No. 1 will cease. An emergency meeting of the Board has deemed that the risk of fatality to coronavirus troops is too high and that their valuable efforts could be better focused elsewhere. In addition, while the Board appreciates that at some point we will have to offer accommodation to the man, relocation of Target No. 1 at this point in time would serve as a serious detriment to both ambiance and property values in our dominion. Chief Executive Satan, along with the rest of the Board, unanimously agree that the best strategy would be to keep the target alive as long as possible to preserve what we can of our culture.

Grimbold set the memo down, squeezing his eyes shut, fending off a blinding headache. "Well. Looks like you and your ... men are off the hook, Bob. The issue's been resolved by our frightful leader."

"Thank you, sir. Thank you very much! Okay, lads, about-face! Let's not take any more of this gentleman's time." They shuffled around to leave.

"Don't mention it," Grimbold replied. "No, seriously. Do *not* mention it."

BABA YAGA'S APPRENTICE
by Louis Evans

Two women sat across from each other in the back booth of a bar. Both were old, but in vastly different ways. The first was old in the way of a wealthy woman from a modern, industrial nation: graceful and well-supported. She wore an antique bomber jacket and a surprisingly adventurous pair of jeans. The jeans looked as if they'd been pulled from a back closet after years of disuse, and in fact they had been.

The second woman was ancient beyond days and wizened like a peasant whose teeth had never known fluoride and whose face had never known sunscreen. Her grey hair had wrinkles, and from her wrinkles sprouted endless grey and bristly hairs.

"Baba Yaga has not had a customer in many years," said Baba Yaga, her voice creaky, her accent theatrically Slavic. She was perfectly capable of using the first-person pronoun, but she liked the sound of her own voice saying her own name. "How did you find Baba Yaga?"

"It's what I do. I'm a journalist. Or, I was." The other woman, whose name was Grace, smoothed the front of her shirt, feeling naked without her press pass. She'd worn this outfit to cover the Democratic Convention in 1968; the smells of weed and tear gas and hippie blood were still baked into the thing.

"And you want Baba Yaga to return you to the heights of your profession, yes? A scoop, a Pulitzer, an editorship? This can be done, but be warned—all Baba Yaga's spells come at a price."

"No. No, I gave up on that years ago. I'm not here for me. I'm here for the kids."

"Kids are Baba Yaga's specialty! She has done this since before the Old Country. Your sons and daughters, Khans and Tsarinas!"

"Not my kids. I don't have kids like that." Not many men had wanted to be a stay-at-home husband to a crusading lady journalist in the sixties and seventies; at least, none of Grace's four husbands had. Four divorces, zero children. Grace was not looking for a love potion.

"Speak, child. Baba Yaga will stop jumping to conclusions."

"I'm a journalism professor these days. Politics writing. And I'm worried for my students."

Baba Yaga nodded. The process—chin down, chin up—took the better part of a minute, and produced the creaking of a wooden ship in a hurricane as her wrinkles, wattles, and warts rearranged themselves tectonically.

"The newspapers have been dying for two decades now. No ads, no subscriptions. And all everyone wants to read is lists of quizzes about period dramas set in Imaginary England! Even the surviving papers are only hiring television critics. No jobs for political journalism, real journalism.

"And the news itself is just as bad. Do you remember the debt-ceiling crisis?"

Baba Yaga cocked her head thoughtfully, then spoke, "In the third year of the reign of Ivan the Irritable, Baba

Yaga loaned him an emerald the size of a boar's heart on the promise of repayment in four chests of pure gold, but when the prince's treasure fleet—"

"You don't remember it! Precisely my point. The debt crisis was the biggest political news last year and nobody cared. Because there was no story there, no villain. Just a bunch of unmemorable squares in suits shooting themselves in the foot for reasons the reading public doesn't understand and then pointing at each other and shouting 'he did it.'"

Grace took a huge swig of the beer in front of her. "Ahh. Now Watergate, that was a story. Crime! Lies! Secrets!"

Another swig. "Not that I want another Nixon! That bastard was too clever by half. Too clever."

Another swig. These microbrews were surprisingly strong. "What we really need is some utterly bankrupt idiot. Morally bankrupt. Too egotistical to really hide anything. That would do it. Gravy train for the journalism school class of twenty fifteen, woo-hoo!"

Another swig.

"Ah, I'm full of shit. Forget it."

"Is not shit, and Baba Yaga does not forget. You will have your spell."

"Really? I don't have to like, find wing of bat and eye of newt? Newt Gingrich once gave me the elevator eyes in this jacket, does that help?"

"Is not necessary, and please do not mention Gingrinch again. Some things Baba Yaga does not touch."

"Just to be clear, Grace didn't touch him either," said Grace.

They shared a firm nod, two female professionals at the top of their respective fields, each one knowing the price she had to pay to reach this point and guessing that the other's price was just as high.

"Baba Yaga is the greatest witch in the world," said Baba Yaga. It was a statement of fact, not a boast. "All she needs is intention, power, and faith. Three ingredients, three participants to make the spell. Let it begin."

Baba Yaga was silent a long time, and when she spoke again her pitch was not a crone's high rasp but the deep bass of good jazz.

"What is Grace's intention?"

"To create successful careers for graduating political journalists."

"Whatever the cost?"

"Whatever the cost."

"Good. What is Baba Yaga's power? It is the power of ice and snow, of bear and hawk. The power that moves the thrones of the world like a child moves his toys." Grace was nailed to her seat. Nothing physical was happening but the spell was working, throwing off more power than Indiana Jones's Ark of the Covenant.

"And faith. Not Grace's faith, for a journalist turns her face from faith to seek the truth. Not Baba Yaga's faith, for a witch cannot trust in the gods. The faith of another. The sublime, self-confident man who was born to riches and believes he has Midas's touch, who lies in ruins and claims they are a great palace. That faith of man's arrogance called hubris, called narcissism, this spell binds thee—"

Baba Yaga's voice gave out. She panted in the whirlwind, and then, all at once, the spell departed.

"It is done," said Baba Yaga.

Grace smiled, not sure what she believed. But hundreds of miles distant, in a green room in a taping studio, which bore the name "Apprentice," in a skull with hair like threads of stolen gold, the spell struck home. A single whisper split the silence.

"It'll be yuge."

CHARISMA

by Dan M. Kalin

Simona looked carefully around the garden she had been working all afternoon. *Good! The weeds are almost entirely gone.* Next to her, two small squirrels played while she worked. *They weren't much help today, except perhaps as comic relief.* Simona suspected they were mostly there to make sure she didn't inadvertently uncover their horde of winter food. The other reason was they liked being close to her when she was outdoors.

"You two are ridiculous. I'm kneeling all day in the hot sun while you play and play." Simona always talked aloud to the many small animals living on or next to her four-acre, wooded property. One of the squirrels shook its tail as if to refute her words before coming next to her leg and placing one paw on her jeans in a tentative fashion. "No, I'm not really angry with you. I suppose you want me to refill your nut dish, hmm?" Their answer was a frenzied tail-up running about, bravely bouncing off of her leg to make the sharp turns.

Simona stood straight up, stretching her back muscles out of the hunched-over posture gardening required. Placing her hands on her lower back she looked straight up at the light blue sky which was now beginning to darken with approaching dusk. Creaking a little, she said a quick prayer to the goddess, before going back into the house. Her cat, Tango, was there to greet her along with Orson the rat. Most people would expect some friction between the normally antagonistic species, but in this case harmony prevailed. Simona expected nothing less, after all. Tango rubbed himself around her legs, while Orson investigated the smells her jeans had picked up from the earth. Moving cautiously, Simona shuffled in to her small but comfortable kitchen and started the tea kettle.

Tango gave an odd vocalization which almost sounded like human speech, ending as always in cat talk with the 'owwweeerrrrr' sound. He was a large, yellow-striped tabby cat, who could easily place his paws atop the countertop when standing on hind legs. Orson was grey-furred and, while big for a rat, was not in the same class as Tango.

"Yes, yes. Dinner will be served shortly. I'm doing it now, see?" Simona prepared their respective food dishes while waiting for the tea water to boil. Soon, Simona was forgotten altogether as her friends feasted.

Tap, tap, tap, insisted a noise from the kitchen window. Outside, a young male crow from her woods stood proudly with a gift: a shiny marble, doubtless lost by a careless child. Simona opened the window and accepted her prize.

"My, this is so beautiful. Thank you, my young friend, it is truly a treasure!" she said and continued praising the young crow. He puffed up and strutted back and forth before allowing her to stroke gently underneath his beak. "I have something for you as well, where did I leave it?" The script was always the same, she would look and look until finally finding a small bag of peanuts. Taking two she offered them up to her young admirer. "Don't eat the shell this time!" Her friend quorked, took one peanut in its left claw and the other in its beak before leaping off of the window sill in flight. Simona watched him for a few seconds smiling, until she heard the teapot announce completion of its task.

Simona sat down at the kitchen table, drinking tea as the sun completed its descent on the horizon. Looking at the calendar, she determined there would be no visible moon tonight, at least not in her little corner of the world. *Good, I'm tired already and don't need to go traipsing in the woods for moon-herbs tonight. I'll log on to my social media and see what family and friends are up to. Maybe a little television after.* Tango lazily swatted at the tea-bag tag, making her scold him half-heartedly. "You keep that up and maybe it will be time for your annual bath quicker than you think, young man!" Tango flicked his tail as if he didn't believe the threat, even for a second. Orson lay stretched out on the table with a full belly, in the final remaining patch of sunlight.

"I'm going to take a long, warm bath before dinner. You two stay in here please, I don't want to share my bathwater tonight!" Neither one bothered to respond.

After her bath, Simona made herself a nice dinner omelet with mushrooms and herbs from the garden. Taking a glass of wine afterwards she sat down at her computer to check on her social media accounts. Ever since her son Ian had set it up she, quite to her surprise, found it to be addictive. Her circle of friends spanned early childhood to more recent, work-related ones. Even relatives she barely knew began to be known online. Sharing pictures and memories had once been a delight for her. Recently, however, a new politician had entered the national scene, dividing friends and family as seldom before. Simona did her best to ignore all of the hyperbole, she didn't care about him one way or the other, but her friends all seemed to be seized by a collective insanity. They either loved or hated him, no matter what issue was being discussed. Worse than that, the divide appeared to approximate halves, so a plurality was never formed. Just two sides endlessly sniping and provoking each other online.

"It's almost like a spell, what's happening, boys," she said addressing Tango and Orson, each of whom had commandeered an arm of her easy chair. "Something like this can be truly evil and set off real wars if it is not addressed early. The amount of power to cast such a spell would be ridiculous, affecting everyone in the world. Even I am affected by it. I dislike the man and I don't even know him." Tango and Orson held their peace on the topic.

Simona threw up her hands finally, "I can't look at this anymore tonight, let's just watch some Discovery Channel, shall we?" The boys were amenable and soon the trio was happily watching a rerun of Shark Week.

***

The next day, Simona decided she should go speak with her coven master, Leopold. If there was a spell affecting everyone in the world, surely he would be aware of the situation. Leopold ran a small shop selling essential oils and fragrances in the arts district. In the last few years, his business had gone from a sleepy concern lucky to see more than a couple of customers a day, to a thriving business. In fact, he employed several coven members as clerks during the weekends when demand was high from tourists.

CHARISMA

As it was a weekday, she found Leopold, a grey-bearded man fully owning the look of a prosperous hippie, behind the counter explaining the wonders of essential oils to a potential client. Seeing Simona, he smiled in greeting and nodded her towards the back of the store to a small sitting area stocked with makings for tea. She settled in to wait.

"Thank you for waiting, sister. What brings you to me?" Leopold asked a few minutes later. Usually the only time he saw Simone was at communal worship meetings.

She proceeded to speak of her concerns about the country's new president, which was generating so much strife between people. He nodded as she detailed her suspicions.

"Yes, I believe you're right, there is a spell behind it. I have had to maintain a shielding spell in my store so the effect would not contaminate what we do here. Check it yourself, is the shield working?"

Simona addressed herself internally and found that while she was still aware of her concerns, she no longer felt an irrational dislike for the man. "Yes, the shield works. I was affected by the spell outside, but now it is only an annoyance."

"I initially created it to maintain a calm atmosphere here, but the result is what amounts to a safe psychic space. I need to also treat my residence. Unlike you, however, my effect is that I believe he is doing a good job. The base spell must be very powerful, as I don't vote red for obvious reasons," Leopold explained.

"Do you have any idea who might have created it in the first place?"

"No, I don't. I did look to see if there was any locus of force centered on the man himself, and there isn't any evidence he is directly responsible. It seems to draw its power directly from those affected, in a feedback loop, so those responsible no longer have to maintain it. There are maybe a thousand of us worldwide who could do something like this, but finding them would not be easy."

"How can we stop it? Should we? I don't think this is an ethical use of power: creating division, sowing hatred," Simona said.

"I agree, but there isn't much we could do to stop it. The spell is now self-powered. It might end when or if someone kills the politician, but it might not if the spell finds a new host. Now, there is an idea! It might be easier to shift the spell onto a more acceptable vessel: to someone who doesn't inspire the same extremes in opinion."

"So the extremes are not generated by the spell itself?"

"I don't think so. This guy inspired the same kind of discord before he became president, but it was on a smaller scale. He was famous before, but people had no trouble ignoring him when they felt like it. I know I didn't give him a second thought."

"How would someone shift the spell? I think it's something which needs doing," Simona asked respectfully.

Leopold looked sharply into Simona's eyes and confirmed her resolve. "I can research it over the weekend, and maybe have something back for you next week. Don't expect formal coven support on something this politically sensitive, though, we have to treat both sides equally. Are you planning or willing to do this alone?"

"Maybe. It disturbs me to see everyone fighting like they are, it cannot be good for our community. Dangerous even. What if he whips up a crowd to come after us again? I know we're in better shape this time around but it would still be an ugly situation. I'll think about it over the weekend and decide once I see what you have for me, it might be something I couldn't even do," Simona said.

"I'll tailor the spell or procedure to what I know of your strengths, which are significant," He said with a quick smile. "Promise you won't just rush into anything before understanding all of the ramifications, please! I like having you with us," Leopold urged.

Surprised Simona colored, "I won't. I have too many responsibilities to casually make such a decision. Why, my animal friends alone will keep me focused on the most important thing: hearth and home."

"Do me a favor, will you? If you come across any comfrey and damiana in your woods, can you harvest some for me? I'm running low."

"Certainly, I was going to ask. There will be a nice moon tonight, so I should be able to find a good selection."

A bell from the front of the shop chimed. "Ah, here comes another customer. I'll take my leave and look forward to seeing you next week, go in blessed peace, sister," Leopold said in benediction.

As Simona walked back to her wooded home, she pondered whether the spell could be transferred to something innocuous, a rabbit perhaps. No, that might be problematic if a predator was to kill the rabbit and the spell escaped to something else. Try as she might, she couldn't think of any one of her friends she would want to burden with what she considered a curse. As she entered her land, the forest creatures gathered as usual in greeting. All wanted to reassure themselves of her health and be loved in return. If you were to survey the health of the resident skunks, possums, armadillos, bobcats, foxes, raccoons, and coyotes it would surprise the uninitiated. In Simona's four acre woods, every creature tolerated every other creature: harmony ruled. Outside in the wide world other rules applied, but having a safe place without parasites, predation, and disease makes a difference.

Simona could sense the stain of national hatred and strife working its way even into her domain, now she was aware of it. That evening, she picked the things Leopold had requested, but also spent time collecting ingredients to create her own shield, similar to what Leopold had deployed in his shop. By the next evening, she had marked the boundaries and invoked the goddess successfully, creating another zone of blessed peacefulness. Once more she was bone-tired, but there were mouths to feed before another bath could be drawn. As she worked to satisfy Tango and Orson, the mobile phone began beeping in an alarm notification.

"I wonder what this is, boys. Let me check," Simona ran over and read the text message. It was a national notification of emergency being declared by the president using the national alert system. The emergency was to announce his decision to contravene the will of the sitting congress by building a wall on the southern border, using emergency powers. Simona threw her phone onto the couch in anger. Moments before, she had felt peaceful and now the cad had reached past her shield to further aggravate. Tango looked ready to vanish if more sudden moves were being contemplated by Simona, and Orson was always ready for a turn in fortune, all rats have that gift.

Noting the alert status of her animal friends, Simona calmed her breathing saying, "I'm sorry to let him upset me, I'll be better now," she said as she went back to making their meal and set two dishes down with a flourish. She then busied herself preparing and packaging herbs for Leopold while her mind raced. Maybe she could transfer the spell to a tree! They were strong, slow of mind, and benign for the most part. It was hard to hate a tree, wasn't it? Unless you were a developer or lumberjack, who would as soon cut a tree down as look at it. No, a tree wouldn't do after all. Even rocks were alive in a sense to someone like Simona, but they too were ruled out for similar reasons.

A long soak in her bath accompanied by a glass of her favorite wine put the final touch on releasing tension. Once more the trio sat down and watched several episodes of a new show about the life and times of the current British Queen. It did its job of distracting Simona from the issue she was determined to remedy. The issue of the American President could wait another day or two.

***

Simona woke the next day filled with determination, somehow in her dreams she had come up with a plan. She decided no one else should bear the burden of the spell if she was not willing to do so herself. It had to be her. As Simona considered the situation, it seemed obvious a mild-mannered witch who never hurt anyone would defuse the curse. Having made the decision, her life regained the normal rails of its existence. The week passed quickly and, due to the protective field or perhaps her decision, Simona wasn't unduly concerned by outside influences.

Packing up the herb packets for Leopold into her walking bag, she set off once more for his shop. Once she exited the lines of her property, the irrational thoughts poked at her insistently again. The amulet she made as protection for short trips worked, but its power was less than needed for full immunity. Simona gritted her teeth and walked faster. An hour later she entered the store once more and relaxed in the field Leopold had installed. As before, he was occupied with a customer so she made herself a cup of tea as she waited.

"So, sister, do you have my herbs?" Leopold asked with a smile.

"I do, they are right here," Simona said as she pulled the small package out of the bag and handed it to him.

"Thank you! I needed these sooner than I thought. I want to compensate you and won't take no for an answer." Leopold handed Simona a small envelope holding some cash which she tucked into her pocket

"Good news on another front, I've done the analysis and have a formulation which should work for the task. Here, let's spread it out on the table," the coven master opened a new scroll with the full set of instructions. "As you can see, the shift isn't all that hard, the hard part is that it must be done with the subject within line-of-sight. Have you decided where the curse will be transferred?"

"It's a very difficult decision, Coven Master. Every possibility had issues and I eventually realized the fix might require some personal sacrifice on my part. In the end, I think I should take the curse into myself. I've assumed the fact I am relatively innocuous would help mitigate the worst effects, plus I'm able to work secondary spells to keep it contained."

"Dangerous, Simona. What if the transfer pulls more out of you than anticipated? The President will get something from you in exchange, I doubt you'll be able to choose what goes to him. I'd be very cautious there, what if he gains your powers?"

"I've considered it, and I think it must be done regardless. If he gains my powers, at least he won't know how to properly use them; and he is old enough so there isn't a lifetime left for him to learn. No, I have to do this; he is a threat to our way of life if nothing is done," Simona soberly stated.

"I see your resolve, sister. While I cannot officially endorse what you're about to attempt, I shall pray for its success and your personal safety. Do you have any questions on the formulation?"

"No, the scroll is very logical and straightforward. I'll try to find small ways to minimize the risk, but I think the biggest issue will be finding a way to get within eye distance. The Secret Service will keep me at a distance if they get any indication of ill intent."

"I can help you there, sister. Here's $500; send a donation to his campaign website and ask where or when you can hear him speak. No campaign in the world would ignore the request! I'm concerned enough to support your effort but it has to be our secret! You know the politics of our world," Leopold handed over another small envelope and pressed it into Simona's hands. "If something goes wrong with your workings, depend on me to help set it right. Good luck!"

Her heart warmed from Leopold's support, Simona clasped the envelope to her chest along with the scroll and hurried home to begin the work.

As Leopold predicted, the campaign manager personally responded to Simona's donation submittal and provided a ticket for an upcoming presidential rally, to be held less than

100 miles from her home. Simona gathered all of the ingredients and brewed the potion which would be activated upon recitation of the necessary mystic phrases. The good news was she didn't have to be very close to the President or even make eye contact with the dolt, she merely had to ingest the potion and watch him while conjuring. Simple enough. The potion could be ingested before the rally as it was effective for several hours.

In the days prior to the event, Simona acquired some conservative clothing to cover her power tattoos and charms. Nothing must detract from the fiction that her intentions were those of a true supporter of the President. She even purchased campaign buttons and a hat proclaiming her allegiance to the man.

Riding a bus to the campaign rally, Simona noticed the marked stares of those in opposition. Looks of pure hatred and muttered comments about her intelligence were luckily the overt extent of their behavior, probably due to the approximately equal presence of those who vociferously supported the President. *I'm lucky they haven't gone for each other's throats; I'd get caught up in the melee in this outfit,* Simona thought to herself as she averted eyes from both camps.

At the entrance to the hall holding the rally, Simona got in line for the security screening, but first she drank the potion from its small vial and disposed of the glass container. Oddly pleased she had added some sprigs of mint into the elixir, she waited for her turn. A deadly serious Secret Service agent asked for her ticket and ID, which Simona handed over promptly. No one is ever comfortable when going through a security screen, so she didn't worry much about being stiff.

"You've come a long way to see the President," the agent said.

"He wasn't planning to come any closer, so I made a day of it. It isn't that far really, but now I'll have a story to tell my kids," she said thinking of Orson and Tango.

Simona's name didn't set off any flags and she didn't have anything which would pose a security concern, so the agent waved her through, "Enjoy yourself, ma'am."

"Thank you, I will!" Simona managed to respond as she gathered her, now disorganized, bag to her chest and searched for the assigned seating section printed upon her ticket. As expected, it was in a remote section. *Five hundred dollars doesn't go as far as it used to,* she chortled, but it would be sufficient for a clear view of the stage. Above the stage was a gigantic screen which would probably be used to project video of the man himself for those like herself in the very back. *I'll have to be careful to ignore that,* she thought, *the spell wants line of sight to the actual person.*

The venue filled up quickly, and the atmosphere was much like a pep rally in high school. Soon Simona had people on either side of her. The man to her left wore work clothes and the same hat as her. The raucous and sweaty fat woman to her right kept telling everyone around her how the President had changed her life for the better. Simona wondered what her life must have been previously if this was an improvement, but kept it to herself. She was a little bit wary of the man, as he exuded an air of silent menace, although he hadn't done anything to justify the concern.

The rally started with about thirty minutes of local politicians patting themselves on the back for bringing the President to their fair community. The crowd was in a mood to applaud, so they jumped on their cues as directed.

The auditorium felt more like a sporting event than anything else. For an introvert like Simona it was all she could do to stay in place and follow everyone else.

The fat woman shouted out the President's campaign slogan, inspiring the crowd around them to chant it over and over in unison. The chant was picked up and spread throughout the large room, along with synchronized stomping of feet. The floor rumbled under the assault, and Simona felt as though she would faint.

The local party leader got the message and started the windup to announce the President. The noise level rose higher and higher, as the crowd felt their power, reveling in the anticipation. The lights dropped, and a single spotlight lit the President as he strode towards the podium waving to his true believers. Simona thought the sound level couldn't increase, but soon found it could. The President was wearing an expensive suit with a strangely long tie covering what must be a very large stomach. He also wore the same hat which was sitting on Simona's head. The fat woman leapt to her feet, screaming her love for the President at the top of her lungs, which were considerable. The silent man was now energized as well, shouting along with the crowd and making arm movements looking something like a salute. The video screen showed a close-up of the great man himself, his hair flying in the breeze provided by the venue air conditioning. He had flung his cap into the crowd, like Elvis, and a fight for the precious relic ensued in the VIP section.

Simona could see the President from where she stood and started the invocation as she stared at the tiny figure on the stage. The overall noise level drowned out the words as soon as they were uttered and if anyone were to be watching Simona it would appear she was another true believer caught up in the rapture of the moment. As the final words were spoken, Simona felt a weight settle in somewhere high in her shoulders, *Nerves, I'm fine. Just fit in until I can get out of this mess.*

Strangely, the crowd began to subside, and the President began to speak. Like many of his speeches, it was calculated to fire up the crowd and included many pauses for applause. Simona knew the spell had worked because the crowd response was desultory at best, with only smattering of applause and none of the whooping and hollering which had greeted his appearance. She sat down and told herself to clap when appropriate.

The President began to notice a difference too, getting more and more animated as he strove to whip up what was previously his crowd. None of it worked, the applause was expected and it was there, but nothing like before. As he closed out his speech, a service dog broke free of his client and rushed the stage towards the President. Clearly wanting to play, the Labrador Retriever rolled over, play-bowed and danced away from the Secret Service agents as they tried to capture it. Finally the President waved them off and approached the dog himself. Immediately the dog rolled over looking up at the President with adoration in its brown eyes. Knowing when he was upstaged, the President bent down and petted the misbehaving pup as it wagged its tail nonstop. The owner was brought up to reclaim his dog, who clearly wanted to stay with the President, but the entire episode brought the most applause from the now-jaded audience. In what was meant to be a big finish, the President waved his arms, shouted his slogans, and ended by running for the stage exit. The dog broke loose once more and ran after him, generating more laughter than cheers or applause.

by Dan M. Kalin

"Quit hogging the armrest, Bitch!" Sweaty fat woman said viciously to Simona.

Simona started and moving her arm apologized, "I'm sorry, I didn't mean to crowd you."

"Your type never *means* anything, do you? Just think you're better than the rest of us," sweaty fat woman spat out and punctuated her words with a hard push on Simona's shoulder.

"Leave her alone, you fat cunt!" the silent man broke silence viciously, stepping in front of Simona's seat to address the fat woman's provocation. The fat woman sized up her opposition, including the right fist the man held ready for use, and decided to exit noisily to the right.

"I'm sorry about that, ma'am, but you can't reason with people like her. My name's Gary, and I'll see you safely out of here if you'll allow me to help."

"Thank you, Gary. I must say her reaction came as a shock, it never happens to me. If you can just get me outside, I think I can walk back to the bus station."

As Gary took her arm above the elbow and navigated the crowds, she learned Gary was a HVAC technician and greatly disappointed in the President's speech.

"Don't get me wrong, ma'am, I still support his politics for the most part, but when you see him in person I don't know what all the fuss is about. He's just another lying politician. I thought he was more than that, but glad I came if only to help you."

Simona carefully edited what she told Gary, sticking to generalities on where she lived as well as what her political views actually were. Before long, they were outside the bus station and it was time to part. Gary shyly offered up his business card, swearing he would drive the extra miles without charge if she needed any air conditioning work. Nonplussed, Simona thanked Gary and boarded the bus. Watching out the window she saw Gary standing and waving as the bus left.

On the drive home, Simona came to know Gary and the fat woman were under the influence of the curse which she had claimed. The point was driven home by the evenly split welcoming versus dirty looks from the other bus riders. The good news was Simona was not a proper home for the full power of the curse, engendering fans and detractors who mostly maintained their distance. *Ah well, there was almost certainly going to be a price. My solitary lifestyle can adjust to this situation and I can go mostly go on as before. No more large groups, but I'm fine with that,* Simona thought to herself.

As she walked up the hill to her home, she looked for her friends, but they were nowhere in evidence. Simona unlocked and entered the front door, "Boys, I'm home from the wars. It's time for dinner!"

Normally, Tango and Orson would scramble into the room all over each other, but today there was no scramble of furry paws. She walked into the kitchen, the only evidence of her two friends were empty bowls and a swinging pet door.

Odd! Simona walked outside to her garden, *maybe they are out playing with the squirrels?* Simona called for them, but no response came back. She heard a scrabble on her oak tree and she saw the squirrels sitting on a branch watching her.

"Hello, my friends. Have you two seen Orson and Tango?" Simona asked as she approached the tree. The squirrels watched her closely, retreating higher up the tree as she approached them. "What is wrong with you two?" They didn't answer, and definitely didn't want to get any closer.

At the edge of the garden, there was a bloody rat tail left in the dirt along with a trail of blood headed for the brush at the edge of the clearing. Simona picked up the tail, it looked familiar, and followed the trail. There in the brush, Tango sat eating a large rat which had to have once been Orson.

"Tango, what have you done?" Simona scolded. Clearly, Orson had put up a fight as one of Tango's ears was cut up and tattered.

Tango directed a look of pure, feline hate at Simona, hissed, then retreated further into the brush with his dinner.

Shocked, Simona collapsed onto the recently-tilled soil and cried as if her heart had broken.

***

The President leaned back in his executive office chair, then addressed the Chief of Staff and Press Secretary, both standing sheepishly in front of the Resolute Desk. "What the hell happened out there, Simon? We were going great guns and the whole thing just dried up. Shoot, I even saw empty seats in the last four stops. That shit only happens to Democrats!"

"I don't have an explanation, Mr. President," Chief of Staff Simon said. "Edgar here says the polling took a dive after the service dog incident. Nothing is trending even close to what we saw previously."

"That's right, sir! The tweets aren't being read or complained about and you're losing followers in huge numbers. Right now you're neck-and-neck with the Prime Minister of India, which represents a 30% drop," Edgar read from his notes.

"Edgar, you need to check your attitude at the door. If you can't be loyal, you won't see the six month mark on-the-job. I need can-do people, not excuses," the President chewed.

"With all due respect, Mr. President, this feedback is purely data-driven and loyalty has nothing to do with it. For some reason, people aren't reacting positively or negatively to your activities. No reaction means a loss of trending."

"Look, you useless piece of shit, great data; what the fuck do we do about it?"

"This useless piece of shit resigns, effective immediately. I'll show myself out," Edgar turned and exited the door closest to the President's assistant.

"No one quits on me, you're fired! Not only that, I'm announcing it right now on Twitter, citing lack of competence," the President shouted at Edgar's back.

"Sir, please don't send that, it will only give the press a reason to give Edgar coverage for his side of the story."

"Too late, bitches. I get things done, I don't sit around making excuses. Maybe we'll regain some momentum on the back of it."

Simon sighed and stood ready for the President's next edict.

"What about that other matter? Have the White House exterminators dealt with the rat issue? I had one run over my foot at breakfast, the room was full of them."

"The exterminators have traps out and expect to regain control of the situation very soon. They mentioned it was very strange for the rats to follow wherever you go, it is almost as though they love you."

"I don't love them, spent my whole life in the city and never had a need for any pets. Now it seems every damn cat or dog I see wants to crawl onto my lap. They haven't attacked me yet, but I think it is a security risk. Make sure the Secret Service knows I want an animal-free zone centered on me at all times," the President directed.

"On that, the Head of Detail asked if you would look out the window to see what they are dealing with."

The President of the United States looked out his window onto the lawn. "Goddamnit Simon, it looks like more than a thousand squirrels are out there, all looking at me."

"More than five thousand, according to the Secret Service. As quickly as they are removed, more come in. There are even more birds sitting in the surrounding trees and bushes, it is beginning to be a problem for the landscaping crews."

"Fuck this! Light up the helicopter, I'll head down to Florida to play some golf."

***

The next few days of news coverage were quite unusual: a sitting President being chased off a golf course by resident gators, entire flocks of birds sitting on top of the Presidential golf cart, and many incidents of dogs slipping their leads just to be closer to their Commander-in-Chief.

SUPERLATIVE
by Robert Morgan Fisher

She loved words. A writer. Words weren't just her stock and trade, they were her very reason for living. Like a jeweler with gems, painter with colors, junkie with pills, so was she with words. Or take any other analogy one might care to create, because apt analogies are merely precise word clusters and therefore as invaluable as any bejeweled crown, perfect shading or illicit stash.

For years, a certain word had come to mercilessly gall her.

The word initially lodged itself in the soft tissue of her brain like an oyster's grain of sand. But instead of accreting into a pearl, this particular qualificative had metastasized into a vicious tumor. One she could no longer ignore. It grated, so to speak, on her nerves. Tarnished and contaminated anything with which it came into contact.

To remedy this singular logophobia, she chose the radical surgery option. She needed to cut losses, cosmetics be damned. Henceforth, each time she reached for an adjective to denote the transcendent, the optimal, the most magnificent, whenever she wished to express ultimate approval—whether as a single-word utterance or to simply modify a noun—she would, at all costs, eschew... the G-word.

She performed a search & replace in every unpublished manuscript...

Burned T-shirts, any stupid hats celebrating the adjectival affront...

Forbade her children and students to use it...

She wasn't messing around here.

You wouldn't think it'd be that hard. Yet so ingrained was the G-word that at first, she had trouble sticking to the plan. Her saving grace, however, manifested itself in an alternative adjective:

Grand.

Easy to recover from a verbal misstep with:

Grrrr...and!

She flavored her Grand with a slight Irish inflection, a comic brogue. It wasn't hard; felt familiar and correct. In time, it confidently and completely replaced the G-word in her vocabulary. She'd blurt without hesitation:

Grand!

Additionally, she invested her vocabulary with a plethora of alternate pluperfections. She dug deep. There were, it turned out, so many interesting ace adjectives readily available in search engines and thesauri:

Tremendous!

Colossal!

Superior!

She also effectively employed understatement:

Superb...!

Excellent...!

Splendid...!

(This last little quiet throttle on hyperbole did not go unappreciated by those weary of the New Nationalistic Grandiosity from which G-word worship had arisen.)

SUPERLATIVE

A newfound sense of originality returned not only to her writing but also to every conversation and interaction. She grew more verbally... tolerant. To be sure, she still involuntarily cringed or flinched upon reading or hearing the G-word, but was less inclined to indulge in any absurd, futile, mental substitutions:

The *Grand* Lakes
The *Big* Depression
Alexander the *Gnarly*...

***

As it so happened, she sold a novel. Finally. The publisher was very excited, asked to see what else she had in the hopper and turned the acquisition into a multi-book deal.

In reviewing manuscript notes, the writer saw where the editor had made an innocuous suggestion that, instead of saying *his grandfather's father*, she use the conventional, more concise G-word descriptor.

The writer flat-out refused.

It became a point of contention and almost blew the entire deal. After a prolonged, mystifying back and forth, the editor caved.

A week later the editor called.

He said, I got to thinking... and I did a search of your other manuscripts. And you know what?

The writer knew what was coming.

Not once do you use the word—

I know.

Why?

Because it's overused, unearned, banal and lazy.

Then—
You know why.
The editor teasingly accused her of being OCD.
Perhaps.
Then the editor jokingly called her a grammar Nazi. This was inaccurate, of course, but it pushed a button.
Okay, since you went there, did you know that… in the years following World War II not a *single* newborn male child in Germany was named Adolf?
The editor chuckled and muttered, You're crazy.
Perhaps.
The editor chortled a small chuff of bemused acceptance then said: Whatever.
Okay, so… we good?
A considerable pause. At last the editor spoke:
Yeah, we're good. In fact, this might be something we can use.
How's that?
Well, it's a marketable quirk. Something you'll be *known* for. A stylistic conceit. Like Perec—you know he wrote an entire novel without using the letter E?
I'd rather people discovered it on their own.
No, trust me. This is a thing. It'll sell books.
Hmmm.
Well, that's what you want, isn't it—to sell books? You do want to be rich, right?
What a stupid question, thought the writer. Nothing to do with the issue at hand. Words were the only thing, ultimately, that held any value for her. From an early age, she'd filled spiral notebooks with words that pleased her. She still read those notebooks, coveting certain words, dreaming of a story she might decorate with language she

loved. Sometimes she'd repeat a word in stormy sleep over and over, tossed on waves of dreams until morning, when the word would dive back into her subconscious like a played-out seal.

But don't you think announcing it will make me look insane? You don't think that's... trying too hard?

Well, you're a writer. You *are* insane, the editor laughed. But it's fine.

You think?

Oh yes. It's *more* than fine... said the editor with an almost audible smile.

The writer held her breath, body tensing. *No No No No No—*

As a matter of fact, he said, it's *great*.

A GREAT GOAT

by Peter Ntephe

The meeting of the Alpha Tau Omega Fraternity of the University on the Niger was called to order.

"Great men!"

"Great, great, great!" resonated around the hall.

You had to be a great man to have qualified for admission into the fraternity and you were certified great by having been so admitted.

"I greet you all, great men," continued the Grand Liege.

Another round of "great" was loosed upon the hall.

"We are gathered here, at short notice, to discuss a matter of paramount moment."

The black-clad men with white ties all nodded sagely in acknowledgement, shoulders squared in what they considered appropriate poise for the dignified in mind and body.

"That matter, as you all know, concerns the goat which should have been the centerpiece of our yearly banquet."

"Yes, great, unh-hunh."

"Despite our having found and contracted *aboki* of appropriate skill as would handle the requisite barbeque and despite there being only a few hours to the banquet, there is still no goat."

"Where is our goat? *Kedu* our goat?" The cry came from the back of the hall.

"Precisely," said the Grand Liege, looking in the direction of the query, "where is our goat?"

"Yes, where is it?"

The Grand Liege furrowed his brow.

"Did we not at the last gathering delegate to the Grand Scriptor the task of procuring the said goat for us?'

"Yes, we did, Great. We did."

More furrowing of the brow.

"And did we not, in the presence of all great men gathered then, present to the Grand Scriptor in cash, the sum budgeted for the said procurement?"

"Yes, we did. We did o."

"May I therefore crave your indulgence, great men, to call on the Grand Scriptor to explain to us why there is yet no goat tethered to a grazing post for us to behold in advance of the arrival shortly of *aboki* with sharp knives to commence the process of barbequing."

Alozie Okezie, the Grand Scriptor, stood up and adjusted his tie. He was tall and fair, looking every inch an *aje butter*, a child of privilege, despite a vastly different reality. It was not the polish of a pampered upbringing that manifested in such fulsome looks. Rather, fate, as quirky as ever, had decided randomly to compensate the pecuniary sleight of hand by conferring a most striking visage.

The senior Mr. Okezie, reputed to have been even more handsome in his youth than Alozie, was a court janitor. His regular interactions with affluent lawyers made him determined that his offspring would acquire the best education and transform the lineage from have-nots to have-a-lots. He drove his two children to study hard from

A GREAT GOAT

an early age, an endeavor which had so far been rewarded with the best of intended outcomes.

On the strength of exceptional grades, Alozie had gone to King's College, that most elite of boarding schools, on a scholarship. With As in all his SSE subjects, Alozie easily repeated the scholarship feat for university. Relatively straitened circumstances at home thus negatived for most part, Alozie was duly admitted on account of his looks and renowned intelligence into the Alpha Tau Omega Fraternity where he had become, no less, the Grand Scriptor for the year.

"Great men," the handsome Scriptor began.

"Great, great, great," came the reply, although there was also muttering, from the back, of "where is our goat?" If Alozie heard the muted protestations, he did not show it. Instead, he spoke up confidently.

"A great man went to a great market in search of a great goat."

It was an opening worthy of the best Grand Scriptors and the hall responded accordingly.

"Say it, great! Say it!"

Alozie smiled expansively.

"Upon getting to the great market, your Grand Scriptor made his way to what he perceived to be a great merchant in great goats. This merchant was clearly of Patrician bearing, despite his being attired in humble clothes suitable for the daily rigors of his trade."

The assemblage was loving the narration and responded cheerily once more. Alozie cast his gaze around the room, smiled again and continued.

"Great men must understand that getting to this point was no easy task for a great man – your Grand Scriptor had to overlook the aggressive jostling, noxious odors and general uncouthness of the hoi polloi whose habit it is to throng such markets across the land."

This time, there was not only vocal approval but applause. The Grand Scriptor was in full flow.

"In any event, after haggling with the said goat merchant, in a manner most auspicious and befitting of men of unimpeachable countenance, a fair bargain was struck."

Applause. Pounding on tables. Shouts of "Great, speak that English *biko!* Fire on!"

"Thus did I hand over to this merchant the great money which great men had aggregated for purposes of an ennobled purchase. To consummate the transaction, the merchant in turn handed over, at the end of a sturdy length of Indian hemp rope, a he-goat of the most magnificent proportions, sporting a mane as immaculate as if it had been polished by the gods themselves."

"Great, you done win! See English."

Up to this point, the Grand Scriptor had been a picture of amiability but his face now turned serious and his tone took on an urgency.

"Thereupon Great men, I made my way out of that great arena of traders and trading, onto the main road which I intended to cross in other to join a befitting means of conveyance back to the distinguished company of great men in this great citadel of learning."

"Yes, Great?"

"As I waited patiently for the cars to pass, being of such dignified composure and upright bearing as only great men can muster amid a surrounding chaos, guess what happened, great men?"

"What happened? Motor hit you?"

A GREAT GOAT

Pregnant pause.

"Ah-ah, talk now, Grand Scriptor?"

Alozie affected an expression of distaste before proceeding.

"To my shock and amazement, great men, this goat, this outwardly magnificent specimen which I had assumed to be of Patrician stock and expected to comport itself accordingly, revealed itself without warning to be a most contemptible Plebian. It suddenly broke loose of the rope and bolted into the congregating hordes which, as I had earlier told you, save for me, were composed entirely of barbarians as far as the eye could see."

"So? What exactly are you saying, Great?"

Alozie's voice now rose.

"So, great men, I ask you, would any of you, in all good conscience, have deigned to descend into that abyss of the proletariat, abandoning all dignity and superior bearing to pursue this goat, now revealed to be a Plebian of the highest order, through the multitude of the unwashed and unlettered? Would any of you have taken that risk, to be identified as a Plebian rather than a great man? To drag the name of the Alpha Tau Omega Fraternity in the mud perhaps not only metaphorically but also literally given the perilous state of the walkways following the rains that morning? Would you?"

"No, Great! How can? Of course not. *Tufiakwa!*"

Alozie smiled grandly now, revealing a brilliant set of white teeth.

"Yes, of course not, great men. Your Grand Scriptor has sworn, like all of you, to uphold the five letters of the Alpha at all times, forswearing all distraction and resisting all temptation to the contrary, whatever they may be and wherever they may occur. It was therefore with a heavy heart at the loss of the goat but with immense pride at having lived up to the hallowed code of conduct of all great man who have gone before us and those who will come after, did I make my way back to campus to report the sad events which occurred as aforesaid."

There was an uncertain silence but the Grand Scriptor moved quickly to fill it with his denouement.

"In the circumstances, Great men, I inquire – did your Grand Scriptor not acquit himself as creditably as any of you would, given a similar turn of events? Did I not? I say unto you, did I not?

An outburst of approval greeted the rhetorical challenge.

"Yes of course, Great."

"You are truly a great man!

"Great, great, great!"

"Great, if it is only for this English *sef*, you done win!"

"Na you biko, Grand Scriptor!"

There were a few dissentient protestations of "*Bia nwokem*, you this man, where is our goat or where is our money?" But they were swept aside as most of the great men rushed forward to pump the Grand Scriptor's hands and pat him vigorously on the back.

And that was how it came to be that the twentieth annual banquet of the Alpha Tau Omega Fraternity was conducted bereft of the traditional barbeque but otherwise in good cheer and dignified gaiety befitting of all great men past and present, and those who were yet to come.

AN OFFICE PARTY

by Nicole M. Pyles

Inside the damp dark office,
The workers wanted the party over with,
But their leaders gathering in the front
With their foolish, fiendish grins,
Hadn't even begun to celebrate.

Eyes burned from computer screens,
Crumpled clothing on their tired skin,
Slouched with exhaustion,
And high gray walls pressing in,
They had forgotten anything else existed outside.

One of the leaders snapped his fingers
"SMILE!" he jeered at the crowd.
Half smiles and tired grins appeared
On their solemn, broken faces.
No one dared challenge the leaders in charge.

That's when the leaders buzzed with excitement,
Their party was about to begin.
One of them hissed at the workers to sing.
No joy was heard among the workers,
Who sang happy birthday.

by Nicole M. Pyles

The leaders with their wide grins and sharp teeth,
Clapped with delight as one of them,
A fat and spoiled leader
Waddled to the front of the room,
Laughing gleefully in surprise.

Oh you shouldn't have, the leader called out,
As the birthday song concluded,
But one very tired soul
In the back of the crowded room.
Muttered under her breath, *we didn't.*

TEAM BUILDING AND OTHER HORRORS

by Jill Hand

Our world changed overnight. On Tuesday, after we put the paper to bed, we threw a retirement party for Vince McClung at the Tugboat Inn. The following morning, upon entering the newsroom, I found it so dramatically altered from what it had been the day before that I stopped dead in my tracks, astonished.

Vince was a crusty old-school newspaperman. He'd been in the business since Lyndon Johnson was president, starting out as a cub reporter and working his way up to managing editor. A heart of gold lay beneath his snarling veneer. Everyone who worked at the Post-Observer loved him, from the news editor on down to the truck drivers, the janitors, and the compositors. The compositors had their own union and they usually detested management on general principle, but every one of those tough, cheerfully profane men would have given their lives for Vince without hesitation, if the need ever arose.

As was customary, Vince's sendoff was awash in alcohol, as well as reminisces about natural disasters resulting in death and dismemberment and massive destruction of property as well as political scandals and lurid murders going back forty years or more, all of which are topics dear to a reporter's heart.

I'd had too much to drink the night before. As a result my head felt like it was about to split in two, sending my poor, quivering brain tumbling onto the floor, splat! I'd hoped for a languid day of making a few phone calls and putting the finishing touches on a feature story for Sunday's paper about a woman who bred prize-winning Afghan hounds.

Too bright! That was my first thought as I stepped through the door of the newsroom and recoiled like a vampire confronted by sunlight. The flickering, buzzing fluorescent tubes in the smoke-stained ceiling panels had been replaced with coldly efficient lighting which shed a merciless illumination, like that of an operating room or a police interrogation chamber. The yellowed ceiling panels themselves had been replaced with brilliantly white ones. The newsroom no longer smelled cozily of Vince's cigars and news editor Hugh Curran's cherry pipe tobacco and Darlene the receptionist's hairspray. It smelled like cleaning chemicals and efficiency and high expectations. It smelled like professionalism. I didn't like it.

The partitions which used to separate the workspaces had been removed, leaving the entire room exposed to view. There was now no privacy, no way we could put our heads down on our desks and take a nap without being seen. Gone were the battered metal desks. Gone, too, were the rolling chairs upholstered in green vinyl, patched here and there with silver duct tape.

The desks had been replaced with ones made of what appeared to be white particleboard, giving the room the appearance of an ice floe, and what the hell? Was this some kind of a joke?

"I see you noticed the ergonomic seating spheres. They encourage good posture. I'm Jackie. Welcome! And you are?"

The person addressing me was a woman who looked to be in her early thirties. That made her a few years older than me. She had a trendy haircut and wore about a dozen silver bangle bracelets.

"What the hell's going on? What happened to the old furniture? Who are you?" I said.

She smiled poisonously.

"I am Jacqueline Campanile, the new managing editor," she said sweetly. "As for the old furniture, it's been taken to the dump."

"Jesus Christ," I said. "My desk went to the dump? It had all my stuff in it. My Rolodex, my files, my notebooks, all my stuff."

She raised her eyebrows. "Profanity is not tolerated at the Post-Observer. It's in the rulebook. Your rulebook is in your new desk. Your Rolodex and your other things are in your new desk."

She held up a clipboard. "Tell me your name and I'll consult the seating plan. That way you can find where you'll be sitting from now on and acquaint yourself with the rulebook."

Her chilly gaze swept me from head to toe, zeroing in on my Doc Martens. "The company dress code is on page five. Pay particular attention to what it says about footwear."

I knew then that Jackie and I weren't going to be best buddies.

by Jill Hand

There were similar cries of dismay when the other reporters began to trickle in. Some of them, the ones who quickly figured out which side their bread was buttered on, changed their cries of dismay to cries of admiration, congratulating Jackie for making our workplace so much cleaner and nicer.

She beamed, enjoying being showered with praise. Clearly, she was a different sort of manager than Vince McClung, who would have called anyone who sucked up to him in a blatant attempt to curry favor something so blisteringly obscene that the offending party would have slunk away in shame. Sadly, Vince was no longer in charge. He'd moved to Boca Raton, Florida, where he'd told us he planned to do nothing all day but fish and play cards and smoke cigars. Jackie was in charge now. It was a whole new ballgame.

"We'll have a meeting in the conference room at 11 a.m. There'll be one every day, at eleven sharp. Please be prompt. Everyone must attend unless they have a valid excuse," Jackie announced, as we went around, discovering where our desks were located. My fellow reporters had the dazed, incredulous expressions of people who'd been in a bad car accident. Some were better at hiding their feelings than others. Marion Delaney, for instance, had a big grin pasted on her face. She kept saying, "Wow!" and "How cool!" and "I love how open everything is now."

Steve Horowitz sidled up to me where I was trying out the posture ball at my new desk. He leaned down and murmured, "Marion's going to be Jackie's Igor."

"What?" I said. I was trying to sit up straight, but the ball kept rolling out from under me.

"Her Igor, like the hunchback who was Dr. Frankenstein's assistant. Wait and see. Marion's totally going to brown-nose her, hoping for a promotion. You watch."

Steve was correct. Marion and a small contingent of others hung on Jackie's every word, lavishing her with praise. Most of her ideas were so ridiculous that it was obvious to even the copyboys and the stringers. For example, she announced that our focus from now on would shift from hard news to what she called "happy news." That consisted of puff pieces about local businesses, and stories about people who'd grown exceptionally large vegetables, and about senior citizens who'd had books of sentimental poetry published by vanity presses.

I had to write a story about the latter. One poem in particular haunts me to this day. It was by an ancient lady named Rosetta Dibble and was titled, simply, "Kittens."

Jackie, like many managers in the early nineteen-nineties, when these events took place, was enthralled by Japanese business practices. A few years before, Japan's economy was booming. Tokyo real estate had the highest property value of any city in the world. The bubble had gone up and businesspeople in other countries were scrambling to figure out how the Japanese did it, so they could do it, too.

By the time Jackie entered our lives Japan's economy had begun to falter, but Jackie didn't know that; nobody knew, except for certain economists. That's why, at one of her eleven o'clock meetings, Jackie presented us with our very own Japanese: Hideo Watanabe. He was, she told us, a motivational speaker and efficiency expert who'd come all the way from Osaka. We would have him with us for a week. He would observe us at our work and make suggestions on how we could improve.

by Jill Hand

Sandy Moscatto was sitting next to me in the back of conference room. She began to sing "Japanese," by the Vapors. "I Think I'm Turning Japanese," she sang, softly.

"Shut up," I hissed.

I was glum because we'd been forced to wear the new company uniform of chino trousers and navy-blue blazers with Post-Observer written across the breast pocket in bright yellow thread. Blue and yellow were the paper's new colors. They were on everything from the masthead to our coffee cups to our business cards. We even had a company song, which Jackie made us sing at the beginning of every newsroom meeting. It was called, horribly, "We're Your Friends." It went, "We're Your Friends, at the Post-Observer! We keep you informed by telling you what you need to know. From Pawling's Corner to Lohasset, we bring the news to you! With a smile! Yes, we bring the news to you every day! We bring the news to yooooou!"

Lohasset and Pawling's Corner were towns on our circulation area's northern and southern borders, respectively.

Charlie O'Keefe, who wrote a column about state and local politics, was sitting on my other side. He pushed his bifocals up on his nose and leaned forward, observing Hideo Watanabe with interest. "Hey," he called out. "I ran into guys like you on Saipan, back when I was in the Marines."

Oh no! I thought. He's going to mention the flamethrowers. Charlie, don't! For the love of God, please don't mention the flamethrowers.

No luck. Charlie launched into one of his gruesome war stories.

"Yep, I was with the fifty-two-eighties, the Fighting Bobcats, we were called. We had these flamethrowers, see, and since there's a lot of caves on those Jap islands, we blasted 'em with our flamethrowers, in case there were any Nips in there, which there often were," he said cheerfully. "You shoulda seen how they…"

"Thank you, Charlie," Jackie cut in. "Let's get to today's topic, shall we?"

Watanabe's forehead wrinkled as Charlie told his tale. He was an earnest young man with thick eyebrows and full lips. He was probably translating 'bobcats' into Japanese and puzzling over what Charlie meant by 'Nips.' Then his forehead smoothed out and he smiled. "Oh, yes. My father told me about these unfortunate incidents. Very unfortunate. All water under the bridge now, as you say, correct?"

Surprisingly, Charlie and Watanabe became boon companions, with Charlie introducing our visitor from Japan to the delights of Country Western music. There was a bar down the street from the office that we liked to frequent called The Last Roundup. The jukebox was loaded with songs by both Hank Williamses (Junior and Senior), as well as by Johnny Cash, Patsy Cline, and many more. Watanabe took to it like a duck to water. He asked me one time, "What are your thoughts regarding Waylon Jennings-san. Are you enjoying his music?"

"I am," I told him. "I am enjoying also the music of Willie Nelson-san, and that of Jerry Lee Lewis-san."

"All very fine musicians," he agreed.

After he left us Watanabe quit the motivational speaking/efficiency management business and opened a Country Western bar in Osaka. He used to send pictures of it to Charlie O'Keefe, who passed them around to the rest of us.

"Maybe I oughta take him up on his invitation and go visit him, over in Japan," Charlie said, ruminatively. "I bet it's changed a lot since I was there the last time, back in July of forty-four."

We told him we thought it probably had.

Bad as being forced to wear the company uniform and sing the company song was, there were worse things we had to do. Tai chi, for one. Every day before lunch we had to go outside on the crabgrass-choked front lawn and go through a series of movements that resembled slow-motion karate. Passing vehicles honked at us and drivers rolled down their windows to jeer.

"Tai chi is Chinese. I thought we were supposed to be Japanese. Ow! I've got a cramp," Darlene the receptionist complained, reaching down to massage her calf.

"Tai chi is good for you," Jackie told her. "Come on, everyone, graceful movements. Let your mind relax. Breathe! Let it flow! Ten more minutes and it's time for lunch. Today we're having mini quiches and pigs in a blanket!"

"Yummy! I love pigs in a blanket!" Marion Delaney enthused.

"You are a pig in a blanket," Steve Horowitz muttered, not loud enough for her to hear.

That was another thing: we had a catered lunch every day. No more going out for fast food or bringing a sandwich from home and eating it under a tree in the park. Our lunch hour was now spent trapped in the newsroom, where steam tables were set up, servers in white jackets standing behind them, dishing out food.

It was supposed to be a perk, but it didn't feel like one. Attendance was mandatory, unless we had a good excuse. We had to punch in and out on a timeclock now, like factory workers, every minute of our day accounted for.

And our days didn't end when we clocked out at night. Jackie expected us all to go out with her for dinner and drinks, one big, happy work family, the way the Japanese did. This went on for hours, night after night. It was exhausting, pretending to be having fun.

Weekends were no longer our own, to do whatever we liked. Now there were company trips to the beach, and to batting cages, and to amusement parks. One time, we went camping. We slept in tents, two to a tent. I had to share a tent with Marion Delaney, who snored.

It was like a summer camp from Hell. We toasted marshmallows and Jackie made us sing "Kumbaya, My Lord" and "We're Your Friends." We had a "rap session" around a fire pit, with the person whose turn it was to speak being handed something called a "talking stick," indicating that they held the floor. It was a Native American tradition, as I recall. Jackie was nothing if not eclectic.

The worst part of the camping trip was the team-building exercises. There was a trust walk, with a blindfolded person being guided through a trail in the woods by a partner who wasn't blindfolded. I was partners with Marion. I guided her through a patch of poison ivy. It wasn't deliberate; I was too tired from sleeping on the ground and listening to her snore all night to pay attention to where we were going.

Marion got back at me by "accidentally" failing to catch me during an exercise in which you're supposed to fall backwards into someone's arms.

"Oopsie! Sorry about that," she said as I landed flat on my back, the wind knocked out of me.

by Jill Hand

I think we would have all up and quit (with the exception of Marion and a few others) if Jackie's reign hadn't come to a sudden end in a spectacular way.

It was a boat race, a competition with other newspapers and magazines from around the state. The object was to build a watercraft from scratch and pilot it into Hatapechee Inlet, around a series of buoys and channel markers and back to the starting point.

Jackie had us all working feverishly on the Post-Observer's entry, the Nellie Bly. It was a sailboat, fashioned out of wood from a kit, using a diagram from a magazine called Boat Hobbyist.

"Are you sure this is right?" I asked Steve Horowitz. We had the Nellie Bly up on sawhorses in the newspaper's garage and were busily sanding the sides. "It seems kind of wobbly."

"It'll probably be fine, once it gets in the water," he assured me.

Jackie insisted on sailing the Nellie Bly herself, with no one permitted to help her crew. This was her moment in the spotlight and she was going for it, ferociously. She wore a captain's hat on the big day, like the Skipper on "Gilligan's Island." A reporter from a local affiliate of a major TV news station interviewed her. She boasted about how she had captained the Post-Observer into a new era, one in which the paper was experiencing an unprecedented rise in circulation.

A portion of that footage was replayed later, when the Coast Guard was searching for her, after the Nellie Bly had been swept out to sea. Neither Jackie nor the Nellie Bly was ever found. The last we saw of them, we stood on the dock at the marina, cheering, watching as the little boat with the blue and yellow sail rounded the final buoy. That's when it was caught in a riptide and speedily whisked out into the Atlantic.

It turned out that the rise in circulation that Jackie had bragged about had been slight. Certainly no one would call it "unprecedented," the way she had.

The publisher was an octogenarian who spent most of his time golfing. He took little interest in the day-to-day operations of the Post-Observer and was horrified to discover that the paper was mired in debt. The round-trip airfare and week's lodging for Hideo Watanabe had cost a mint in itself, let alone all those catered lunches and after-work drinking and dining get-togethers and the field trips for fifty people.

The publisher almost had a stroke when he saw the bill. The upshot was that he sold the paper to our competition, the Daily Intelligencer, making our new name the Post-Observer-Intelligencer. We no longer had to wear blue blazers or do tai chi or punch a time clock or sing "We're Your Friends." We went back to our old, comfortable way of doing things.

Sometimes, when I run into one of my former coworkers from those days, we reminisce about our brief time under Jackie's leadership.

"That was really something," one of us will say.

"It sure was," the other will respond.

THE ELVES' REBELLION
by N.E. Griffin

It is one hundred eighteen days till Christmas when Tweenee proposes the idea. "What if we just stopped working until they meet our demands?" The idea feels dangerous, and a contagious shiver runs among the elves.

"Could we?"

"Should we?"

"What would happen if we did?"

"Dasher would never allow it," Footoo whispers. "Remember what happened to the last Seetoo?" (The new Seetoo shifts uncomfortably. It's awkward for the new ones when we talk about the disappeared ones. I will have to talk to Footoo about his poor manners.)

"But she made the mistake of stopping work alone," Tweenee says, her eyes gleaming like a glacier in spring. "If we all did it, the reindeer would have to listen. They must have toys to deliver on Christmas Eve. What choice would they have?"

I keep my head down, tapping my chisel against a block of wood that will eventually be the head of a doll. *Tap, tap, tap*, that nose is coming along quite nicely, isn't it? Yes, indeed.

Around me, the other elves whisper.

"What should our demands be?" Tweenee asks.

by N.E. Griffin

"Better food!"

"12-hour workdays!"

"Weekends!"

"Holidays! I hear there's this thing called 'Labor Day' coming up."

Their dreams make me queasy. They think Dasher is the problem, but I know like none of them do that Dasher is just following orders. The real obstacle is the Big Guy, and the Big Guy would never allow us to stop work, not even for a day. Fewer elf-hours of labor would mean fewer toys, and for him there will never be enough toys, because toys earn him the adulation of the children. So it is always, more toys, better toys! The best toys in the world! His ego is as insatiable as his temper is terrible.

Why do I know this? Because I am Eenie, the chosen First Elf. The one blessed to accompany the Big Guy on his annual flight. It is the greatest honor an elf can aspire to, and to the other elves it elevates me almost to the status of a reindeer.

But there is a burden that comes with being Eenie—or Number One, to the Big Guy and the reindeer. That burden is knowledge.

I don't remember much about my life before I was chosen to be one of the ninety-nine elves in the workshop. None of us do. I don't remember why I was granted the honor of being Number One. Probably I was just "ready"—by whatever standard the reindeer judge these things—when they found themselves in need of a new Number One.

I do remember the day I was chosen. The extra-fuzzy red hat the reindeer gave me, still damp with the sweat of the Number One who came before. The praise from the other elves, telling me what an honor it was to be chosen as Eenie, as if I didn't know. (How did I know? I don't remember. It's as if we pop forth from whatever womb bears us with such knowledge.) They all expected a full report next Christmas about the wonders I saw.

There's no denying, I do see wonders on that yearly voyage. We elves rarely leave the workshop, and when we do, we look out on a barren tundra. Only a few months of summer grey break up the interminable white of winter. But in a single Christmas Eve, I see all the world, or at least all the world that venerates the Big Guy in some form. The annual sleigh ride takes us across oceans and continents, over thick forests, swamps, grasslands, deserts, fjords, and mountains. I see it all under the luminescence of the moon, which gives the world a ghostly pallor.

But I also get to see up close the man who is our God. The way he gorges himself that night, literally and spiritually, on the altars the people build to him. The massive lawn ornaments bearing his form. The intricately embroidered stockings hanging by the fireplace, showing him with a jolly belly and rosy cheeks. The plates of cookies left out with adoring notes. (He eats every single one.) The twinkly lights and the candles and the ornaments and the wreathes—he relishes all of it. "Look, Number One," he says, "At that ten-foot-tall blow-up Me. They really love Me here." Invariably, the house with the most garish decorations gets the choicest presents.

But the way he takes obscene pleasure in the praises of those houses that worship him is less troubling than the vengeance he exacts on those that don't do so to his liking. It doesn't take much to earn his ire. Failure to leave a note, or perhaps an inadequate plate of cookies—Little Johnny doesn't get that train set. Too many decorations with that poseur, Frosty—Betsy's doll is not the kind that can walk and talk. Worst of all, a house that seems to think Christmas is about that other God, with his sad little manger attended only by herdsmen. For those people, he reserves his cruelest, most depraved punishment—a stocking full of coal. The horror!

I have little sympathy for the reindeer who lord over our days. But I must admit, as abysmally as they treat us elves, so he treats them on Christmas Eve. "On Dasher! On Dancer! Faster! Faster!" he yells, whips snapping mercilessly.

On my first Christmas Eve, I thought he was fearful of disappointing the children if he could not make it to all the houses in one night. But now I understand: the hours extend themselves indefinitely for him. It is days and weeks in normal time that we spend flying around the world, so no child ever needs to be left out due to poor weather. So when he bellows through a fog, "There are children down there exalting me, we must find a way!" it is his narcissistic need for their praise that propels him on. The rest of the year, he gorges himself on food to maintain his famously doughy physique. That one magically prolonged night, he gorges himself on their adoration, and after a full year he is desperate for it, so desperate that he would risk the lives of all of us, even his most loyal reindeer, to reach the next destination, to feast his soul on the next idol erected in his honor.

Tweenee pulls out a contraband pencil and an envelope clearly purloined from the cache of the Big Guy's letters. She starts jotting down the list of demands. I wonder how she learned to write and recall that she often volunteers for letter-opening duty in the evenings after dinner. She has been planning this for a long time.

THE ELVES' REBELLION

"I want a more comfortable bunk," Elie says. "The reindeer get to sleep on straw, why do we get just stiff boards?"

"Yeah, good one!" Seethee says. "And no more antlering for punishment. I got antlered last week just for dropping a box of nails!" He holds up his shirt to show us the bruises—unnecessarily, as it has happened to all of us at one time or another.

"And maybe…" Seevenies says, her lip trembling, "Maybe we can find out what happened to the ones who disappeared? Because maybe they're all right somewhere—retired!"

I look up from my doll and regard her with pity. Poor thing, she was inconsolable for days when the last Neenoo disappeared after badly botching the tracks for a model train. I open my mouth to say something, but Fietio beats me to it. "Oh honey, I don't think we ever want to know that. But—how about a comfortable retirement? Somewhere with sun!"

I particularly like that demand, and I know just the spot. There is a string of islands I fancy, with little red fishing cottages nestled between sparkling seas and towering stone mountains. It looks like just the kind of place that we elves might be at home. I often dream of the place, even during my waking hours, laboring away in the workshop.

But it is only a dream. All this talk is—a beautiful, mad dream.

Without thinking what I am doing, I climb atop our workbench and pinch my lips together in a shrill whistle. The other ninety-eight elves fall silent and look to me, their eyes wide with some misplaced form of reverence. For a moment, words fail me. In my tiny breast, longing surges. Longing to pump my fist in support of their rebellion, to lead the charge to the reindeers' barn with all our little tools, to batter them and wound them, to scatter their straw beds and set the barn aflame, and then to move on to the Big House, where our real enemy lives.

But that little burning ember extinguishes as quickly as it lit. When words come, it is as if they were once planted on my lips like seeds, now sprouting. "This is madness," I say. "The reindeer can always get more elves. If we rebel, we will disappear like the others, and not to a happy retirement."

I watch as my fellow elves deflate, physically shrinking now that I have dashed their hopes. Tweenee tightly clutches her pencil. I can see fury in her eyes, but she says nothing.

From this angle I can see a grey outcropping of rock through the window. Atop the rock stands Dasher, ears angled alertly forward, antlers majestic against a setting sun. My eyes meet his, and he gives the briefest nod of approval. Suddenly, I understand why I was chosen as Number One, and my belly churns with shame.

REVOLT OF THE TUBAS

by Mark Nutter

Tubby thought he had a pretty good life for a tuba.

He worked steadily, traveling from studio to studio to record funny tuba music that underscored images of fat people, hippos, and other awkward creatures.

One day, after recording twenty-six takes underscoring a fat woman waterskiing, and after the client said, "can't you make it a little funnier?" — something inside Tubby's tuba brain snapped.

Enough is enough, he declared. My ancestors were Prussian and German. I've been featured in works by Mussorgsky, Wagner, Mahler, Strauss. From this moment on I choose dignity over novelty.

He issued a final angry 'BLAT' at the client, stormed out of the studio, and changed his name from Tubby to Julius X.

He began writing pamphlets and leaving them in places where other tubas could see them, in tuba bars and tuba coffee shops, places where you weren't welcome if you weren't a tuba.

Tubas began meeting in secret, in small cells of two and three, at night in high school band rooms and empty concert halls.

The grassroots movement grew. Before long the rebellious tubas were legion.

Things came to a head at a midnight rally in the park, tubas massing by the hundreds, holding torches in their shiny bells.

"Brothers and sisters," said Julius X, "for too long we have been used for the amusement of others. It's time to reclaim our dignity. For ourselves, and for our children, the euphoniums."

"Hey! It's after hours! This is an illegal assembly!" shouted a voice from the fringes of the tuba mob. "You must disperse!"

An overweight cop named Dave approached the podium where Julius X stood. Spontaneously, the tubas began to accompany his splay-footed walk, appropriating the hated funny fat man music for their own, making it a defiant anthem.

"Cut it out," said Dave.

"You don't think it's funny?" said Julius X. "Not even when it's played by three hundred tubas?"

"No!" said Dave. "Now break it up before I haul you all in."

"We have the same right to assemble as any other instrument."

"I warned you," said Dave, drawing his sidearm and pointing it at Julius X.

A sympathetic sousaphone tipped forward, engulfing Dave's head in its enormous bell. The sousaphone stood upright, raising Dave's fat body into the air.

The crowd of tubas played the funny fat man music faster and faster as Dave kicked and struggled and smothered inside the sousaphone bell.

REVOLT OF THE TUBAS

Now that the tubas had tasted blood there was no turning back.

Word of the revolt reached the bassoons. These proud 17th century woodwinds, the darlings of Bach and Elgar, formally declared they would never again accompany Halloween cartoon skeletons.

The musical movement snowballed. Banjos distanced themselves from the hillbilly kid in Deliverance. Accordions demanded apologies from anyone who ever made an accordion joke. In New York City, hundreds of trombones protested being used as a visual gag and threw their slides into the East River. Jew's harps demanded to be called simply 'harps,' and classical harps, fearing for the safety of their families, acquiesced.

The growing movement spoke not only to musical instruments, but also to people who thought they were musical instruments, a rare medical condition.

Julius X, now the most feared instrument in the world, created his own secret police, the SSS (Schutzstaffel Sousaphones) to track down anyone who was now or had ever been amused by novelty instrumentals. Friends turned in their friends, children their parents, high school oboe players their bandleaders.

Offenders were marched down the street while loved ones played slide whistles and kazoos and uniformed sousaphones shouted, "not so funny when it's your own family, is it?"

Attendance at concerts became mandatory. Thousands were herded into stadiums to hear the Music of the New Enlightened Age. Orchestras of a hundred tubas played the classics: Claire de Lune, Prelude to the Afternoon of a Fawn. Giggling was punishable by death. Violins and cellos were reduced to cleaning the urinals.

by Mark Nutter

But Julius X's harsh measures began to have an economic impact. The market for funny videos vanished, because funny videos were not as funny without funny instruments playing funny music. Watching fat people walk without hearing a tuba became an empty experience, like Christmas in Los Angeles.

People stopped going to sports bars, because watching bloopers of outfielders colliding wasn't the same without a muted trombone going, "wah wah wah."

A dark mood descended on the country. Everyone was afraid that if they laughed at anything, anything at all, they could be accused of the thought crime of hearing tuba music in their heads.

Fortunately the gloomy mood would soon end.

At a rally on the National Mall in Washington, D.C., as Julius X gave a speech to his followers who, truth be told, were growing weary of his repetitive tuba rhetoric, a new sound was heard.

Julius X declaimed to the crowd, "never have we been more powerful…"

Tweet tweet.

He paused for a second, then continued, "the sound of degrading funny music has been silenced…"

Tweet tweet tweet tweet tweetily tweet.

"Who's doing that?!" Julius X demanded.

"I am," said Polly Piccolo.

She'd made her way to the front of the crowd, her tiny silver form dancing past the sousaphone goons.

"How dare you interrupt me?!" Julius X advanced on Polly, trying to look threatening, but with Polly playing 'tweetily tweetliy' with every step he took, he appeared ludicrous.

REVOLT OF THE TUBAS

There were scattered titters in the crowd.

"Who's laughing?" demanded Julius X.

A line of sousaphones took what they hoped were menacing steps forward, but accompanied by piccolo music, all they got were chuckles.

A brave trombone, having had enough of the tubas reign of terror, stood himself on end and extended his slide, so that Polly Piccolo could stand on it and address the crowd.

"Laughter isn't evil, it's good and powerful," she said. "If we can help others laugh by providing a funny soundtrack, then that's what we should be doing."

The crowd as one expressed agreement, eager to return to an older happier past.

"I miss poking people in the back of the head with my slide!" said a trombone.

"I'm not a harp, I'm a Jew's harp, and proud of it!"

Like a massive instrumental wave the crowd advanced on Julius X.

The sousaphone thugs saw the turning tide. They played fast funny running away music as Julius X ran away.

He didn't get far.

Normalcy was re-established. With the return of the missing soundtrack, people felt free to laugh at the obese as they bumped into walls, fell into fountains, and rolled downhill. Life was funny again.

And what of Julius X?

Because of his abuse of power, everyone felt he deserved the most extreme punishment possible. His bell was filled with potting soil and he was sold to a couple from the Hamptons who used him as a planter for anthuriums.

Wah wah wah

THE DICTATOR'S DREAM ABOUT PAINTING

by Katrina Dybzynska

Paint it black and white.
Ban other colors. Apply
only an essence as diluted
paint will allow for shades
and grey areas. Classify
the brushes. Forbid thin
strokes. Stick strictly
to the official symbols.
Do not leave blank spots.

Paint danger.
Then, in a centre place – a contrasting
solution, just one. Mark clear
lines. Do not let your hand
to hesitate – aim for right
angles, no leaks or blurs.
Choose an expensive frame
for your painting to last in enforced
respect.

THE FAITHLESS ANGEL
by E. E. King

I've seen it all... and long ago. There is nothing new under the sun... nothing new above the sun either.

I should know, I'm an angel. Oh, not a big guy like Peter or Gabriel; I'm just a guardian. I get assigned here and there, watching my charges until they die. Then I get a new one.

I used to be a believer, but now my heart's no longer in it... that's just a figure of speech of course. I don't actually have a heart – no heart, no lungs, no spleen, no pancreas. I do have a soul, though. In fact, I'm almost all soul. A soul and an appendix. Don't ask.

I try to keep it secret, my lack of faith. If the big guy ever finds out, God knows what he'd do. He's a vengeful sucker.

I can pinpoint the ending of my faith. It was at the very start of my career as a guardian angel. I'd just been allotted to Aliza. It seemed an easy assignment. She was a sweet, pretty, God fearing girl — much good it did her. She came from a big, close knit family who were pretty well set.

So I, not having much to do, was hanging out in heaven, watching God deal cards. God has often been accused of playing dice with the universe, but God favors poker — and he has a hell of a time finding anyone willing to play. That is why on this day that I'm telling you about (in 1650 BCE), God and Lucifer were playing a few hands.

Lucifer? I can almost hear you thinking. Surely God would never hang out with THE DEVIL.

Most people forget that Lucifer was God's favorite, the smartest, most charming and loveliest angel – hell, his very name means "bringer of light."

That is why God occasionally invites him up for their particular brand of poker, otherwise known as "let's fuck with the humans."

Well, that day God was in a chatty mood, going on and on about his favorite new pet – Job. It was Job this and Job that – "Job is handsome, rich, strong and so righteous that after every feast he gets up at the crack of dawn and sacrifices one of his seven thousand sheep, five hundred shed asses, three thousand camels, or five hundred oxen, just in case one of his sons or daughters accidentally curses Me in their hearts," God said.

As far as I know none of Job's sons or daughters ever cursed God… usually that was done by the sheep or ox, but who can blame them?

So, as I was saying, God and Lucifer were playing and Lucifer said, "Job only adores you so much because he's got it all. I bet that Job wouldn't be so uxorious if things got a bit tougher."

"Naw," God said. "Job would praise me no matter what."

"I bet I could make Job turn against you in just one day."

"You're on," said God. "Just don't injure him, that's all I ask. He's got lovely skin and it's rare in the Sinai."

THE FAITHLESS ANGEL

So, Lucifer rounded up some bored Sabeans who were roaming around the desert looking for someplace to pillage and directed them to Job's 500 yoke of oxen and 500 donkeys. Next he found a few Chaldeans and gave them keys to Job's camel coop.

Then he goaded God into firebombing Job's 7,000 sheep. Let me tell you, the sheep's guardian angel was pissed!

I had gotten tired of the game and was watching over my charge, the sweet and pious Aliza. She was at her brother's with the rest of the family when whoosh - God ups the ante. With a mighty wind he destroys Job's house and all ten children. They were torn limb from limb, their body parts scattered like dice over the desert.

I flew up to heaven fast as my wings could take me... "Yahweh," I said, "Lord of Lord, Host of Hosts, Master of the Universe, the Cosmos and Creator of Everything," (God likes titles almost as much as praise.) "Aliza, my ward, a good and God fearing girl as you could hope to find, has been ripped into little pieces by a cruel wind that has blown nobody any good... Surely you can't allow this to happen."

"The sins of the fathers..." God begins. He is a God of few words which he repeats a lot; maybe that's why He is so fond of prayer.

I interrupted.... "Yes, that's fine, Lord." I said. "But, her father is JOB. He has no sin. So perhaps you could just do a little miracle, reassemble my ward and we can forget this ever happened?"

The Guardian angel of the sheep was in a corner pulling his wool out. But he knew better than to complain. God hates sheep. He's not too fond of oxen either.

by E. E. King

Lucifer crossed his lovely legs, grinned and dealt a straight.

God's addicted to praise and poker. He raised the stakes, disregarding his former objections to preserving Job's skin and health, gives Job a horrible case of acne and herpes.

Job wept and prayed and looked around for something to sacrifice.

Job's wife, who had taken the slaughter of their children harder than Job said, "It's time for you to stop offering stuff up to Yahweh, Job. He destroyed all the sheep, oxen, she-asses, camels and our ten children. Now all you have to offer him is okra and brussel sprouts, and you know God hates veggies. Just look what happened to Cain when he offered the Lord greens. The only decent thing for you to do is to curse Yahweh the child killer and die."

"Silence, Woman," said Job. "Don't you know suicide is a sin?"

Just then there was a knock on Job's door, which oddly enough had survived the destruction of his house. It stood like a small hinged monolith rising out of the ruins. Behind the door were three of Job's friends, Eliphaz, Bildad, and Zophar. They had dropped by for a cup of mead and some Matzo. Instead of being welcomed by servants and ushered into Job's lovely home, they were greeted by the charred remains of sheep, oxen, and a few fingers and toes - the remnants of Job's children that had blown into the yard.

"What evil have you wrought," they cried. "You must have sorely offended The Lord our God to make him punish you thus."

"I have done nothing wrong, praise the Lord," Job cried. "For no known reason I am become desolate, lacking cattle and kin. I curse the day I was born. My birth should have been shrouded in darkness. Light and life only intensify my misery and make my skin itch."

"Well, Job," said Eliphaz, "you always made out like you were so holy, telling everyone who had ill luck to 'bear up' and praise Yahweh. But now it's clear to me that you've never really understood their pain. A few pustules and you fall to pieces."

"Is that contagious?" asked Zophar, rubbing his cheek.

"No," said Job, "I love the Lord with all my heart and all my…"

"Herpes, "said Bildad and the three fled as if bad luck were catching.

"How, God," asked Job, "can you judge people by actions since you, oh Lord of Lord, Host of Hosts and all that, can easily alter their behavior? How can we appease you oh Omniscient One, you who are beyond all comprehension. Why do you let the wicked people flourish while I suffer?"

Job looked around hoping for an answer, but no one was there. He was talking to himself, a sure sign of madness.

"Talk to me, Yahweh of Yahwehs, Don't just inflict all this shit on me and remain silent."

But the day was still as death. In fact, the sun blazed more brilliantly than ever, making Job's abscesses ooze.

Out of the desert a wind arose, circling and swirling like a gigantic dust bunny.

"Hey," said the voice of Yahweh, calling from inside the whirlwind, "Do you realize who you are talking to? How dare you question me? Not only did I create the world in seven days, I also made the Behemoth. He eats grass like cattle, the Big Behemoth. His strength is in his loins but his power is in the navel of his belly. It's all in the core; it's where I got the idea for Pilates. You couldn't make anything like that could you?

"You never even invented the wheel, let alone a Behemoth, or an entire discipline that exercises every single part of the body.

"I also created the leviathan. You couldn't catch the leviathan with a fishhook if your life depended on it. Could you make a pet of him or put him on a leash for your girls… or rather could you if you had any living girls… Which you don't…

"No - You know nothing! I am God, motherfucker – QED, bitch."

(QED 'Quod Erat Demonstrandum', is Latin for 'I haven't actually proven anything, but believe me anyway.)

Job wasn't satisfied, but no one wants to argue with a whirlwind.

"Sorry, Yahweh," he muttered, "You are of course right. I could never even draw up plans for a behemoth or a leviathan, let alone make one."

Thus, God won his bet with Lucifer. It put Yahweh in a generous mood. With a wave of his hand he cured Job's herpes and gave him a tube of Clearasil, clearly a miracle since neither acne cream nor tubes would be invented for centuries yet to come. He deeded Job twice as much property as he had had before, some new children, and one hundred and forty years in which to enjoy them. In fact Job's new daughters were so beautiful that he even put them in his will… which was most unusual.

But Aliza, my sweet, loving, innocent girl was still dead, her dust blown to the corners of the earth along with her siblings. For her there was no return from the beyond and no forgiveness.

A NIGHT OF RAPTURE
by Margaret S. E. Smith

It started with the disappearance of the catering staff; or more precisely, with Senator Avory's lament at the disappearance of the Pairpoint silver serving tray with the creme-filled puff pastries. This unhappy announcement was followed by the senator's wife's discovery that her champagne flute hadn't refilled, and Reverend Jeremiah James' declaration that his assistant, to whom he'd been giving notes on his upcoming "Rolling In the Dough for the Lord" telecast, had vanished. It snowballed from there.

The partners from Linderman, Linderman, and Cayse were forced to retrieve their own coats, as the house servants were nowhere to be found, the Vanderhewns took to milling about like lost lemmings upon realization that their Chauffeur, Schulzi, had disappeared with the keys to the Rolls, and Nina Trent, Au pair to Lady Canton and her family, had vanished from the upstairs nursery…along with all three Canton children. It was generally conceded by all that something was seriously amiss.

Keller Thompson – who started the night straight-backed and spit-polished from head to toe in a black tux (rented), Giorgio Brutini patent leathers (borrowed), and French Silk ascot (polyester) – had, by this time, wilted slightly, allowing a bit of his unfortunate natural state (eBay

by Margaret S. E. Smith

whoring college student) to show through. Foster Hewitson, whose father was hurriedly approaching while explaining to the automated recording on his Gold Edition Nokia that he had "been holding for the 'next available operator' for the better part of thirty minutes, dammit!", stood crisply beside his U of M roommate, attempting to tidy him up as the senior Hewitson strode over. He wanted his father to know his advice had been heeded. "Find yourself a lackey son. Someone hungry to climb the social ladder. Befriend him, groom him, train him to the Hewitson standards. One who'll beg to be indebted to you. Remember Foster, if you ever have to do things yourself, you are not living up to your full potential."

At Foster's urging, Keller – fluttery hands pinching, pulling, smoothing, and jiggling himself back into a semblance of faux-couture – sprung to attention. This was the man Keller aspired to be; a captain of industry, leader of men, never settling for second best – unlike his own father, who happily settled for a mom & pop restaurant and three acres of vegetable garden in some backwater Florida town. Keller refused to settle after Foster began showing him what he could have; only 19 and he was hobnobbing with important people who mattered…people like the Hewitsons. He eagerly awaited his idol's astute observations on the strange goings-on.

"Well, we've all agreed; something is seriously amiss."

Keller stared at Hewitson Sr. in awe, eyes begging, "Please adopt me" as he basked in the heady glow of the man's presence. Foster, who didn't bask so much as perspire after 20 years orbiting the gravitational force that was his father, responded as he had been trained to. "Tell me what to do father, and I'll make sure somebody does it". That

A NIGHT OF RAPTURE

had been nearly a month ago; and so far, nothing much had gotten done.

The Hewitson estate (also known as La plus belle maison à Palm Beach), had in that month become headquarters for those in attendance that fateful January night. It was on the Hewitson's 71" Plasma that the group heard the news: it was official; people were suddenly disappearing for reasons unknown... and it was global. Within hours, vital operations that kept society running were screeching to a halt. Within days, power plants began to shut down. By weeks end... the grid went dark.

Before the loss of power, the group gleaned certain facts about THE EVENT, as it had so cleverly begun to be called. Firstly, the disappearances coincided with sightings of bright lights in the sky, and secondly, the upper echelon of society seemed to have been spared the fate of the lower masses. After the loss of power, speculation became the game of the day. The consensus among Linderman, Linderman, and Cayse, was that it was The Rapture – which the corporate attorney's took in stride, seeing as they never truly expected to get into heaven anyway. This theory, however, didn't sit well with Reverend Jeremiah James, who favored a "Reverse Rapture" concept, in which only the most deserving was left to inherit the earth. This idea pleased Senator Avory and his wife. The Vanderhewns, as well as Foster, favored an alien abduction scenario. As the debate raged – The Rapture or Alien Abduction – Keller, his belly rumbling painfully, could only think to himself that the two were basically the same thing if looked at in a certain light. He sighed. Yes, the shine had definitely worn off as the group failed time and again to accomplish anything useful. Still, he was certain Foster's father was

by Margaret S. E. Smith

working on it and would soon stand forward to lead the charge toward survival. Why even now, Mr. Hewitson stood by the French doors looking out over the flower garden, no doubt conceiving his master plan. More time: that was all that was needed.

By dusk, Keller decided to gather some wood, and that night the group enjoyed a cozy fire and a meal Keller cooked from their dwindling food stock. The next morning, he rose to find Mr. Hewitson once more in deep contemplation by the beautiful, and no doubt expensive, French doors. Sighing, Keller decided to rut around the pantry. He found some potatoes and smiled, suddenly remembering something his father had once shown him. Laughing, he ran to the gardener's shed to get what he would need.

At sunset, Foster joined his father where he stood observing Keller in the garden. He squinted and crooked his head quizzically to the side as he watched his lackey-in-training down on all fours, moving piles of earth this way and that. "What on Earth is he doing, Father?"

"He's toiling, Foster," his father replied in a rather board voice. "Did you know that you could grow potatoes right from cuttings of the vegetable itself?"

Foster laughed. "Now why would I know something like that?"

"You wouldn't," his father chuckled, "it isn't your place to. But see, everything falls back into its proper place given enough time. Others like Keller will answer their nature and begin toiling once again, and we shall answer ours by running things for them. It's the order of the universe."

Satisfied, father and son turned and joined their friends inside, just missing the flashing of bright lights as they lit the darkening sky over a now empty garden.

A FEAST TALE

by Cathy Adams

When the white missionaries first came to our island we were friendly but a little skeptical. That approach turned out to be correct. All six of them insisted we change our horizontal drainage ditches at the periphery of our hill crops to a vertical direction even after we explained to them that we had been planting our crops our way for 7,000 years. We lied about the 7,000 years part. In truth, we had no idea how long our hill lands had been cultivated that way, but not one of us could remember the crops being laid out any other way, so 7,000 years sounded like a respectably convincing claim.

The missionary with the bald head, the small round glasses, and the sharp nose did not believe us and told us we were doing it wrong. After more arguing and many pictures drawn on both the man's paper and in the sand, one of our villagers and some members of his family became convinced that this foreigner must know more than we did, even though I fervently protested the idea and reminded all listening of our 7,000 year planting history. Against my wishes, the farmers and their families changed the direction of the ditches. At the first heavy rain the water backed up and washed all of the top soil along with the newly seeded crops down the hillsides into a useless mess in the valley below. The bald man and the other missionaries stood with us in the rain and said it was their god's will that we were being punished for our wicked ways. We were facing a harvest season with no crops, but we told the missionaries we were having a feast and they were invited. They all came, and we ate them.

That turned out to be a serendipitous year because only a few weeks earlier several of the missionaries had written letters which they managed to get out on the last exiting boat to the mainland. They wrote to their missionary friends back in their home country of our bountiful hills, our white sands, our warm air, our many island animals, and most of all, our heathen ways. Later that year a boat full of eight missionaries came, and we ate them, too.

By this time, some of our people had developed a real taste for missionaries and suggested we send word that we wanted more, but only one of us had paid attention to their lessons enough to write in the missionaries' English. We tried copying the little picture lines from the only book they had brought, but we had no idea if the message made any sense. One of our women who had learned some of the writing managed to get onto paper a single line.

come to we eat

We sent out the message with the next boat to the mainland, but apparently this was an insufficient invitation in the English because no missionaries came that season. We had to settle for eating the villager and his family who had insisted that we follow the missionaries' agricultural advice. There were six members in his family, and most of us had never liked them much anyway.

A FEAST TALE

By the next planting season we were back to our 7,000 year old irrigation and planting methods. After that we had plenty to eat except late that summer a new problem was visited upon us. A trading party from the nearby island of Wahmudadata arrived with animals that proved almost as detrimental to our landscape as the missionaries had been, except they tasted better. Pigs.

At first we ate only a few of the animals for a special feast. The plan was to raise the pigs and keep a steady supply for eating, but the pigs regularly escaped the pens we made for them and rooted up our gardens and crops. Keeping them fed required an enormous amount of vegetation. One small boy was eaten after he wandered into the pig's sleeping quarters. Found buried deep in the mud was a shell bracelet his mother had made for him, and her wails could be heard across the island, or so it seemed. We ate all the pigs.

Then we came full circle back to the missionary problem. One very hot morning a boat arrived with seven missionaries, all men, and we had hardly got our boiling pots and knives ready before a second boat came with six more, except these must have been from some other tribe because they spoke a different language from the English. Three of them were women, and they wore uncomfortable looking dresses that went from their necks to their ankles and fit so tightly around the middle they stood up straight as trees all the time. The men wore equally horrible pants and shirts, all tightly fastened to the necks and made from material the color of dirt. These missionaries would hang their heads down and not look us in the eye when we spoke to them. We had to dip our heads down too and look up at their pale faces when we tried to talk as it was considered rude to speak to the top of someone's head. The first group appeared visibly bothered by the arrival of the second one, and it seemed there had been some terrible breach of etiquette for both groups to have shown up at the same time. They had many words with one another, but no one could understand what the group in the uncomfortable clothes was saying. The first group yelled at the tops of the heads of the muddy clothed group who then yelled down at the ground, and thus it went until the sun was high and everyone was tired and thirsty. Soon the groups separated, one to the east and one to the west of the island. For the time being, we quietly put our pots and knives away.

It was the hottest season of the year, and no matter how politely we suggested the muddy clothed missionaries dress as we did, they refused. To make matters worse, they had brought with them bands of cloth with strings attached that they insisted our women tie around their shoulders and wear over their chests. After some time we figured out that their unwillingness to look at us when they talked was connected to these bits of cloth. They shuddered like dying fish if they accidentally caught a glimpse of our women's bare chests. We accepted the bands of cloth, thanked them, and took the cloth into our huts where we used them to store nuts. Then we returned to our discreet preparations for the next feast, which, thanks to the dual arrivals of missionaries, would be the largest ever.

With all the noise and commotion, soon both groups came sniffing around to see what we were up to. As it turned out, the muddy clothed missionaries must have been clued in to what we were doing when they saw us chopping up roots and vegetables, setting up big pots, and loading up firewood underneath. No matter how many times we said,

A FEAST TALE

"Fish, fish, fish," and pointed at the pots, they were suspicious. This may have been because some of the children had pulled at the hands and barely exposed wrists of the muddy clothed women trying to feel their flesh. It was a logical deduction. The uncomfortable missionaries scurried to the farthest end of the island.

The first group of missionaries seemed pleased that they had left and took it as some kind of personal moral victory. The men all held hands and performed what we had long ago learned was called a prayer. We stood back, respectfully, and let them finish their words before we clubbed them on the backs of their heads. Then we ate them. Everyone slept well that night on a full belly of missionary.

The muddy clothed missionaries remained in what they thought was hiding for a full two weeks in caves on the far side of the island. We secretly watched them. The men tried fishing from the ocean but not one of them had any fishing skills and sometimes the women, who never strayed far from the men, ended up crying at the water's edge, their heavy skirts so bogged down with sea water they had to gather the heavy folds under their arms to walk away. They tried to eat from the island foliage, but none of them seemed to know what was edible and what was not. Our people could not understand how these know-nothing, unhappy, overdressed people had ever survived anywhere. We intervened only after seeing one of the woman gathering leaves that would have left them all with severe diarrhea followed by eventual death. In frustration over their helplessness, we began delivering food to them daily: berries, fish, roots, greens, and coconuts. They took this to be benevolence, but in truth it was for our own benefit. We liked healthy meat.

by Cathy Adams

The plan was to let them be throughout the remainder of the growing season. We did not try to talk to them because we could not understand one another anyway. I began to think they were the most useless missionaries on our island to date. They could not take care of themselves in the slightest. Except for the nut holders, they had brought nothing of use to us. Of course that changed later that season on the night they began singing. Our people like singing. We sing on all special occasions: wedding feasts, burial feasts, holiday feasts, birthing feasts. Their singing was nothing like their clothes or anything else about them. The sound was loose like island birds and the melody fluttered high and light. The music flowed around us and went straight up to the stars in the sky above us. Their voices lifted our hearts into the night as none of the missionaries before them had ever done. Their singing was like what the other missionaries had tried to do when they performed their prayers, except none of us had ever felt power in their prayers the way we did with the singing of the uncomfortable and straight as trees missionaries. The sound lured more and more of our people until soon we were all gathered in the firelight of the missionaries who stood in an arc behind the flames, as there were not enough of them to make a circle around the fire. They held hands and sang, their chests rising and falling with the effort. Our faces lit up in the fire before them must have appeared a fearsome sight to these missionaries who had rightly figured out that as long as they kept singing we would not move any closer. The singing went on into the night. The children fell asleep in their mothers' arms on the warm sand in front of the fire. The elders smiled and folded their hands in their laps while they listened. The missionaries sang and sang until one of the men fell down before the fire. The others stopped, breathless, and in a few seconds one of the women resumed the singing. Soon the others joined in once more and it went on like this for some time until another fell out. The remaining four resumed their singing until the sun was beginning to rise over the ocean and their voices became thinner and thinner. The sound no longer reached the stars but stopped just at the clouds and then soon only at the tops of our trees. The last woman faltered and her singing faded out, the six of them now collapsed in silence on the sand behind the embers of the fire. For the first time they did not look as tall as trees.

The day was fully upon us all. We thanked them for their song, though they could not understand our words. Their voices had been the first good gift any of the missionaries had brought us. The ones before them had spoken of love, of consuming the body of their god and even his blood. It made sense to me now, and I thought it was all very beautiful. So we carried them back to our pots and fires and took their second gift. After every man, woman, and child was full, for the first time we thanked their god for what he had given us. Then, sated, we slept away the afternoon. More would always come.

IDEA DOLLY BOSS

by Warren Brown

She camped in Bora Bora
took spaceships to the moon
wrought swordfish into plowshares
cavorted with the loons

The stories they are endless
and mostly semi-proved
and most who've been
too close to her

Are pretty glad they moved.

CORVID-19: THE CROWS! THE CROWS!

by Andrew Jensen

"Whose turn is it to tell him?"

The President's PR advisors looked around the room. Their immediate boss had long ago ordered them to be the bearers of bad news, so they took turns putting their jobs on the line.

"Let Enrique do it. He's the bird watcher."

Jerks! As everyone laughed, Enrique gathered up the summary he knew would go unread, and went to the briefing room.

"Mr. President, we have to deal with a slight mispronunciation. You called the pandemic CORVID-19, instead of COVID-19."

"Who cares? That's not a big deal. In fact, I like it better that way."

"But sir, CORVID-19 makes it sound like it has something to do with crows. That's what Corvids are, sir: crows."

The President looked delighted. "So it's a new kind of bird flu! I'm brilliant! This is terrific, we have to get it out there. Listen, do I have to do all your work for you? Put out a statement about it . . . no, never mind, I'll just Tweet it. It's faster."

"Of course, sir."

"Did you get that one, Enrique?"

"Get what sir?"

"I'm 'Tweeting' about bird flu."

"Oh. Very clever, Mr. President."

"You people have no sense of humor, do you, Enrique?"

"Not at work, Mr. President."

***

One of the rules of the PR office was that if you started something, you had to finish it. There was no passing the buck.

"What's the fake news this time, Enrique?"

"Mr. President, the left-wing media is calling your CORVID-19 disease theory 'idiotic.'"

"What did you expect?" The President furrowed his brows in deep thought. "You know, Enrique, a crow couldn't fly if it only had a left wing. I like that. It's profound. I'm gonna Tweet that one too."

"Sir, don't you think they'll point out that the same thing could be said about the right wing?"

"Who cares? The people who matter won't be listening by then. Watch and learn from your master, Enrique. Watch and learn."

***

"Okay, Enrique, how are we doing spreading the news about the Crow Flu?"

CORVID-19: THE CROWS! THE CROWS!

"Mr. President, you wouldn't believe it. People all over the country are out in the fields, shooting crows. I had no idea so many people hated them!"

"Believe it! They're creepy. Think about those old movies with a crow sitting on skull."

"Those are ravens, sir. But they are related. Ravens are also Corvids. Well done, Mr. President."

The president glared suspiciously. "My point is that people have always been afraid of black birds. That's just common sense. You can always trust the American people to do the right thing. That's why we have the Second Amendment."

"Mr. President, there's a new health risk. There are so many dead crows that not all of them are being collected. Some have fallen into reservoirs. There's worry that infection might spread."

"I see. The crow corpses will spread CORVID-19. We can't have my base getting sick by picking them up. I've got it! A brilliant solution! I want you to put together a program of Crow Corpse Collectors. We'll call them the CCC for short. They can wear those all-white Hazmat suits."

"Uh, Mr. President, I'm in PR, not policy."

"Then tell someone else to write it for you. Delegate!"

"Yes sir. And where will the money come from?"

"This is a public health thing, so take it from them. Oh, and it's a job-creation thing too, so take some of that money. It's about time the rural people got some of that money that's always going to New York and Washington."

"Of course, sir."

"They're good people, you know, Enrique. Terrific people. I'm proud to support them in this difficult time."

by Andrew Jensen

"New Yorkers, Mr. President?"

"Get out, Enrique. God, you're stupid. Who hired you?"

***

"Mr. President, there are more problems. The media has compared the CCC to the KKK! Farm fields have been plowed under to bury the corpses, and the health officers won't let them be replanted for a whole year. The Agriculture department is taking a lot of flak."

"Enrique, you panic too easily. Who cares about fake news? Shooting crows as about as All-American as we can get. Just remind people of our roots: give them something to cheer for. Make a joke out of it."

"Really, sir?"

"Yes, and I have just the thing. Find me a scarecrow suit."

"A scarecrow suit?"

"Is there an echo in here? Yes! Like in the Wizard of Oz. It'll be a great thing to wear to next Tuesday's rally. I'll show them who the crows should fear."

"Mr. President, is that wise? Think of the dignity of your office."

"I create my own dignity, Enrique."

"The costume will ruin your hair."

The president paused. "Good point. Tell the Vice President he can wear it."

"Is he going to your rally, sir?"

"He is now."

***

CORVID-19: THE CROWS! THE CROWS!

"I have good news and bad news, Mr. President."

"There's no such thing as bad news, Enrique, just the opportunity to stick it to my enemies."

"Hundreds of people are taking to the streets and country roads in scarecrow suits, carrying shotguns."

"Good for them! Are they all shooting crows?"

"Apparently they're shooting anything with feathers, and a few things without."

"Well, I'm sure they deserved it."

"One was a Rolls Royce."

The president's eyebrows shot up. "Phantom or Silver Cloud?"

"Silver Cloud, sir. Vintage."

"That's a tragedy. See if the owner wants to sell it. It can probably be restored."

"Yes Mr. President."

"Wasn't that rally great, Enrique? The vice president looked terrific in the scarecrow suit. Pay attention, and you might learn something. I don't know why I bother with a PR office."

"The media didn't like it. One even suggested you should have dressed as the Cowardly Lion, for not wearing it yourself." Enrique stood with his eyes closed.

"The Cowardly Lion? I'm not fat! Wait, they're calling me a coward? Who said that?"

"It was the reporter you said looked like the Wicked Witch, sir."

"I should have said 'bitch.' I'll get her."

"Of course, sir."

"This is your fault, Enrique. I let you talk me out of wearing that suit, and now look! I should fire you!"

"Yes sir." It would be a relief.

by Andrew Jensen

"Anything else, Enrique?"

"Well, Mr. President, some animal behavioral scientists are concerned about the strangely coordinated ways the crows are responding . . ."

"Let them worry! You know I don't trust those guys. Who would be dumb enough to worry about birds?"

"Scientists, Mr. President?"

"Get out, Enrique. And make sure that reporter never gets near the White House. Ever."

***

"What the hell is going on with the crows, Enrique? Why don't you have this CORVID thing under control?"

"They're fighting back, sir."

"That's impossible."

"Crows are smart, sir. They can count, they can recognize guns. In some States they could probably pass the qualifications to vote."

"Don't try to be funny, Enrique. Just tell me what's going on."

"Well, sir, they seem to have found ways to drop dead mice and other small animals into our grain supplies. So much food has been contaminated we're facing shortages. And with all the contaminated fields, it'll be at least a year before we can produce enough to feed everyone.

"Then there's the airports: the crows are chasing other birds, like pigeons and starlings, into the path of jets as they take off and land. There've been so many accidents the FAA is shutting down the skies again.

CORVID-19: THE CROWS! THE CROWS!

"And they've managed to knock out a lot of the electrical grid. They fly up to the high-tension cables and peck through the insulation."

"Doesn't that kill them?"

"Yes, Mr. President. They seem to be willing to die."

"The crows are terrorists! Are they Muslims?"

"I don't think so, sir."

"It sounds like they are. I'll have a tweet ready in a moment. This is a national security crisis!"

"There's more, Mr. President. With the power down, the hospitals are having trouble treading the COVID patients."

"You mean CORVID. I discovered it, remember?"

"How could I forget, Mr. President? The point is: people are dying."

"Americans are dying, and these terrorist crows are killing them."

"Not only crows anymore, Mr. President. Scientists have observed ravens flying down from Canada in greater numbers than ever before. They seem to be advising the crows."

"Didn't we close the border? Anyway, it doesn't matter. Canadians are weak. What can a bunch of Socialist Ravens do?"

"The vikings had great respect for ravens, Mr. President."

"Vikings? They were tough guys. Why did they respect them?"

"They believed ravens were the messengers of Odin, the god of the battlefield. They carried his thoughts and memories."

"That's just religion. I don't believe in that stuff."

"Many Native Americans have stories about ravens too. In some cultures, the raven is a trickster: really good at making people fall flat on their faces."

"They've tricked you, Enrique. That's all fake news! Ravens don't vote. They don't read Twitter. They don't Tweet. Who cares about ravens?"

"I care. I'm a birder sir. I watch birds. I have an impressive life list."

The president looked surprised. "I didn't know your people did that sort of thing. You're not gay, are you?"

"No sir, as it happens, I'm not."

"Then I don't get it. Tell me, has all your bird-hugging taught you anything we can use against these ravens, or crows, or whatever? I need to Tweet something right away."

"Sorry, Mr. President. I can't help you."

"Can't, or won't?"

"Won't sir. I can't help you in good conscience. If I had to place a bet between you and these birds, I would bet on the Corvids every time."

"These birds are terrorists! This is treason!"

"I wouldn't call it that, Mr. President."

"You're fired! Get out of my office!"

"I can give you one useful piece of information, Mr. President."

"It's too late to grovel, Enrique. You're fired."

"You're right about them, sir. They don't tweet."

"So?"

"Corvids are stronger than tweeters. They chase them away, and sometimes even kill them. Remember that."

***

CORVID-19: THE CROWS! THE CROWS!

Many hours after the Secret Service had hustled Enrique off to an undisclosed location, the president tried to go to sleep.

He couldn't. His mind was full of large black birds, flying in organized waves, pecking their way relentlessly into the White House.

He wondered how long the nightmare would last.

MINUTES

by Buzz Dixon

"Russell?"

"Thirty."

"Mr. Whitman?"

"Sixty." The executive sounded rather panicky.

Freefall, no simulated gravity. Minute particles of ice and debris floating in the absolute zero vacuum.

Corpses, too.

"I have ninety," said Baker, the yacht's new captain by virtue of being the highest ranking surviving crew member. "Mr. Pyrite, sir, how much oxygen do you have?"

Pyrite felt irritated. Baker could read all the suits' status, why bother him?

"One hundred and twenty minutes," he said.

"Thank you, sir," said Baker.

"What about us?" Amber said. "What about our suits?"

Baker, as gently as possible, asked, "How much oxygen do you have left?"

"Fifteen minutes," said Amber, her voice rising in hysteria. "The children only have ten and twelve!"

"We'll try to think of something," said Baker. To the ship's computer, the portion that survived the explosion, he asked, "Have you located the leak?"

"Not yet," it said in a cool, flat voice that only added to the tension the humans felt. "The main seals are intact. The life support system should be able to repressurize the surviving compartments and keep you all alive until help arrives, if you can find and seal the leak."

"Why can't you do that?" Pyrite demanded. "I paid good money for you!"

"Yes, you did," said the computer. "But the maintenance droids were in the other portion of the ship when it exploded. I have not been able to communicate with them."

"How long before help arrives?" Baker asked.

"I'm sending a repeating distress call to Bradbury Base," said the computer. "Assuming they have a ship ready, help should arrive in seventy-two hours."

"We'll be dead by then!" said Amber.

"If you don't find the leak, yes. You will be dead," said the computer.

***

The emergency lights stayed on, and there was enough battery power to keep them warm if they could restart the life support system.

"What caused the explosion?" Whitman asked. "Sabotage? Malfunction? Meteor?"

"It doesn't matter now," said Baker. "We either find the leak or we're dead. Find it, then we can debate what happened."

"What about the children?" Amber was shrieking now, and even with the suits' communication system muting her shrillest tones, her voice sounded piercing.

MINUTES

"They're not important," Pyrite said. "I'm important. Me. I own this yacht. I command this company. You all work for me. You serve my needs.

"Earn your pay — seal that leak!"

***

Russell laughed. He sounded bitter. As the lowest ranking crewman, his suit carried only half an hour of oxygen. "Yeah, right. Earn my pay.

"You pay less than half standard spacer wages, fat man."

Pyrite seethed. Floating in the middle of the wrecked cabin, his bulk seemed like a miniature planet with all the others orbiting him like lesser moons. "I'll see you ruined," he said, uttering one of his infamous catchphrases.

Russell laughed again. "That won't matter in — " he checked his suit meter "— twenty-seven minutes."

"What about the children?" Amber screamed again.

"Computer, shut her up," said Pyrite.

***

Baker and Russell, the yacht's two surviving crew members, were not part of the actual engineering and astrogation teams; the explosion blew those spacers to oblivion with the rest of the ship.

Rather, they served as liveried servants, wearing fancy dress uniforms that imitated those of the legitimate spacer ranks.

They focused their attention on maintaining Mr. Pyrite and his staff and any guests in the fashion to which they felt entitled.

Despite this, Baker and Russell still knew enough about basic ship operation and emergency procedures that they could stop the leak…if they could locate it.

"We're all going to die if you don't do something!" Whitman said. He enjoyed only thirty minutes more oxygen than Russell.

"I'm thinking!" Baker said. He glanced at his own meter: Eighty-five minutes remaining. "Computer, can you locate the leak?"

"No," said the computer. "My sensors are damaged. I can tell you the size of the leak — no more than six square millimeters — by the rate at which the compartments' atmosphere spews out, but as to where it is located…sorry, not a clue."

***

Amber screamed silently, clutching the two youngsters. As one of Pyrite's numerous concubines, she was allowed to bring her children with her.

Two of her children floated dead in the cold hard vacuum. Her surviving child, Violet, nine standard years old, stared numbly out the faceplate of her custom child size suit.

The boy, Sammy, three standard years older than Violet, looked stoic, trying to be a man despite the fact his mother, Beryl, another of Pyrite's concubines, floated dead only a few meters away.

While the computer muted Amber's screams over Pyrite's suit, Baker and the others could hear her.

"If we don't find the leak in the next five minutes," said Baker, "the children will start dying.

"Let's start looking!"

Pyrite remained floating in the center of the compartment, of course. As lord and master of the Kaleidoscope he did not deign to perform such mundane tasks.

Baker and Russell started examining the outer hull bulkheads as closely as possible.

Problem: The ship's hull packed a good half meter of insulation, circuitry, and life support systems between the cabins and space.

The leak might not be a single easy to find hole, but perhaps a series of hairline cracks, none linking directly to the other.

Still, they looked.

After all, they had the rest of their lives to dedicate to the task.

***

Amber calmed down enough to explain to the children what they needed to do and the three of them began searching for the leak.

Even Whitman joined in, though he really didn't know what he was looking for.

Pyrite, from his vantage point in the center of the compartment, watched them all at work.

Lacey, his personal fashion assistant, designed the suits that the crew and passengers of the Kaleidoscope wore. Fashioned after old European military uniforms of the late 19th century, they were a riot of colors, each hue precisely defining the wearer's status in the Pyrite interplanetary organization.

The concubines, little more than chattel property even in the enlightened 23rd century, received skin tight suits that emphasized their bosoms and posteriors, but with a niqab-like faceplates and wholly useless high heel boots.

Their children wore simpler pastel suits patterned after school uniforms of the mid-20th century.

Baker and Russell's uniforms shared the same basic design, but with different color variations and more ornate piping depending on their rank.

Whitman, as befitting a high ranking executive in Pyrite's interplanetary enterprises, received an opulent suit with large cuffed gloves and knee-high boots, but Pyrite himself, ah, Pyrite himself wore an ornate uniform of royal purple crisscrossed with gold piping and silver braiding, neon orange epaulets, corporate emblems displayed across his chest like medals of old, thigh high folded over shiny black boots with buckles fore and aft, intricately fashioned elbow length gloves, an elaborate crested helmet, and a short scarlet half-cape floating uselessly behind him.

"And it's not merely enough that you are more important," said Lacey. "Oh, no, no, no. You must look more important.

"After all, what good is status if nobody recognizes it, hmm?

"Therefore your suit's oxygen reserve must be more than that of the Kaleidoscope's captain, which must be more than the senior officers, which must be more than the junior officers, which must be more than the common spacers, and so on and so on.

"This must even extend to your concubines — especially your concubines — and their children. Never ever deign to acknowledge the possibility they might be of equal status to you. Keep them — and their oxygen — down so they'll know their place.

"And it's important you demonstrate to others how important you are by avoiding any appearance of plebian, practical, proletarian function in your suits.

"No tubes or nozzles, everything self-contained!"

"What if they need more oxygen?" Pyrite asked.

"That's the delicious point," said Lacey. "If, for whatever reason, you need to venture forth into a vacuum, your staff and crew cannot last as long as you! They will be forced to acknowledge their inferiority by returning to the ship before you. It's genius, I tell you! Genius!"

Pyrite smiled when Lacey said that several standard years earlier, but now in the grim reality of survival in space following a disaster, he wished he could tell his personal fashion assistant that he was now his former personal fashion assistant and that, true to form, Pyrite would ruin him.

Saying such now would be wholly superfluous, of course: Lacey floated less than two meters from him, dead eyes gaping in terror as the absolute zero temperature flash froze his body before he could don his own spacesuit.

***

Lacey's strategy and Pyrite's vanity guaranteed that there was no way to recharge their suits short of taking them off in a pressurized compartment.

To gain their elegant look, Lacey removed all external connections from the suits.

Once donned, there was no way to get air, water, food, or power in, or sewage out short of stripping the suit off and letting the recharging crew prep it for future use.

That trapped Pyrite and his crew and his concubine and the brats with just the oxygen Lacey deemed worthy of them.

Violet, the little girl, died first.

Pyrite paid no attention to Amber and the children, but the trio broke off their search for the leak as Amber grabbed Violet's shoulders and shook her.

Had he looked, Pyrite would have seen the child desperately gasping for air within her suit, her lungs working furiously as she tried to find one last molecule of breathable oxygen in the fetid carbon dioxide of her helmet.

Terrified, she clawed desperately at her faceplate like an ancient deep sea diver trying to open his helmet as water rushed in.

She was dying.

She panicked and kicked and struggled more and more and Amber tried desperately to hold her, to comfort her, but Violet thrashed in absolute mindless terror, her lips turning blue, tiny blood vessels in her eyes rupturing as she tried harder and harder to breath…

…and then it was over.

She didn't go limp — there was no gravity to pull her limbs down — but she floated aimlessly, lifelessly, like a wooden puppet dunked into a pool of water.

Pyrite did not hear Amber howl but he did see her suddenly launch herself at him like a human guided missile, hands extended, reaching for the neck seal on his suit.

***

MINUTES

Pyrite grabbed her wrists before she could tear his suit open, but he couldn't stop her from banging her helmet into his and holding it there so he could hear her voice carried through the vibrations of the touching faceplates.

shesdeaddamnyoushesdeadshewasjustachildtheywereallchidrenwhydidntyougivethem enoughoxygentoliveyoufatheartlessbastard

— and then Baker yanked her off Pyrite and flung her away.

Amber spun across the compartment, colliding with the frozen form of Lacey then hitting the bulkhead near Sammy and Violet's inert form.

Sammy grabbed her shoulder to keep her from bouncing away, and she swept him up in her arms then pulled Violet's lifeless body over as well.

I should have never brought her along, Pyrite thought. To Baker he said, "Well? Find anything?"

"We're looking," Baker said. "This is a big compartment, there's a lot of debris. We're taking up the side paneling—"

"Stop talking and get back to work!" Pyrite said. "What do you think I pay you for, anyway?"

Pyrite couldn't see Baker's face clearly in the emergency lights and that probably was just as well. Baker pushed off and resumed his search for the elusive air leak.

***

The Kaleidoscope carried more than enough suits to go around.

by Buzz Dixon

Problem: The disaster hit so fast that most of the surviving crew and passengers couldn't get their suits on quickly enough.

Like Lacey, most of the frozen corpses drifting aimlessly about were partially suited up: Another two or three seconds and they would have lived.

But the icy cold of absolute zero robbed their fingers and hands of feeling and mobility, and fumbling impotently, they couldn't complete the necessary seals before death overtook them.

If Pyrite relied on his own efforts, he would have died, too.

Fortunately, two employees put his safety above theirs, and helped him don his elaborate suit before they died in the cold.

One had been Beryl, Sammy's mother, another of Pyrite's numerous concubines, and she died with one last haunted look on her face as she tried to glance in her son's direction for the final time.

***

Sammy died next.

He tried so hard to be a brave little man to the very end, but he was only a child: His terror broke him and he started crying, his faceplate filling with tiny drops of tears.

Like Violet, he instinctively clawed at his throat and face as his oxygen ran out, his air becoming hotter and hotter and staler and staler with each breath.

And then he, too, passed from the living to the dead.

Amber clutched both small corpses to her tightly, her own tears filling her helmet.

She looked at Pyrite and screamed silently, shaking the bodies in her arms as if to say, "These are your children!"

They were Pyrite's bastards.

When Amber and Beryl and all the other now dead concubines signed onto Pyrite's organization, they willingly forsook all claims to kindred and inheritance.

They were flat salaried employees, independent subcontractors if one wished to get technical about it (and Pyrite and his phalanxes of lawyers and solicitors and attorneys certainly did want to get technical about it).

They paid for their own clothes and their own food and their own pensions and their own health insurance and if they ever ran afoul of Pyrite, he would indeed ruin them with an incessant barrage of lawsuits filed on every inhabited planet, moon, colony, and space station until they were reduced to dire poverty.

As was only just.

Pyrite, after all, possessed wealth and power and status, and what good is wealth and power and status if one can't use them to dominate others and protect oneself?

***

Baker continued searching, but he kept one eye on Amber.

Unlike Pyrite, he could hear what she had to say over the suits' com link, and despite the awfulness of the situation, he still possessed a sense of staff loyalty to Pyrite.

But Amber seemed spent. She recognized the futility of striking at Pyrite and accepted her own death with quiet resignation.

Still clinging to the two dead children, she drew her legs up under her in a fetal ball, then her body shuddered briefly as she ran out of oxygen and expired with them,

***

"Any word from Bradbury Base?" Pyrite asked the computer.

"None," said the computer, "but that is to be expected. We're a light hour from them."

"I could be dead before I know if they're coming or not."

"Yes, that possibility exists."

"It's not fair," Pyrite said after a moment's silence. "It's not fair. I've amassed so much, I've bought out so many, I ruined so many others. It's not fair that I die this way, alone and from lack of oxygen."

"You should have thought of that before relying on your custom suit," said the computer.

***

Ten minutes later, Russell said, "I'm going to try something."

He grabbed a free floating suit, checked its size and setting, then opened it up and flipped its helmet back.

"I'm going to try to get out of this suit and into the other one before the cold freezes me," he said.

"You'll never make it," said Pyrite. "Keep looking for the leak while you have a chance."

"No! I'm going to do this! If I succeed, well, that'll give me an extra thirty minutes to keep looking."

MINUTES

"He has a point, sir," Baker said to Pyrite. "The longer he lives, the better all our chances."

Pyrite looked dubious but gestured for Russell to try.

The empty suit floated like a ghost beside Russell. Baker and Whitman held it steady so it wouldn't drift or bunch up while Russell attempted the transfer.

Russell took several deep breaths, pumping his lungs full of oxygen, then unsealed his helmet and began stripping off his suit.

Had the Kaleidoscope orbited closer to the sun, had the temperature not been absolute zero, Russell might very well have succeeded.

But as soon as the air in his suit leaked out, as soon as the power shut off, ice crystals instantly formed on the surface of his skin from his minute beads of sweat.

His fingers slowed and stiffened, the skin turning dark blue as the blood coagulated and froze inside them.

His eyes began freezing over, first the moisture on their surface then the vitreous fluid inside them.

Blind and unable to move his fingers or hands, Russell felt the burning cold of absolute zero freezing his limbs, solidifying his stomach, squeezing his head like a vise as his scalp tightened while it froze.

It took him several long, agonizing seconds to die, and during those final moments he cursed himself for not staying in the relative warmth and safety of his suit, enjoying one last minute of oxygen, one more minute of life.

"Well, so much for that idea," said Pyrite. "Now get back to work."

***

"Time?" Baker asked.

They stripped loose as many panels as they could, going over every square centimeter of the remaining compartments, trying to find the damned leak.

No luck.

"Sixty-seven minutes," said Pyrite. He really felt irritated that Baker barked orders at him like an underling.

"Thirty-seven minutes here," said Baker. "Mr. Whitman?"

"Mr. Whitman?"

"Seven minutes, damn you!" Whitman sobbed. "We're never going to find it, we're never going to find it—"

"You won't find it if you keep whining like a little baby!" said Pyrite. "Get back to work, slacker!"

"Go to hell!" Whitman yelled. "We're going to die out here! We're going to die because of you and your stupid space suits. 'Everybody needs to know their place.' Yeah, great idea."

"You liked it when you were informed of it," Pyrite said coldly.

"Because I never thought I would die as a result of your vanity! I thought it was just going to be another one of your damn fool stupid ideas."

Pyrite's eyes narrowed. "'Another one'?"

Whitman laughed bitterly at him, floating over to confront his employer faceplate to faceplate.

"You're an idiot," he said. "A damned idiot. You never had a workable idea that you didn't steal from somebody else. When you did come up with something, it typically blew up in our faces."

"The only thing that kept you going was your lawyers — they could throw up screen after screen, shield after shield, keeping you away from the consequences of your own actions."

He turned to Baker and said, "Hey, you want to know why we're headed to Charon? Way out here on the edge of the Kuiper Belt?"

"It's an investment opportunity," said Pyrite.

"It's a lawsuit!" said Whitman. You finally ticked off enough people in the Neptune system to have to flee further out again in order to avoid being bankrupted.

"First Earth, then Luna, then the inner planets, then the asteroid belt, then Jupiter, Saturn, Uranus, Neptune.

"What did you have planned after Pluto? Eris? Sedna? How far are you going to flee? Do you think you can reach Alpha Centauri?"

"Whitman, calm down," said Baker. "We still have time. Keep looking — "

"No," said Whitman. "I'm tired. I'm tired of his lies, I'm tired of running, I'm tired of cleaning his messes and kissing his ass.

"I quit, Pyrite. Hear that? I quit."

And with that he shut off his com link, turned his back on Pyrite, and crossed his arms and legs.

He looked like a levitating yogi from ancient lore, and he stayed in that position until he died.

***

To his credit, Baker wasted no time trying to dissuade Whitman; he kept looking for the leak.

Many long minutes passed.

Pyrite seethed in rage at the incompetence and failure of his staff. When he reached Charon — "if" was something he refused to consider – he would hire tougher, stronger, more resolute people.

Or rather, he'd have somebody in his company hire them for him.

***

"I found it!" Baker said.

Pyrite stirred from his self-pity and lethargy. "Don't talk, plug it up!" he said.

A pause, then: "I can't."

"You can't? The computer said it's only six millimeters square!"

"It is," said Baker. "It's a small pipe, just a little nine millimeter tube to drain condensation off the main life support system, but it's broken and the other end empties into space."

"Then stick something in it and plug it up!"

"I can't reach it," Baker said. "I can see it, but there's a support strut between me and it. I can't squeeze past it."

"Computer, can you shut that tube?" Pyrite asked.

"No," said the computer. "It's broken on the wrong side of the automatic shutoff valve. One of you will have to do it yourself."

"How many minutes do we have left?"

"Baker has three minutes," said the computer. "You have thirty-three."

"I have an idea," Baker said. "I'm going to try to disconnect one end of the strut and bend it back. If I can squeeze in close enough, I can jam the finger of my glove into the tube."

"That should be sufficient," the computer said. "Once you plug it I can repressurize the rest of the compartments. You will be stuck there until help arrives, but that's better than dying, I suppose."

"Stop talking and do it," Pyrite said,

He could see Baker's legs hooking themselves around part of the wreck to gain leverage, then he could see his lower body straining to pull against the strut.

"…it's…moving…" Baker said.

"Keep pulling!" Pyrite said.

Baker's legs tightened again and again, then they relaxed.

"Baker is dead," said the computer.

***

Pyrite frowned.

"What now?" he asked the computer.

"You can either finish what Baker started," said the computer, "or you can die. The choice is yours."

Pyrite cursed under his breath. "If you want anything done…" he muttered.

***

Pulling Baker loose was the hardest part; the stupid crew member got himself entangled in the strut and other wreckage.

Pyrite worked harder than he had worked in over fifty years. It took a lot of effort but he finally pulled Baker's corpse loose and set it floating off to join the others.

by Buzz Dixon

He peered into the passage Baker created by removing access panels, internal mechanisms, and bending back the support strut.

It didn't look very big.

In fact, it didn't look big enough at all, but it was the only option he had.

Pyrite crawled in.

***

He ran into problems immediately, little bits of loose debris and circuitry snagging his suit and slowing down his progress.

The strut couldn't be broken free, and he wasn't strong enough to bend it further back, so Pyrite slowly squeezed his bulk around it.

It was long, hard going, progress measured in millimeters, millimeters measured in minutes.

Still, what other option had he?

***

"I…I can't do it," Pyrite gasped. "I can't reach it. Computer, is there any word from Bradbury Base?"

"None so far," said the computer, "but we're still several minutes away from the earliest possible reply time."

"How much oxygen do I have left?"

"Thirteen minutes," said the computer.

"I can't make it," Pyrite said. "It's impossible. Nobody could make it."

"Actually, several people could have made it," said the computer. "All your concubines were slim enough to reach it. All their children, too. Sammy could have reached it easily, Violet most definitely."

"They failed me again," said Pyrite.

"They lived as long as you allowed," said the computer. "You chose the custom suits, you decided how much oxygen reserves they should have.

"If you had given everyone a full two hours, Violet or Sammy or even Amber could have reached the leak, plugged it with tape or even a wine cork, I could have repressurized the compartment, and you could all have lived in relative comfort until help arrived."

Pyrite blinked in disbelief. "That's ridiculous," he said. "They were children — bastard children. Their status didn't earn them two hours of oxygen."

"And yet, here you are," the computer said.

Pyrite cursed under his breath again and tried backing up. The braid and piping on his suit became hopelessly entangled in loose wires and circuitry; he couldn't retreat.

"I'm receiving a message," the computer said, then without asking if Pyrite wanted to hear it: "Space Yacht Kaleidoscope, this is Bradbury Base. We have received your distress signal and are launching a rescue ship immediately. Arrival time is estimated to be seventy-one hours from now. Space Yacht Kaleidoscope, this is Bradbury Base. We have received your distress signal and are launching a rescue ship immediately..."

"It keeps going on and on like that," said the computer. "If you want, I'll keep playing it, but I think you'd find it repetitious."

"Help's coming?"

"That's what they said, yes. Of course, it won't matter to you if you don't plug that leak."

"How many minutes do I have?"

"Five minutes…no, now it's four."

Pyrite strained his right arm as far out as he could reach, coming agonizing millimeters short of the broken tube.

If I can just reach it, plug it with my finger, the compartment will repressurize, I can open my suit, wait for help to arrive…

He tried again and again, stretching his army further and further, pulling against the wreckage and debris holding him back.

Slowly but surely he closed the gap between his glove and the tube. Now he could feel the jagged broken end of the tube through his thick glove, and if he could just reach out another ten or twelve millimeters he could plug it.

"I'm sorry, sir, but you're out of time," the computer said.

"No!" Pyrite screamed, and stretched and stretched and stretched, straining with all his might against the debris that held him back, desperately trying to move his fingertip over the open end of the tube.

He could feel his lungs working frantically, trying to find any oxygen left in the foul, fetid air inside his suit. In his ears he could hear a roar, his vision grew blurry, then dark.

Just a little further! He thought. It's not fair! It's not fair! I have wealth and power and status! I have wealth and power and status! I have wealth and power and status!

He kept repeating that thought like a mantra until he became equal with everybody else.

A MORALITY TAIL
by E.E. King

One thing was certain, that the white kitten had had nothing to do with it: — it was the black kitten's fault entirely. The white kitten you see was just a young cat, but the black kitten was an ancient demon in a fur suit.

Oh he was cute alright. Everyone loved him. He'd roll on his back and let his tummy be pet just like a normal feline, but that's the way with devils, they're never what, or whom, you might expect.

The black kitten had been housed in a cage with the white kitten at the humane society, just waiting for an owner, or so it seemed… But of course he wasn't really waiting at all. His master had already arrived.

It was early 2018. The rapture had come and gone, unnoticed. No one had qualified.

Many had believed, and still believed that someday, probably soon, Jesus would secretly return to Earth and transport all true believers up to Heaven.

But sadly, when Jesus had returned to earth, the very few who were eligible were either too young to have been told about the rapture (in fact, they were infants), or they lived on remote isles in tempest tossed seas and had never heard of the rapture. And, as any god or devil will tell you,

you can't get to a place you don't believe in and you can't believe in a place you never heard of.

Part of the problem, though unintentional, was Jesus' fault.

HE had been up in heaven leafing through some earth catalogues when a picture caught HIS eye. It showed a handsome man in a sleek all-black suit with long coat and red lining. It was no one's fault that it was a Hugo Boss catalogue from the 1930's. It was no one's fault that not only did Jesus not realize that Hugo Boss had been the designer and supplier of uniforms for the Nazi Party both before and during World War II, Jesus didn't even know what a Nazi was. Oh, HE checked in on humans every few thousand years or so, but HE couldn't be expected to keep up every anomaly, could HE? HE'd been too busy counting all those God-blessed sparrows.

So, when HE returned to earth, clean shaven and in a brand-new 1930's BOSS uniform, complete with nifty armband, the only people who followed HIM were boisterous, bald, white men. Tattooed on their fleshy arms was the same spiffy logo Jesus had on HIS attractive armband. The emblem looked much less prepossessing when inked into fat.

"Beating the Nazis was our biggest mistake," said one.

"What's a Nazi?" asked Jesus.

"That's a good one," chortled a pale man. Spittle shot from the hole made by a missing front tooth. A profusion of red veins fanned across his nose, abundant as deep-woods fungal mycelium. His shirt, raised over his protuberant belly read: Master Race.

A MORALITY TAIL

Jesus had heard of races, but HE thought they involved speed. This dude didn't look like he could outpace a crippled tortoise.

Christ interviewed these people, but it soon became clear they didn't qualify for rapture. So, after a quick visit to the Audubon society to verify the sparrow count, HE returned to heaven alone.

Those remaining on earth, everyone that is, were left to endure seven years of filthy, nasty tribulation under the tiny thumb of the Antichrist, who was disguised as the leader of the most powerful government on earth.

Most did not recognize the Antichrist, even though he possessed all the characteristics detailed on the "How to Recognize the Antichrist List", popular on most Rapture Ready Websites.

- The Antichrist will not be so called; otherwise he would have no followers.
- He will not wear red tights, nor vomit Sulphur, nor carry a trident, nor wave an arrowed tail.
- He will be materialistic.
- He will talk prosperity. Beware. Remember there is always free cheese in a mousetrap.
- The Antichrist will not believe in God, but he will be religious.
- He will deceive even the elect and the electorate.
- He will be almost as, or possibly even more, charismatic than Hitler.
- He will become a military leader.
- He will have a gigantic ego and will be the most arrogant person of all time.
- He will pretend to love Israel.

by E.E. King

If life had been fair and the universe just, the white kitten would have had some power too. Maybe he'd have been an angel or at least some minor jinn, but as most deities know, fair is whatever the ruling gods decide it is and the ruling gods of the moment were black and furry and orange and almost hairless.

Orange and black are not good god colors. They are the colors of Halloween, a time when witches and spirits roam the earth with impunity.

For two months, the kittens roomed together in the humane society, sleeping in each other's paws, playing with string and lasers, and supping out of the same food dish. And for two months, the black kitten whispered commands into the white kitten's ears as he slumbered.

Thus, when the white kitten was finally adopted and sent to the house of a person-too-important-to-be-named, he knew what he had to do. And he did it.

Firstly, though it nearly killed him, the white kitten ate a whole sprig of lavender to sweeten his intestines. Secondly, he peed on the very important person's computer keyboard, creating a short circuit between the letters B and M, W and I, and others as well. Due to the fragrant odor of his urine, the very important person never realized that his computer was compromised.

Sadly, this very important person was the only human standing between the Antichrist and the bomb.

And so, when the very important person sent out a fluffy Mother's Day memo to the News, saying: 'We should honor our moms,' it went instead to the Antichrist, saying: "I agree to launch the Bomb.'

While the earth went up in flames and ash, the black kitten laughed as he, being a demon, was immune to fire.

But, though the black kitten had fomented the plan, the white kitten had peed on the keyboard. Without him the world might still be here. Are we responsible for our actions even if brainwashed? Who was really responsible for the world's end? The Antichrist, the white kitten, the very important person, the black beast who loved tummy rubs, or Hugo Boss? Which do you think it was?

DAMAGE CONTROL

by Will Isenberg

"Ugh, did you take one of those Ubers?" Kathy Jade says with a shudder as she opens the front door. "I'm a Lyft gal myself. My husband says I'm crazy, but if it's crazy to not want to be dragged into a ditch by some stranger I've never met, then call me queen of the mental hospital. Hi, my name is Kathy. Kathy Jade."

Kathy's leopard print shirt is so tight that it looks like she is trying to self-asphyxiate. She brings me into the house, and sits me down at the kitchen counter.

"It's hotter than a gorilla's armpit out there. Water?"

Before I can tell Kathy that I brought my own water bottle, a plastic bottle of Fuji appears in front of me.

"The city water tastes like a plumber's toe fuzz," Kathy says. "And I'd buy Dasani, which is cheaper, but you can just taste the child labor when you drink it, you know? I read that article last month about those poor children in Kurdinistan, it's just awful what that company's done to their village."

I nod enthusiastically. It's a habit I picked up from listening to my dad argue with the evening news.

"Ok, I don't have time to go over the contract, but did you read what I put in the Facebook group?"

by Will Isenberg

Kathy's post asked for a teenage girl to help care for a six-year-old who would be competing in the Little Miss St Louis beauty pageant. Qualifications included CPR/Heimlich maneuver training, a clean drug test, and the ability to be social media savvy.

***

"I read the post. I printed out a resume—" I hand her my resume. It's the first one I've ever written, and I made sure to tailor it to the job description. I included a list of friends and dummies I'd practiced CPR on, a comprehensive list of every illegal drug that I've never taken, and a printout of my five best tweets.

Kathy glances through it. "Perfect, thank you so much, you are a godsend Emily—"

"Amelia," I correct her with a smile. A habit I picked up in pre-Algebra class whenever the teacher writes the wrong equation on the board.

"You have braces?" Kathy says, fanning herself with my resume, which she has already folded up. She opens the Fuji she had set in front of me and downs it in one swallow. "Where did you get them? Not Dr. Gupta's office I hope? I've heard all sorts of nasty things— lead poisoning, orthodontic cancer— Jocelyn, sweetie, come down, time to meet Emily!"

Still fanning herself, Kathy picks up her phone. "Oh, look at this," she says with a sympathetic pout. "Check out this good boy here!"

I'm expecting to see a dog, possibly also drinking designer water and wearing a leopard print shirt. What I actually see is Kathy herself, holding a small African boy.

"His family was just the sweetest you'd ever meet. Zanzmania. You've heard of that country right?"

"Of course—"

"It's a shame— Jocelyn, get down here!— so many kids your age don't know geometry. Can't even find Alaska on a map, it's terrifying."

"I know where Alaska is. It's that island below California."

Kathy looks at me aghast. "No dear, Alaska's not an island. Hawaii and Panama are the islands."

"No, I was making a joke, because on a map— never mind, it's—"

"Also I don't— Jocelyn!— have cash with me, do you have Venmo or SquareCash? I don't use Facebook cash, they track all your purchases and god knows I want some government agent snooping on my grocery shopping."

"Venmo's great," I say, pulling out my phone. "And your original post said fifty dollars, that's per hour, right?"

"Oh!" Kathy gives a big laugh. "That's good, I like that one. Let's make sure it works, how about you send me a dollar real quick?"

"Me send you money?"

"Well sure, we want to make sure it works. I'll Venmo it right back, of course."

I send the dollar to her Venmo profile, which has the same photo with the orphan from the alleged nation of Zanzmania. Kathy's phone dings. "Oh perfect. Now I'll just send it right— Jocelyn!"

I turn around, but instead of seeing Kathy's daughter I see what appears to be an oversized weasel charging and barking. It runs to me, sinks a row of needles into my leg, and urinates all over my shoe.

"Oh nooo, Jocelyn, don't be a bad girl, nooo you didn't mean to do that did you?"

"I— my shoe is soaked—" I'm trying to remain composed, but my foot is hot and wet like a summer day when the AC goes on strike.

"I'll get you a towel. Now I'm not blaming you, dear, but Jocelyn can sense human fear, it's in her blood—"

"And filtered out with her urine?" I ask, standing still as Kathy tosses me a towel.

"Oh there you are!" Kathy says, looking up the staircase, as a six-year-old girl comes bouncing down.

My jaw dangles like a flaccid willow tree. This girl has a spray tan so dark it's borderline racist. She has heavy eyeliner, makeup, and lipstick, like a cursed doll that crawled out of a horror movie and decided to model luxury clothes for kindergartners.

"Come down here, Cinnamon, you need to meet Emily."

"Amelia." I wave and smile at the girl. When I first saw Kathy's ad on Facebook, I assumed Cinnamon was the chihuahua and Jocelyn the daughter. We all have some learning to do.

"Oh, Emily, don't touch that towel with your shoe, you'll get the carpet dirty."

"What?" I look at the towel in my hand, which I had naively assumed was for cleaning the cat piss off my own sneaker.

"Your shoe is filthy, they never clean those Ubers, and then you're just wiping it all over the carpet."

"Right. Could I have a different towel for—"

"Oh, we're running late," Kathy checks her watch. It's tiger print, and has large fake crystals that flash like leering paparazzi cameras. "Cinnamon, Emily, we've got to go. Don't want to be late!" she sings.

***

Then Kathy is driving us in a Prius. I'm in the backseat with Cinnamon.

"So, Cinnamon, what do you do for fun?" I ask.

"Oh, she likes posing for photos, and dressing up, and doing her makeup," Kathy says, looking up at the mirror at her daughter. "Don't you, sweetie?"

Cinnamon shrugs. She hasn't yet learned how to fake a smile. She must not yet have worked at a McDonald's with a manager who likes giving shoulder massages to his staff. But I digress.

"Oh I forgot," Kathy says. "Would you snap a quick photo? Gotta boost that social media presence. Her fans are waiting!"

"Fans?"

"Here, take out your phone. I'll log you in to her account." Kathy reaches back for my phone.

"Hey, maybe I can do that—" Our car is swerving like an aunt holding two-for-one margaritas.

Kathy tosses back the phone and it lands on my shoe. "Ok, Cinnamon, so for this one, I'm thinking a big smile, maybe even kissy lips, and maybe make a heart with your hands? You know, like you love your audience?"

"Wait, are hearts typically associated with love?" I ask innocently.

"Of course," Kathy says, turning around as the car switches lanes on its own. "What else would a heart mean?"

by Will Isenberg

I point my phone at Cinnamon, who proves me wrong about fake smiles. An enormous grin that would put Marilyn Monroe to shame stretches across her glossy lips. Her wide eyes reflect everything around us, and her manicured nails form into a perfectly symmetrical heart.

I take the photo, and feel a bit icky. Like I've eaten fish at a restaurant without checking its Yelp reviews first.

"Ok, so for hashtags, I'm thinking 'Getting ready for our big day.' What do you think, Cinnamon?" Kathy asks.

"Getting ready for our big day. Getting ready ready ready for our big big day." Cinnamon is looking out the window, singing to herself.

I post the image. We're getting closer to the theater. I can smell toddler angst in the air.

"Hey," I say. "I'm looking at her followers. Um. Good news and bad news. A lot of her fans are men? In their forties and fifties?"

"Lots of my co-workers. I tell them about Cinnamon, and they tell their friends. They're very supportive."

"I bet they are. Any of them a manager/amateur masseur at a local McDonald's?" I ask to no one in particular.

***

We arrive at the theater, and I'm carrying five bags of costumes, makeup, and aerosol cans. The handles from the bags cut deep into my palms.

Kathy is not the only mom wearing some feline-inspired article of clothing. The crowd is a jungle of tiger shirts, cheetah scarves, and leopard yoga pants which have never been anywhere near a yoga studio.

"I hope none of these exotic cats are attracted to the scent of chihuahua urine," I say.

"Ugh, you should see some of these moms," Kathy whispers to me. "So many get into it for the absolute worst reasons. It's almost like they're trying to make up for their own boring lives by living through their daughters' success."

"Yikes. I'd never thought of it that way. Good thing we're doing this for the right reasons." I scratch at a neon green bracelet which reads "Little Miss St Louis Volunteer."

"Oh, Cinnamon's tan is rubbing off. Emily, would you get the spray can from the bag?"

"Which bag?" I ask, looking at the five that I'm holding.

"The black one."

"Ok, not to drag this out one second longer than it has to, but which black bag?" Two of the bags I'm holding fit that description.

Kathy sighs with a vengeance. "Here, this is black, this is off-black. The can is in the black one."

"Sorry." I'm rooting through the bag. "I'm colorblind. It's genetic. For the past three generations, none of the women in my family have been able to tell the difference between black and off-black. It nearly bankrupted the family rock-sorting business."

I spray the tan on Cinnamon. It's more of an off-tan, but I decide to keep this to myself.

Then a man who is definitely an amateur masseur leads us to our own dressing room, which smells like a perfume bottle grew antlers and gored a scented candle to death.

"Ok, Emily, you'll have to adjust that seat. They always make them so low, it's like they've never heard of a

by Will Isenberg

six-year-old before," Kathy vents to her own reflection in the wall mirror.

"Maybe they should speak to Cinnamon's Instagram followers. They seem to be well educated regarding six-year-olds."

"What? You're not making any sense. Come adjust the seat please, what am I even paying you for?"

"If we want to get technical about it..." I trail off. The seat raises as I locate the pedal. When I pull my hand back, it's smeared with black grease. "I have some good news and some bad— Kathy?"

Kathy walks out of the room, but I can still hear her voice, blaring like a flight attendant over a plane intercom, asking the general public if they have a bottle of Fuji water.

"Moon beams on the lily pads,

Stardust in your eyes,

Swing down from a silver rope,

And catch me by surprise..." Cinnamon is singing to her reflection.

"That's very nice," I say.

"I wrote it myself."

"It's pretty. Are you singing it for the pageant?"

She shakes her head. "I don't sing. I dance." She hands me her phone. It displays a song titled, "Shake Dat Nasty."

"I remember this song. They sang that to us in nursery school," I say, pressing play.

I'm not sure if the sound I hear is electronic dolphins being tortured with piano wire, or just my own ear drums committing ritual sepuku. But I am sure of one thing: Cinnamon is suddenly gyrating her hips like she's trying to grind out parmesan cheese at a cheap Italian franchise restaurant.

"You might want to be careful," I say, rubbing my forehead. "Health insurance typically doesn't cover hip replacements for six-year-olds."

I pause the music, and Cinnamon ceases to shake the nasty.

"Ok", Kathy is back in the room, dabbing sweat from her forehead and downing another bottle of water. "I got the list. They're putting you up as number five. I tried to get them to change it to number four, but apparently they are a bunch of control freaks who have to have everything their own way. Emily, what is on your face?"

I look in the mirror on the wall. The grease is smeared all over my cheeks and forehead. I look like a chimney sweep at a BBQ joint.

"Gross. I'll wipe this off—"

"Nevermind that, I need you to get another selfie of Cinnamon. It's Mental Health Awareness week, and it would be great for her brand to post about it."

"In support of it, or…?"

"Yes, in support of it— what else is there?"

I lean next to Cinnamon and point the camera towards us.

"Emily! What are you doing?"

"You said to take a selfie—"

"Of Cinnamon! Not of you."

"Ah, the latest trend of taking selfies of other people," I say. "I forgot."

I post the photo of Cinnamon with a poignant essay about mental health and relationship boundaries. I throw in the word 'toxic' a few times for effect.

"Is that gunk still on your face?" Kathy asks with exasperation.

by Will Isenberg

"No, it's a fresh coat. Good for exfoliating."

***

The first three girls go up and perform their routines. I don't have the heart to watch too closely, but there are lot of pop-it-and-lock-its and hip-sockets.

As the fourth girl is performing, I lean towards Kathy. "Seems like all these girls are doing the same type of routine. Too bad Cinnamon isn't singing."

"Singing?" Kathy scoffs and gives me a look. "Girl can't sing. No one in our family can. All tone-deaf."

"You've never heard her sing? Ever?"

"She doesn't sing."

"Not even something random in the shower?"

Kathy shakes her head in disbelief. "I think I'd know if my own child could sing."

Cinnamon's routine is up. Shake Dat Nasty blares, and what's left of my ears flee to Argentina faster than a war criminal.

"Hey Kathy," I say with my fingernails stuffed in my ear sockets. "It's fifty dollars an hour, right? Not for the whole day?"

She gives me a look of confusion, and I infer the worst. But I can't judge. Maybe she needs the extra money for Cinnamon's inevitable therapy in four years.

The remaining girls do their dance numbers. The rest of the afternoon is a blur of swimsuit contests, photoshoots, and so many costume changes I wouldn't be surprised if we caused an international sequin shortage. The grease is dried to my face, but it doesn't matter. I'm posting photos of Cinnamon, capturing each powerful moment like I'm photographing the moon landing. One small dance routine for Cinnamon, one giant leap in her Instagram following.

The final round is over. The judges tally the score, and announce third and second place.

"And coming in first place, after sweeping every category: Cinnamon Jade!"

Cinnamon curtseys and lets the judge put a garland of plastic flowers around her neck. I feel proud of myself, although I'm not really sure why. After a day full of aerosolized melanin and plastic eyelashes, all I want to do is go home and practice Heimlich maneuvers on myself unless I get it all out of my system.

Kathy is screaming like an ambulance siren outside a frat party, and as she throws her arms up in victory, her elbow dents the side of my skull. Eyes watering, I hold up my phone and take several photos of Cinnamon wrapped in the first place sash. I post them with the hashtags #waytogo #teamcinnamon #winnamon.

***

Then we're in the car heading home. "Hey, Cinnamon. Congrats," I say.

She shrugs. One of her fake eyelashes is dangling off her eyelid.

"Do you want to sing that song for your mom? The one about moonbeams and stardust?" I prompt.

"Emily, we've been over this. She doesn't know how to sing."

But Cinnamon opens her mouth.

"Moon beams on the lily pads,

Stardust in your eyes,

by Will Isenberg

Fly me on a pair of wings,
And through the diamond skies..."

Kathy's jaw drops. "That's beautiful! Emily, are you hearing this? Get the phone out— quick, catch it and do a live stream!"

I'm pulling my phone out and opening Cinnamon's Instagram account. That's when I notice it.

"Uh... Kathy? Something's wrong with her account. Looks like a lot of... hate mail?"

"That's— that's impossible, give me that—"

Her arm bends back and snatches the phone. One of her fake nails gouges my wrist as she grabs it. Then she's scrolling, both on the phone and between the lanes of the highway. I lean forward, trying to make out the messages and endless reposts. A single hashtag recurs, and it doesn't bode well at all.

"Hashtag Cancel Cinnamon?" I ask. "What— that makes no sense."

I take the phone back. People are already writing articles about it. Buzzfeed and HuffPo are both cranking out updates on this emerging story.

Then I see the photo in question. The one that has everyone so infuriated.

It's a selfie of me. When I was trying to post the photos of Cinnamon winning the pageant, the camera was facing me for the first one, and I accidentally shared a photo of me with dark grease all over my face.

A selfie of me, on Cinnamon's account, wearing what the entire internet has decided is blackface. In my defense, it's more of an off-blackface, but I keep that to myself.

DAMAGE CONTROL

"So… good news and bad news," I begin slowly. "Remember how you wanted me to boost her social media presence?"

She is losing followers by hundreds with each passing minute. Except the middle-aged male segment of her fanbase, which has actually doubled in the last hour. A significant portion of their profile pictures involve Confederate flags. Oh boy.

Kathy pulls over her Prius to the edge of the highway. "Oh no oh no—Oh shit—Emily, what do we do? You're social media coordinator, what do we do?"

"Ok, so this is damage control now. We should definitely stay calm, maybe issue an apology or an explanation video, make a large donation—"

"Give that to me—" Kathy grabs my phone again. Within minutes, she has shared that photo of her and the African orphan, using the caption #ServingInZanzmania.

The post does not control the damage.

I'm back in my own room now. It's evening. My foot is itchy from where the chihuahua marked its territory. My head is swollen from Kathy's elbow, and the cut on my wrist from Kathy's nail might be infected.

The story has made national news. The Little Miss St Louis organization has announced that they believe hate and prejudice are not good things at all, and that the organizers would be suspending next year's contest pending an internal investigation to ascertain whether the type of lubricant used in their dressing room chairs perpetuates any type of bigotry or injustice. And they have made several strategic donations, a sort of social Alconox to reduce the tarnish on their reputation.

by Will Isenberg

Kathy deleted Cinnamon's account several hours ago, and then posted about their account being hacked by their babysitter. There's a mob of internet sleuths trying to find out who I am, but since Kathy told everyone my name was "Emily," I'm safe for now.

I'm working on updating my resume. I edit the phrase "social media savvy" to read "experienced with social media."

My phone buzzes, and I look at my Venmo account. There's an alert from Kathy, right underneath the dollar I sent her earlier today. Kathy has sent me a request for $50.

FEMALE GOD
by Mike Ekunno

Clik-clok, Clik-clok
And here comes female god
Making a high-heeled entry
To the tiled floor of victims' souls.

Pii-poo! Pii-poo!! goes the alarm
Female god is in bad mood
All them rats scamper in the hood
As big cat pans her jittery prey.

With face overlaid with mascara
And mascara covered with a scowl
Female god sure knows her sandwich fillings
But I'd rather mortar for a spread.

From her swivel throne
Regina roars for sacrifice
A daily haemovorous menu
Savaging the flesh of tender egos.

Here comes red-lipped termagant
With voice like shrill thunder
And eyes with singeing rays
Baring dentition, hoping on a smile.

by Mike Ekunno

Clik-clok, Clik-clok
And female god exits
Like a blast of harmattan
With scorched egos in her trail.

HEREDITY

by Paul L. Bates

Our King is Mad.

Young Cedric believes himself afflicted, like his father before him, by a budding set of ram's horns. I see nothing, of course, nor do any other in attendance, yet none will gainsay the king.

How well I remember his father. I can still see the old man pulling back his stringy grey hair, once thick and blond, to display what he was certain was the sign of his birthright. "Do you see them?" he demanded. "Do you see the horns? Soon they will be large and curved. Soon they will appear in all their glory. But for now, they are just bumps. Do you see them?"

Young Cedric, Cedric IV, has said much the same to many of us, and there are those, like me, who hear the echo of his father's voice in his exhilaration. But it is only his madness, I know. I have served his family since I was a lad, as have most of the others. I see the growing fear in the eyes of those who dare not even glance at one another to share their concern.

The boy's great grandfather, however, known by the sobriquets of Cedric I, Cedric the Great, Cedric the Ram of the Mountains, and Cedric the Ram of the Gods, wore the likeness of a pair of ram's horns upon his battle helm when he expelled the invaders from our lands and founded our kingdom. And that, we are all quite certain, is the root of the boy's madness—although his father's complaint cannot be altogether discounted.

The others look to me for understanding, certain I will show them how to proceed as I am the only courtier educated at the great institutions of higher learning of our former enemy and conqueror. I am the only one with, as Cedric III, before his affliction was fond of saying, an overview. How can I possibly share this with the others? I must put my king's interests before theirs, before my own, and even with this vaunted overview, I am uncertain how to proceed. The weight of their faith in me is crushing. The burden of responsibility is worse.

Our legends tell how Cedric the Great in his youth was, like most of our forebearers, a simple shepherd. When the invaders came, we had neither weapons nor leaders, as we needed little more than our crooks and our dogs to ward off the wolves, the wild cats and the raptors who would prey upon our flocks. True, there were those among us with other skills. Every village had a midwife; every tribe a bonesetter. There were blacksmiths who made knives to shear our sheep and tools to turn the earth in the small garden plots our wives tended. There were millers to grind the wild mountain wheat from which we baked our bread; tanners to turn skins into leather, shoemakers to fashion leather into boots; vintners who made mead from honey, wine from berries—all the trappings that turn men from wandering nomads into landholders.

Our legends tell how the invaders fell upon us with a vengeance, butchering any who resisted. They came riding horses, bearing swords and spears, demanding tribute.

HEREDITY

What could we do? They took half out sheep, saying there were now fewer mouths for us to feed, thanks to them. And they promised to return in a year's time for further tribute. It must have been both terrifying and humiliating for our ancestors. Yet harsh times demand harsh solutions, breed strong willed men, create leaders.

For generations we provided the invaders with half our meat, half our wool, lest we be slaughtered. Our men hung their heads in shame when the tribute was paid, our women hid within their huts lest the invaders find them comely. No one dared oppose these soldiers from the south; no one even dared question their right to claim us as part of their empire.

And then Cedric, whose keen insight and gift of tongues made him more than a simple shepherd, devised a bold plan. One day he disappeared. Everyone thought he had offended one of the surly riders who occasionally kept watch over us and had been killed for the offence. But that was hardly the case.

Cedric, in his wisdom, did in fact approach the riders, catching them unaware one evening at meat around their campfire. He convinced the startled men that he wished to become a soldier, like them, that he was meant for greater things than tending sheep. Impressed by his stealth, affability and candor, their captain agreed. This strong lad would make a fine soldier.

At this point the two versions of the story diverge sharply. Those told by our people are filled with pride and valor. According to our legends, Cedric left his village a strapping lad. He returned a grizzled veteran of two campaigns ten years later as one of the hated tribute collectors. The elders did not recognize him at first, so great were the changes wrought upon him. When he revealed his identity, they were furious, but having the gift of tongues, he soon put them at their ease. He convinced them that everything that had happened during the past ten years was part of a great strategy; that his seeming defection was only the first step toward their liberation. They listened with rapt attention as he explained his plan.

The elders agreed to allow more of the younger men to enlist within the ranks of the hated oppressors with Cedric. He was, by then, well respected in their army for his courage, as well as his good council. The invaders had already agreed to allow Cedric to recruit from the mountain tribes, hoping to have more soldiers just like him for their ongoing border skirmishes with the neighboring empire. Every year, Cedric added more willing young men to his regiment of local fighter. These received the best training, weapons, horses and armor from our conquerors. Little did they realize they were arming those who would one day drive them from our lands.

Cedric was, by all accounts, an astute man. He knew how to listen, how to winnow the truth from gossip, information from chatter. He knew a time would come when the animosity between the two great nations south of us would erupt into a full-scale war, knew when to desert with his entire regiment. That year, those who came for tribute, mostly the fat sons of the nobility, were met not by helpless shepherds but by hardened soldiers. They were stripped of their weapons, their armor, and their horses and sent back on foot with a message for their emperor. *No more tribute.*

Cedric counted upon the fact the invader would be too hard pressed elsewhere to attend to this minor local uprising, at least until matters with the neighboring empire had been settled. By then, he had trained more young men in the arts of war, put others to work making bows and arrows, forging armor and weapons, and erecting a mountain fortification near a tarn, stocking it with provisions. When the invaders returned, after their disastrous war, they were repulsed, with heavy losses, and another message for their emperor. *We will sell you our sheep and the price will be less than you paid for that lesson in bartering, unless, of course, you need another lesson.*

That is the version of the story known by everyone in our small kingdom.

The version I learned at the great university in the imperial capitol was much less impressive. Our people are mentioned only in a single short paragraph in their massive compendium of histories that date back a millennium. They state merely that their enemy, that neighboring empire, invaded our lands and was repulsed by a local garrison. And that in appreciation for military services rendered both at home and abroad we were given our autonomy by an enlightened emperor.

All men are fools and liars. It is hard to know where the truth lies.

Cedric II, first son of Cedric the Great, learned to read, built fortifications along our borders, commissioned monuments to his father, turned the business of ruling the land over to his son when he reached the age of sixty. Cedric III, grandson of Cedric the Great, tended the works of his father until the tumors he mistook for ram's horns drove him completely mad and slowly killed him. His words haunt me still. "Do you see the horns?" he begged. "Soon they will be large and curved. Soon they will appear in all their glory. But for now, they are just bumps. Do you see them?"

by Paul L. Bates

Every day his young son, Cedric, was forced to caress the sides of his father's feeble head, feeling at first nothing, save the old man's conviction. Then the bumps, that grew and grew, curving like a ram's horn. The bumps that made the old king cry out at night, sharing his agony with the entire court. And now the boy, driven mad by his father's hallucinations, echoes the old man's words.

What am I to do?

Tell him there are no ram's horns?

Tell him if he's lucky it's nothing—he's only deluded—otherwise, he'll die in unmitigated torment like his father?

What am I to do?

This morning Cedric IV summoned a war counsel, the first our kingdom has known since the rein of his great grandfather. He is determined to avenge the dishonor our great neighbor to the south once visited upon those simple nameless mountain shepherds. All eyes are upon me.

What am I to do?

THE SCOURGE

by Derek Des Anges

The Scourge, as it was later known, came in the autumn and laid waste to half the population in one fell swoop. The wise-women were laid low; the undertakers fell ill; the charity hospitals filled up with groaning men and women whose numbers were soon added to by those who had served them in their final hours, and the aristocracy cordially withdrew to their country estate for the better quality of air.

The priests, whose intercession to the plainly-offended gods might be counted upon in times of need, locked themselves away in their holy places with a cry of, "Oh how unfortunate," and appeared only upon the high balconies to explain to the waiting masses what they should do.

"It is punishment for being unrighteous," declared Head Priest Bolnara, who felt he was on pretty safe ground with this explanation. Most things were, sooner or later, punishment for being unrighteous. They'd helped themselves in this quarter by ensuring that almost anything was unrighteous when viewed in the right light and by the right person, i.e., one of the Head Priests. "The malaise will not pass until all the wickedness is cleansed from the land."

He went to his high balcony and pronounced this to the assembled masses.

"Too much idolatry," he said, touching the engraved rings on his hands. "There has been too much worship of things other than the Associated Deities, and this is why you—and I—suffer so. For I suffer at the sight of your suffering."

Having made this proclamation, Head Priest Bolnara went back to his sumptuous apartments for his dinner, and forgot all about them.

Dutifully, the people of the town went to their homes and began to destroy anything that might, for example, constitute an idol of something other than the Associated Deities. There was some doubt over this, as the Associated Deities had only recently updated to include a couple of new deities and no one was entirely sure whether they should be counted or not, and the Old Mother had been removed from the pantheon ten years ago and a few people still liked to turn to her when things weren't working out so well.

They dragged the statues to the square below the Head Priest's balcony and piled them high; everyone wanted to be seen to do the right thing.

They stood shoulder to shoulder and clapped each other on the back and burned the statues they'd once loved, and then when the embers had gone out, they went home.

"That should do it," murmured Head Priest Bolnara, when the show was over, and he went back to his sumptuous apartments in the knowledge of a job well done.

By the end of the next week the hospitals were full to groaning and full of groaning, and the numbers of the dead were growing by the day, spattered with the terrible red kisses that came with the illness.

Head Priest Bolnara received a visit from one of his underlings in the closed confines of the holy places.

THE SCOURGE

"I have a theory," said Lay Priest Fauma, who had those quite often and had to be forcibly discouraged from them from time to time, "that this might not be solely the wrath of the Gods. I have noticed that when people come together and greet each other they sicken more than those anti-social ones who keep their distance."

"Our records say you are wrong, and the spiritual wellbeing of the people says that you are wrong," said Head Priest Bolnara, who was preparing to go to dinner and didn't particularly want this weirdo getting between him and his goose. "They are filled with wickedness and until we can determine which particular wickedness has pissed off which particular god, they're going to keep dropping like flies."

He would not, he admitted, have used the same language around the people of the town, but the overall concept was the same.

"Remarkable that no one within the bounds of the sanctuary has caught it so far," said Fauma mildly, with his gnarled hands behind his back.

"No it isn't," Bolnara said, gesturing at the fine things within his private chamber. "We are righteous mouthpieces of the Gods. Of course we are spared."

"Even the cooks?" asked Fauma, raising his thick eyebrows. " Even the servants? How lucky for them that merely by living in the sanctuary and preparing our food they are made righteous. If righteousness can be conferred so easily, perhaps you should go out into the square and lay hands on the townspeople, to absolve them of their wickedness."

"Perhaps," said Head Priest Bolnara, impatient to get to his goose, "we have absolved wickednesses which ought not have been absolved, and this is why the town is punished. Less lenience in future is sure to be the key."

He felt pleased with himself at this explanation. It was surely the case: the townspeople had been treated too lightly in the past and the Gods were irritated with this weakness. More tithes should probably be collected.

Bolnara had almost lost himself in a daydream of the silks he would levy from the notoriously wicked and idle silk-traders when Fauma intruded on his thoughts once more, and not by leaving his chambers.

"In that case why are we not also being punished for our wickedness in misjudgment?" Fauma asked, serenely, his ugly old hands clasped behind his back in deference. "For surely as learned and righteous men it is our duty and calling to make the correct decisions about absolution. And yet, everyone who remains at home and touches none of his neighbours nor servants seems to be spared this affliction. Including idolators and adulterers."

"Well, you'd know all about them, wouldn't you," grumbled Bolnara, and he began mentally writing another proclamation.

The next day he made this proclamation: the priesthood had been too lenient upon the people, and would be giving out fewer absolutions to the masses until the will of the Gods had been thoroughly understood by all. As it was, Bolnara stressed, they were clearly not following the right instructions as they were still afflicted.

He prescribed scourging, and the townsfolk, grumbling and dispirited, went to knit flails for the occasion.

Fauma, meanwhile, went to the Hospice of Charity with his face and tattoos of status concealed, and assisted the Brothers and Sisters of Charity in tending to the

THE SCOURGE

patients who came in speckled with the red kisses of the Scourge. He tended to the ones with the weeping sores, and the ones with the foetid breath, and he observed how those who were consoled by their families were usually swiftly joined by them. He observed how those who were not visited brought no neighbours nor kin to join them later. He observed which ailed, and which recovered, and he observed, in particular, the red marks upon their bodies.

He remained for three days.

When he returned, Bolnara invited him to watch the scourging from the balcony. Fauma stood with his gnarled hands behind his back, and watched the people of the town gather together and beat themselves and each other with knitted flails, wailing in their agony to be absolved by the Gods, if the priests would not do it.

"I notice," said Fauma pleasantly, "that you are not scourging yourself."

"I don't have the pestilence," Bolnara said with an equally pleasant smile, "Because I am not wicked. I have coveted nothing that I should not covet; I have taken nothing that I should not take; I have worshipped none that I should not worship."

Fauma didn't remark on Bolnara's hunger for power, hunger for cooked goose, and hunger for fine silk. He only nodded gravely and said, "I see. Have you given any further thought to the possibility that calling the people together like this so that you can see them suffer just makes the pestilence worse? I have been in the hospitals and—"

Bolnara, vexed by the conversation, leaned forward and placed his well-groomed forefinger across his subordinate's thin lips. "I will not hear another word of your silliness,

Fauma. We are insulated from the wrath of the Gods because we are worthier, and you may thank me for that."

"You?" Fauma asked, startled out of circumspection.

Bolnara, exasperated, slapped him gently on each cheek. "I and I alone intercede with the Gods on their level, Fauma, and it is not my fault if you are too arrogant in your own assumptions to notice! Now, look down there! That man's trousers have been scourged so many times they're falling off!"

"Don't you think it remarkable," said Fauma to his favourite among the servants, "how pristine and untroubled the holy places are by the Scourge? Why, even those of us who dwell within, regardless of our wickedness or lack thereof, are not touched by it."

"Yes," said the servant, who had recently asked for, and been denied, leave to bury her younger sister.

"And yet those without suffer regardless of their wickedness," Fauma added, watching her face. "If only there were some way to change Head Priest Bolnara's mind about this red-painted death that stalks the land. To paint his mind a little more favourably towards, perhaps, urging our brethren in the square to keep away from each other until the Scourge has passed?"

"Yes," said the servant, unwavering, as Fauma toyed with a bowl of terracotta shards meant for the muralists' mixers. "If only."

Three days later, Fauma found a series of red spots on the backs of his hands. Although this troubled and indeed frightened him somewhat, his first thought was not to pursue some sort of cure, but rather to take the proof of his hypothesis to Bolnara—making sure, of course, to tell all the other Lay Priests along his way.

THE SCOURGE

Bolnara was sitting down to a very fine dinner indeed when Fauma begged an audience, and was inclined to hostility even before the man took out his gnarled hands with their red kisses and showed them to him.

"Gods alive!" hissed Bolnara, leaping backward. "Away from me! Out of my chambers! Would you bear pestilence in my own quarters?"

"But you said it was caused by wickedness and depravity," Fauma said peacefully, holding up his red-kissed hands in surrender. "Surely you have not erred so in the last few days that you will be struck down merely for association with me? Or is it my touch that you fear?"

"Out!" Bolnara barked, filled with distemper and the beginnings of indigestion. "Get to the infirmary and stay there."

As Fauma left with a hearty wave from his besmirched old hands, Bolnara regained a little of his composure.

He added as something of an afterthought, "And I shall pray for the gods to intercede with you."

As Fauma lay on his lonely bed in the infirmary, speckled with red but quite without sweat or shivering, he enquired as to whether he would be seeing Bolnara in his isolation. Or, indeed, anyone but the servant who fearfully tended to him.

"Indeed no," said the servant, her hands wrapped in cloth. "None will come near until you are cleansed."

"And how is Bolnara?" asked Fauma, scratching at the red kisses on his hands. The servant squinted at them. They seemed to be a little less vivid than before. Indeed, the more he scratched, the more they seemed to disappear. "Pass me some soap, please."

"They say he is hiding in his chambers," said the servant, passing the soap with a suspicious look. "They say he has the symptoms of the plague. They say he will not speak to anyone and he gives no more speeches from the balcony."

"Symptoms of the plague, hm?" asked Fauma, scrubbing his hands. "Well, fancy that. Did anyone say when they began?"

The servant watched as Fauma scrubbed off the red kisses from his hands and arms. "No, they did not. Only that he had none before he conversed with you, and by his own account he slapped your face."

"Nothing about any servants sneaking into his chambers while he slept with red paint, I hope?" asked Fauma, washing off the last of the soap.

The servant blushed. "No, they have said nothing of the sort."

"Good," said Fauma, with half a wink. "What an absurd idea that would be."

Shortly after Fauma's miraculous recovery from the scourge, Head Priest Bolnara sent another priest in his stead to stand at the balcony and instruct the masses that the real problem, vouchsafed to them in a vision, was the undue congregation of the afflicted in the square. That their future flagellation and burning must take place in private—that being seen to do the right thing, as Fauma suggested from the back of the balcony, was less important than doing the right thing. It was suggested that the cause of their affliction was pride.

Shortly after that proclamation, a lowly servant washed Bolnara's sores and found they came away at the touch of a cloth.

"A miracle!" cried Bolnara, overwhelmed. "The gods have released me!"

"Gratitude," suggested Fauma, "is the repayment of the mortals to the instruments of divinity."

Bolnara sighed, but he did not stint to pile the servant's arms with rings, necklaces, and fine plate from his own personal chambers.

"Well," said Fauma. "Don't the Gods move in mysterious ways, after all."

And he clasped his gnarled hands behind his back, and rubbed the last of the red paint from his nail beds.

SIX VIEWS OF THE WALL
by Daniel Ausema

I:

The wall is huge. Just plain huge. Towering over the streets on either side. It's like a castle wall made of steel. Galvanized steel. He likes that word, the leader does. Galvanized. It sounds strong. It sounds impressive. It sounds huge.

Let them try to cross that wall. No one's getting over the spikes at the top. No one's tunneling through the deep—very deep—concrete foundation he had them put in. No one.

And electrified. Definitely electric. He hasn't checked to make sure, and no one told him it's electric, but as soon as he thinks it he knows it's true. Currents of electricity, like magic, are running through the wall. Invisibly deadly.

Electric.
Galvanized.
Huge.
The perfect wall everyone imagined.

II:

The wall is sagging.

The leader's buddy got the contract instead of anyone with expertise. The foundation is already wearing away after a few rainstorms. The thin metal buckles inward.

"That was an unusual rain," the contractor states, by phone, for the record. "No one could have guessed a rain like that would come. Unbelievable rain. Anyone else's wall would have washed away. But it doesn't matter. Our materials held up perfectly. No one could have done better."

The contractor's voice is oddly distorted. Familiar, yet distorted.

Workers rush in to shore up the foundation. Sandbags and subpoenas and cement shoes stuffed into the growing gaps beneath the wall. Where the holes grow too big, they hide the damage behind construction barrels and walk away.

Decorative flourishes go up on the sagging wall. Gold-leaf letters to celebrate this perfect wall. Gold-like-leaf, anyway. They announce the strength of the wall, the importance of those who live within its circle of protection.

III:

Graffiti covers the wall from the outside. Tags and pieces and great murals of sprayed art.

The earliest works, still visible in places, are angry. Monochromatic rage mixed with hexes and imprecations. A plague on your houses. May your fabled illusions of gold turn back to straw.

SIX VIEWS OF THE WALL

Later art turns to mockery. Layers of colors and jeers cover the anger. As the artists grow bolder, they make more elaborate works, covering great swathes of the wall. What is there to fear from the gormless leader on the other side? Weak and flailing, his lazy attempts to defend his precious wall glide away into distraction.

Even the mockery fades into the past. Newer works celebrate those who resisted. Great murals of swirling colors cover sections of the wall and resolve into images of the new heroes. They gather in crowded scenes, many people of many places. Sometimes they argue. Some are angry. Yet they forge new agreements.

The murals display it all, the struggle and the effort and the deals they reach. Some paintings show the new lives they work to create as well, those of tomorrow and those that may take centuries to build and flourish.

IV:

The leader gloats about his wall. It will stop armies. The enemies that are all around. His eyes dart into the shadows and back, up to the sun, out to the empty stands. The wall is a promise. It will keep the world within from changing. Let the world outside change in new and scary ways. He will keep the protected spaces from changing, will turn them back to an earlier time when he could get away with even more crimes.

The wall must be paid for, of course. Must be improved. The enemies outside its sturdy confines grow desperate and dangerous. Not strong—only he can be strong in this space—but deadly in their imagined weaknesses. The wall needs to be taller, the spikes on top more threatening.

by Daniel Ausema

He pockets the money to strengthen the wall and brags about the protection it now gives.

V:

The sycophant steals the fake gold leaf mounted on the inner side of the wall. The letters stay behind, gray outlines of incompetence. The sycophant sells the letters to those on the outside, slipping easily between the shambled mess of metal panels that never lined up perfectly.

When he slinks back inside, new words have appeared on the walls.

The sycophant speaks, and gold leaf comes from his mouth. Fake gold leaf, just like the words on the wall, dry and crackling like late autumn. The time has come, each word says, no matter what he tries to tell the leader. The time of endings. The time of frailty. Even a wall cannot protect everything within.

Uncomprehending, the leader marvels at the false gold. Their message escapes his understanding, as words often do, and he delights in twisting the leaves this way and that. He cavorts at their gaudiness. Ooh, pretty words.

So the sycophant continues his meaningless speech, and the leader frames the leaves, places them on the wall so he can admire their proof of his inspiring leadership and strength.

When the leader soon forgets that the words are there, the sycophant slips out to steal them from the wall. He sells them, slinking in and out of the barrier's gaps. And he returns to speak his whispering autumn words of praise and false promise.

SIX VIEWS OF THE WALL

VI:

From above, the wall encompasses a small space. It is not the promised wall, defining a line of many miles. Each plan made it smaller, constricting in on the leader and his fevered mind. It surrounds a building, at least. That much he is able to achieve. Where it bisects streets, the people make do, swerving out to avoid the eyesore. Where it butts against another building, the landlords complain, but is it even worth the effort? They brush the rubble from their ledges and double the rent they charge wherever they can get away with it.

Inside the wall, they might have a better chance getting away with it, but they've seen that movie. A little extra money isn't worth the mindless inanities.

Those who deliver goods to the building within brush aside the metallic-looking curtains that now cover the gaps of fallen sections of wall. They walk in, holding their noses, and walk back out.

Every year the wall shrinks inward, and outside, the people live their lives, freed from the leader's thoughtless whims and outbursts.

Within, the leader sits alone, the wall shrunken to crown a head that always lusted after thrones. Now at last he rules alone.

FREEDOM OVER GOOD

by Devo Cutler

Now don't bemoan the fact he lied to us
Cried pussy to the masses
Your reality show host's mask-our-aide,
'Tis fool's gold in the Encyclopedia, Wikipedia
Or any Pedia, You/we know. Ask the media,
    Grumpy or Humpty Dumpty – They'll say,
"Well, I didn't vote for him."

Yet who can resist the call of
One-click Prime purchase?
Or Pay-your-Pal now;
We listen, like lemmings, to the call.
Bucky Fuller warned us
    We'd occupy the space
Somnamulatory manikins
Robotic to a different drummer,

We do not see ourselves as
Sleepwalkers as drawn into
The next binge debut,
TV Sirens' lips part,
Nightly news wakes us into shock;
Some of our more luxurious neighborhoods

by Devo Cutler

      Now charred, boarded up skeletons of commerce,
Maybe that would get earth's attention,
Or yours... But no.

Firetrucks, police cars and ambulances
Rage against blacktop to stop the blood-letting,
Nighttime glow blankets with litter, frothing
Guilt but painted in graffiti,
Reminds us Black lives, all lives, matter;
Start there, don't stop there,
      What more lynched?
But police have their own drumbeat
Mentors nowhere to be found.

Your bones talk to you above
The noise and one or two of you
Notice a small 2.2 earthquake;
It's out in some desert with those
Penis cactus things,
      Not your problem,
You have enough toilet paper to
Outlast even a hurricane.

You choose to watch instead
The swirling clouds.
Is it a storm approaching?
The pretty white, big chested weather woman
Says it's offshore.
      Not to worry,

As windswept ships
Crash against ancient rocks

FREEDOM OVER GOOD

It rumbles under your feathered pillows
And West Elm Cal king-sized bed
And you dream,

Remember to forget
The lesson
Written on columns
       You/We prance by them,
In your dreamscape
Ancient scribblings on marble
And clay – the yellow-lined tablets
Of wisdom you wrote when you knew
       The truth can be felt
With your hand, your pen
Needs no translation,

As they/we/our freakled orange leader
Herds our minds
And musak drones on
Wafting from cracks
In the ground below
A smell of sulfur
We ignore,

Then, go ahead,
Dance, dance, dance
       Off the cliff you go;
Listen as happy radio songs play
Sing along with your favorites

And you, too, are happy to do so,
The reality show must go on,

by Devo Cutler

Yeah though we are in the valley-of-evil
Pretending to be for our best interests
Family, country and God
Tranced into one soon-to-be-molten
Massive exoskeletal exit,

Suddenly silenced
Without a brand or band to
Celebrate
Democracy

Horse -faced and hair-braided
We step-foot
Into Joe's volcano, or maybe Donald's again,
Does it matter as we march?
Willingly
Forfeiting even soldiers who
Died for your/our freedom,
      Now freedom over good
To be burned alive
For the god of comfort

Our pocketbooks fills with fool's gold
The orange haired despot sends us,
in the form of fake news recycled
And our own tax dividends.
We should thank him.
But,
You/We believe there is an elevator
Waiting to catch us
And
cash us out

HINDSIGHT 2020: THE DEVOLUTION AND HISTORY OF THE NEW BREED

by Kate Maxwell

Hindsight 2020: The Devolution and History of The New Breed

Atticus M Warren

Greenland Academics Institute. April 2051

Author Note:

Atticus M Warren MAnth, School of Anthropology, Greenland Academics Institute.

With thanks to the guidance and mentorship of Professor R. Patel and the generosity of the 2051 Greenland Virus and New Breed Retrospective Grant opportunity which has allowed me to undertake this research.

With thanks to Sue Carmalitto for her assistance with data collection.

by Kate Maxwell

Abstract:

This paper offers new insight into the origins and devolution of the Homo Sapiens sub species, New Breed, which devolved in the years following the 2020 virus pandemic. The issue of origins or devolution remains a debated topic. However, this paper aims to clarify the role of the 2020 virus, as a significant trigger, but not the genesis of the sub species. The paper explores initial symptoms and common defining characteristics of the New Breed using scholarly articles, publications, archival footage, and anecdotal evidence from survivors of the time. Final notes on how the New Breed continues to adapt and may still find its place in society, are relevant to questions for sustainability. Strategies encouraging this sub species to become productive contributors to society continue to be implemented today.

Keywords: evolution, devolution, infection fatality rate, sphincter, cerebrum, species

Background: Virus Origins

It began, like many things begin; a tightening of the throat, general fatigue, and the instinct that something was wrong, but it was best to push on anyway. People didn't know what to call the virus at first. Animal names had been used effectively before, where blame could be conveniently shifted to another species, but a more clinical name was now necessary. 'Bat flu' was used briefly but it had connotations to a Superhero franchise of the time and lacked the correct gravitas that this virus needed. Yet, the biology of bats and our incessant encroachment into the

HINDSIGHT 2020: THE DEVOLUTION AND HISTORY OF THE NEW BREED

natural world, had indeed created this cross species transfer that would change the world. News of epidemics overseas, in countries with populations that did not look like their own, sparked interest in initially unaffected countries. But even before the virus arrived, the earth was parched to tinder; global spot fires of conflict, corruption and decay were daily internet fodder. Although a great fear eventually did spread, populations were accustomed to, and complacent about their own dysfunction. However, nobody could have predicted or prepared for the devolution of the New Breed.

Lockdown's of cities began when the virus' exponential escalation overwhelmed or threatened hospitals. People had started hoarding cans and supplies in the backs of pantries and hand sanitiser and other essential items had apparently run out of stock. Glued to their screens, in morbid awe of the rising death board tally, people watched, waited, and washed their hands. Arguments over economy versus health ruled the airwaves. Leaders scrambled to maintain credibility when the populist methods of bluster and spin were useless against a virus with no political allegiance. Schools shut and ran online instead. Offices too. A raft of new life rules was quickly drafted and revised, depending on the number of death statistics and the influence of wealthy lobby groups.

Devolution Triggers:

But something as deadly, if not more destructive, than the virus had been triggered. It wasn't discovered until decades later, after the carnage of wars and pandemics had run their course, when those left were able to piece together the clues. The virus was initially thought to have mutated into a new strain, resulting in the New Breed. It has since been discovered that the virus itself, although certainly able to exacerbate and feed the rise of the New Breed, was not its creator. These unfortunate people had always been amongst us, but now their full devolution had been triggered. Professor Patel explains in her breakthrough article on New Breed origins, *The Virus was not the Trigger*. 'Obviously survival instinct is in everyone but for some at this time, high degrees of panic irritated the fatty tissues of the cerebrum and, as one of the fattiest organs in the body, the brain's temporal lobe was thus irreversibly damaged. The outer cortex was so compromised that devolution was the only pathway. Thus, the New Breed became more self-serving, aggressive and their reasoning irreversibly impaired.' (Patel, 2042, p. 56).

First Events and Symptoms:

The first real signs that the world was dealing with a completely new breed was during the April 2020 Toilet Paper Carnage. Many people, isolating due to the virus, had prepared themselves with extra stores and supplies. It was inadvisable and later even illegal to be loitering in the community unless acquiring essential goods and services. Professor Patel claims that the rampage may have started as a sphincter reflex travelling through the nervous system to fatty white tissues in the New Breeds' brain. The need for toilet paper hoarding was irrational and, more significantly, the first real step in the devolution cycle. It is thought that the New Breed believed eliminating one risk, in this case the horror of a

HINDSIGHT 2020: THE DEVOLUTION AND HISTORY OF THE NEW BREED

faeces covered arse, was all the cognitive strain they were now capable of expending. In any case, it should have alerted governments to the potential dangers, but as most historians and anthropologists know, hindsight is 20/20.

A few thousand were killed worldwide in the toilet paper stampedes. Sadly, as the virus targeted the elderly and vulnerable, the same occurred in the stampedes. Frail old ladies and toddlers were crushed in supermarket aisles, wheelchairs upended, and trolleys used as weapons. In some of the so-called 'open carry' nations, shootings occurred. Often this created more issues as the toilet paper, then blood splattered, was unable to be used and created more rage in the emerging New Breeds. At the time, psychologists explained this behaviour as the neuroses of panic. Some convicted killers were even exonerated by the new psychiatric term, 'Temporary anal nerve insanity'. As Patel has claimed of these sad creatures, 'their fatty white tissues were now so inflamed that the process of devolution could not be reversed.' (Patel, 2042, p. 71) Of course, some debate Patel's theories still and claim it was merely a mutation of the virus itself which caused the New Breed. However, anecdotal evidence and historical patterns do suggest that the New Breed were always amongst us, but their potential for harm lay largely suppressed through regulations and a dormant state of devolution. Now, the typical bluster and blame ideology of some dominant world leaders at the time, only served to incite and build the New Breed's power and influence.

by Kate Maxwell

Herding and other Initial Characteristics:

New Breeds started brandishing their own theories about the 2020 virus on social media. In retrospect, now that we understand the state of their cognitive decline, it is perhaps, more understandable why they relied on such implausible beliefs. Many of them questioned the rollout of 5G networks that took place at the same time the pandemic hit. The fact that viruses do not travel along the electromagnetic spectrum didn't alter their beliefs. Others also claimed that the virus, now killing tens of thousands worldwide, didn't actually exist but was merely an elaborate plot to remove their liberties. Professor Patel again points out, that by this stage their hippocampus had been directly infiltrated and reason was almost impossible. When they began herding and amassing in the streets to protest health restrictions, enacted to prevent further contagion and death, the psychiatric societies started to take notice. In old images you can clearly see the beginnings of their devolution; the bulging of the eyeballs, the slackening of the jaw and the sallowing of the skin. They draped themselves in flags, refused to wear masks and held placards screaming *'Facts not Fear'* while they let their babies loose among the contagion.

Many of the New Breeds, especially the females, started coughing and spitting at supermarket assistants, transport officials and members of the public. Patel restates that the sphincter reflex was again being triggered. Their urge to expel toxins created by changing chemistry, was increased as they began devolving. In archive footage of these New Breeds, seen coughing and spitting directly at people, it appears to be a vindictive act of aggression to spread the virus. But Patel insists, at this stage at least, this was the

HINDSIGHT 2020: THE DEVOLUTION AND HISTORY OF THE NEW BREED

body's last defence against full devolution; a final effort to expel the new hormonal secretions overwhelming their system. But it was difficult at the time to attribute much sympathy to the hordes who were putting so many others at risk. The divisions between the species had already begun.

In the same way that the cover of night can often soften the debris and squalor of a derelict house, the virus did the opposite. It radiated a harsh light, uncovering the decay of man-made environments and failing social structures, in all their polluted glory. The veneer of civilization was cracking more each day. Inequities, which had always been apparent, now meant the difference between life and death. Despite the risk, many took to the streets to protest racial and economic prejudices. This caused a frightening push in the devolution of the New Breed. The nasal and oral passages were now the next to be impacted. The New Breed could now literally smell fear and distress, and this in turn created a toxic blood lust producing saliva. *My life Matters, Not Yours* was the catch cry of the so called 'White Supremacists' who were devolving the most rapidly. A classic photo of Harold Kesler, one of the main instigators of countless horde attacks against black communities, clearly shows his devolution commencement: contorted face, drool seeping from his mouth, yellow patches in his eyes and the slackening of his jaw. Many of those posing behind him, in Nazi salutes, bear similar characteristics.

The Fall of Liberty:

On the night they brought Liberty down it was full moon. Patel scoffs at the idea this had anything to do with the final steps toward devolution. She claims the adaptation had just run its course and timing was purely coincidental. Some of the *Black Lives Matter* protests had targeted statues of slave owners and other figures of oppression. Harold Kesler mandated that his followers would retaliate and bring down, what he referred to as, 'The biggest symbol of welcome to filthy foreigners and their F#@king virus.' (Steiner, 2028, p. 117). Enough was enough, he said, and they would take down the fraudulent Liberty to reform their own. Due to virus-imposed restrictions there were no tourists on the island that night, but at least five caretakers and guards were killed in the explosion. The logistics are still debated today, as Kesler and the four others, instrumental in the terrorist plan, were shot later in a horde/ police battle. Sixty people on both sides were killed. It is generally believed that they had been stockpiling ammunition and explosives for decades. This wasn't difficult in the US, at the time, because little or no weapons regulations existed. A few eyewitnesses recalled the shock of seeing the statue of Liberty's decapitated head and her torch sinking into the Hudson.

Further and Final Physical Adaptations:

From that day it was possible to recognise a New Breed by sight. It wasn't just the sweaty, feverish pallor or wild bulging eyes. Their jaws had begun to move and were receding into their necks. They also developed excessive hirsutism. New Breeds claimed they didn't need masks because their facial hair, now apparent on both sexes, served as a shield to contagion. Of course, this made no sense as beards, especially untended ones, can harbour parasites and respiratory droplets. Neither did it bear up in the virus death rates of New Breeders, which far outstripped the rest

HINDSIGHT 2020: THE DEVOLUTION AND HISTORY OF THE NEW BREED

of the populous. This may have been the only reason that the New Breeds were eventually able to be suppressed: their numbers were in rapid decline due to their virus self-exposure. They congregated in loud swarms, or hordes as we now call them, and were easy to locate.

Their hysteria was not reserved for the virus. A famous young environmentalist of the day who had campaigned against Global warming, only just escaped a major kidnapping and New Breed terrorist plan, when a bearded infiltrator alerted authorities of the plan. Sadly, he fell to the horde when they learned his true identity as a main species. There were numerous other distracting conspiracies and ideologies that the New Breed relished; The holocaust never occurred, neither did the moon landing, Roswell aliens existed and that the wearing of silver foil aluminium protected them from electromagnetic fields and mind control. Apart from the Roswell theory, all these debunked beliefs were blamed on a faulty code in their DNA largely responsible for their ultimate devolution. They also inexplicably idolised the catastrophically inept leader of the US at the time, who many have since named 'King of the New Breeds.' His name still appears on the Presidential records but he was stripped of his title in later years. Most historians refer to his leadership as the 'Age of Orange Decay,' and liken it to a similar period many years before, called 'The Dark Ages.'

Tagging and Monitoring:

After the Ellis Island bombing, New Breeds were forced to register for identity chips. They may have incurred significant cognitive decline, but many still had enough cunning to initially manipulate this system. At first, they just wrapped their ankle bracelets in tin foil but when they realised this wasn't as effective as they'd always believed, they found different ways to destroy the chips. Unfortunately, some even amputated feet. In rabid internet clips they can be viewed hacking their feet and crying, *'Nobody takes my liberty!'* They also formed New Breed ghettos. Generally reviled for their lack of community compliance, stench, their tendency to violence and an appearance which had become more bear-like than human, they banded together on the outskirts of global cities.

Lemmings:

Towards the end of the virus' reign the New Breeds organised their biggest affront yet. Community Restrictions had been lifted and schools and offices reopened. In a coordinated attack against schools, sports centres, and workplaces, they sent their infected in. Coughing and spitting their way through crowds and backed up by armed New Breeds. The virus took hold and the world stopped again. Patel does not claim that this was another sphincter reflex. She says the New Breeds were well past any reversal of their inevitable devolution. This was simply a terrorist attack led by the largest suicide mission yet. Patel argues that, by this stage, the cognitive state of the New Breed had bypassed basic survival instincts. She describes it as, 'An almost Lemming-like compulsion to leap into danger.' (Patel, 2048, p. 205).

HINDSIGHT 2020: THE DEVOLUTION AND HISTORY OF THE NEW BREED

New Breed Wars, Settlement and Sustainability:

The next decade saw more pandemics, natural disasters and temperature rises brought on by climate change. Without huge societal reform it appeared that civilization would not survive. The New Breeds fought viciously. Further explanation of these battles can be found in my upcoming edition, *The New Breed Wars, 2020-2030*. But they were eventually and decisively quelled. There remains a small population, now exiled to what was once known as the state of Texas in the USA. A massive wall was built around the state and they remain chemically subdued and regulated. From field observations and analysis of current cultural norms, they now seem to have adapted to their new biological transitions, as most species do. A pleasing adaptation has been the way that many have now channelled their fantastical and illogical beliefs into fiction and screenwriting. The famous Science Fiction writer, S. Kingly, back in 2025, apparently stated prophetically, 'These clowns make up better shit than me!' And indeed, without the likes of Caesar Redneck screenplays, or Melania Gold's 'Under the Imperious Curse Series' the world would be a less colourful place.

Obviously, the global population has been greatly reduced since the frenzy of 2020. Sustainability and equity remain the guiding principles of the Global Greenland Foundation Centre. As we are all painfully aware, it was timely and necessary to migrate the larger proportion of remaining populations to the top of the globe. Southern countries were heating up beyond survivable limits. The Guardians remaining, who still inhabit countries such as Australia and large parts of Africa and Asia, continue to live creatively and sustainably within the limit of their resources. Problems will always exist, but without the constant sabotage of the New Breeds, general populations are willing and able to act in the interests of the local and global community. If hindsight can teach us anything, it seems to be that we cannot fight mother nature, in either the environment or our own biology, and our survival depends on cooperation and coexistence.

Warren, 2051

References:

Patel, R. M. (2042). *The Virus was Only the Trigger. Facts not Alternatives*, pages 54-112

Steiner, F. W. (2028). *Kesler and his Final Plan*. Berlin: Free Press.

Patel, R. M. (2048). *Understanding the New Breed*. Nuuk: Greenland Foundation Publications

A FRIEND OF THE WORKING MAN
by J.J.J. Kearns

It was Taco Tuesday in Hell.

Of course, it was the worst Taco Tuesday imaginable. This was Hell, after all, but at least, it was something to stare at on a desk calendar. A ray of hope during those long days of sadism, torture, and conference calls. For the unsaved, it was a reminder of paradise lost and a soothing balm only to be canceled at the last second as a cruel joke. Still, the Dark One did follow through with tacos every so often. He had to; otherwise, the whole scheme would fail. If the damned felt it could never happen, nobody would care about Taco Tuesday, and if people stopped caring about hope and momentary bliss and tacos, well then, what the Hell would become of Hell? It might turn good, which would be bad in a place where only the bad was considered good, and that would make it a big, pristine mess.

Doug never worried about such things. He was a middle management demon, complete with horns, a suit, and a tie. Squeezed into his narrow cubicle, he passed away another day of endless night filling out paperwork which towered high around his outdated and slow Tandy computer. There are many forms to fill out after you possess a mortal. True, Doug enjoyed the possession part.

by J.J.J. Kearns

He was good at it, but he always found the paperwork part rather numbing, which was the whole point.

He tried to focus. It was easy on Wednesday, but as the week shuffled on, he found himself glancing, more and more, at the big, red circle around Tuesday. Sweet, sweet Taco Tuesday.

His phone rang. He clicked the speaker.
"Doug here."
"Hi. It's the Dark One. Come to me."
Doug flinched.
"Yes, Master. I'll be right in."

***

The executive suite of Satan was surprisingly humble and designed for functionality. There were no showy displays of wealth or power; just a desk, a chair, and a filing cabinet. The walls were beige and free of decoration. The carpet was old, and the waste basket was overflowing with discarded coffee cups and human bones.

As Doug cautiously entered, the Dark One looked up and spotted him.

"Have a seat."

Satan gestured to the lone chair in front of his desk. It was a piece of furniture clearly designed for pain and suffering, although the people at IKEA would never admit it. Doug sat down anyway, stifling a grimace.

Satan took off his glasses and rubbed his cold, black eyes. His sleeves were rolled up, and his collar and tie were askew. Normally, he was all chic and GQ. But not today. Today, there was something bothering the man who bothers others for a living.

A FRIEND OF THE WORKING MAN

"Listen, I'll be straight: I'm letting you go."

Doug stiffened.

"What?"

"It's not your performance. I want you to know that. It's just, well…we're cutting back."

"You're firing me? How? I'm a bad worker. I'm late. I'm selfish. I was even awarded 'Most Despicable Employee of the Month!'"

"I know but look at the news. Demons are obsolete. Humans are doing all the tempting and corrupting now. Who needs a big staff when you've got cable news and talk radio to destroy people's souls — for free!?! All I have to do is sit back and collect the damned. Easy-peasy. The truth is there's no use for your kind any more. I'm sorry."

He wasn't really sorry. He was Satan, after all. It was just a quick way to end the conversation so he could move on to more important things, like encouraging a war or tempting a priest to eat meat on Friday.

Doug hesitated. He tried to speak, but instead of words, he made silly faces. It had been a long time since Doug cried, and he didn't want to start now. Usually, he was on the other side of such mawkish displays; the unholy thing glimpsed beyond the veil of tears.

He had long feared his job was headed this way. There were rumors. Whispers. Endless ruminations during the quiet hours. But to be here, in this moment, when the words were said aloud and the betrayal was made real, it was almost too much of a cross to bear — even for a demon.

"Just great," Doug snorted. "Where am I supposed to go?"

Satan breathed deeply.

"Well, you can either get vaporized; blown to bits — or if you want, you can leave your resume with Demon Resources. Sometimes, they call ex-employees if something opens up."

"That's it?"

"Yes. Plus, a fairly generous compensation package. I'll give you a week to look it over, and if you like it, sign it, return it, then take a seat in the lobby for all eternity — or until they call you back. Whichever comes first."

"Wait. You want me to sign a contract…with you…the Prince of Darkness?"

"Trust me. There was a lot of bad PR with that Daniel Webster thing, but the truth is I keep my word. Sure, I love breaking the rules as much as the next guy, but I still have to obey a few, or the whole system goes off the rails."

Doug had stopped listening. He was focusing on the knot slowly twisting in his gut. True, Hell wasn't a charity, but you'd think that after all this time he'd at least get a crumb of thanks, instead of a swift kick and a cold goodbye.

Satan offered him the paperwork.

"You've got a week, but think it over. It's a big decision."

Doug stared at the parchment as it dangled limply in front of his face. It was your standard severance form inked from the blood of a thousand satanic paralegals. He took the unholy contract.

"And don't worry," Satan continued. "I'm sure you'll be back to work in no time. After all, with your talent and abilities, you can possess and control any mortal. Am I right?"

And here too were a few more simple words. Only this time, they reversed the gears in Doug's ol' brain noggin and spurred a funny thought.

"You know, you're right. Maybe I'm looking at this the wrong way."

"That's the spirit," Satan replied. "Now go. Begone demon! I cast thee out — and no, I do not validate for parking."

Doug stood up. He thanked his former employer for his lack of generosity, wished him the worst, then marched from his office. As Doug crossed the lobby, he attempted to hold his head high — while straining to prevent a sinister smile from overtaking his face.

***

Jennifer Plum stared at her husband.

It had been a busy day, a busy week, a busy year. It gets that way when you've been soldiering forth, trekking across the country, inhaling fried what-nots at state fair and town hall meetings filled with simplistic questions and rage filled tweets. A rally here. A rally there. Then an apology for the first rally and a well-timed back pedal for the second. It can grind you down, and poor Jenny didn't have much left to grind.

"I…"

"Quiet, woman. I'm thinking."

Mark Plum wasn't thinking, of course. He rarely did, and when he did, it was usually under protest. He did enjoy staring at himself though, which he was currently doing, as he attempted to straighten his finely lacquered hair while gazing at his reflection in the limousine window, completely oblivious to the desperate hordes struggling to get his attention outside just beyond the transparent jowls of his distorted image.

Jennifer and Mark had been together twenty-seven years. Maybe even twenty-nine, if you count the long courtship. They had met at a party. A charity fundraiser for underprivileged rich kids pretending to care about poor kids. She was sincere in her empathy. He was sincere in his lust. They met, fell into something love adjacent, and eventually got married (after much prodding from their friends and financial advisors). There had been good times and bad, and bad times posing as good ones, and all the while, she had somehow continued to care. In her eyes, he was so strong, so confident, so sure of himself, even when he probably shouldn't be, which was most of the time.

"I...."

"Listen, woman. Your job is to smile and look pretty. And stand behind me this time. What are you trying to do? Get elected instead of me?"

Jennifer recoiled nervously, retreating across the squeaky, Corinthian leather, until her tiny frame was pushed hard against the other side of the back seat.

"No, of course not."

Jenny blamed his gruff behavior on the stress. It was always the stress. It had been the stress for almost three decades, since the day they first met. It was something that befell all great men - and Mark Plum. She understood this until understanding became all that she did, after every lie and apology and inexcusable lapse of moral prudence inflicted upon their marriage by the man she called "Lover."

Mark returned to the reflection of his big, pumpkin-like head as Jennifer returned to her silence.

A FRIEND OF THE WORKING MAN

"Focus, Mark. Focus." George Lester spoke up. He was sitting across from them, twisting a thick cigar in his crooked mouth.

"Chill. I've got this," Mark replied. "Flag, guns, Jesus, patriot, freedom, blacks, Mexicans…."

"No. We agreed you'd go, 'Patriot, freedom, then Jesus, freedom, freedom, patriot, guns, blacks, freedom.'"

"George, it's not that hard. Insult the brown people. That's all and the votes are mine."

"And the gays? What about the gays?"

"Don't worry. I'll insult the gays, too."

"You better. This isn't a game. If we don't deliver tonight, every billionaire will ban us from their golf course."

"Trust me. After tonight, I'll have all the rubes happily voting against their own economic interest. Have a little faith, man."

George nearly bit through his cigar as the dark puddles beneath his arm pits began to grow.

Mark smiled. It was fake, of course. There was no joy behind it, only anger, piss, and vinegar. Still, he continued to flash it at his reflection.

And Jenny. What of Jenny? Well, she did like she always did in situations like this. She stared at her overpriced shoes and tried not to throw up in her mouth.

***

They were fifteen minutes into the Presidential debate before Mark had a chance to speak. His opponent, Paul Hayes, had gone first, prattling on about blah, blah, blah. He played all the hits: education, wages, and health care. Mark pretended to pay attention, as he periodically scribbled notes and doodled a drawing of Paul's face complete with crossed eyes and buck teeth just for flair.

Backstage, George watched a monitor in the green-room. He wasn't beneath the hot lights, but he smelled like a locker room none the less. True, the polling had their team in the lead, but it didn't matter. George was always an anxious garbage fire on debate night, and he would continue to remain unconvinced of a win despite the throngs of rabid believers blindly salivating over their mad messiah's every commandment.

Jennifer was in the auditorium a few feet from the stage. She was sentenced to the family section and surrounded by strangers. She had met a few of them before but quickly forgot their names - by choice. Now, her focus was solely on her husband and the precarious, high wire act he was about to inflict.

Eventually, the steam ran out of Paul Hayes' righteous filibuster, forcing Walter Shaw, the famous news anchor and moderator, to turn his furrowed gaze toward Mark's podium and deeply intone, "Mr. Plum. You now have two minutes to reply."

Mark immediately answered...by doing nothing.

He just stood there.

In silence.

His eyes were open, but they found no target. No landing.

The audience waited and anticipated, making the occasional uncomfortable noise to pass the time, but still, nothing was spat out from Mark's normally caustic mouth.

He just stood there.

George leaned in toward the monitor. "Come on, you knucklehead. Talk."

Mark's hands were trembling. With spastic excess, they reached up and firmly gripped the podium. In fact, they shook it, pulling it back and forth as if he were having a seizure. That's when the unthinkable burst forth from his mouth....

"I LOVE BLACK PEOPLE!!!!"

A woman screamed.

The audience froze.

And George Lester peed his pants.

"AND I LOVE...MEXICANS!!!!"

Mark's face was contorting, as if he were losing control of his muscles, as if he were struggling to stop the very words from fleeing past his undulating lips.

And his voice was strange. Normally, it was arrogant and nasally, but now...now, it sounded akin to Mercedes McCambridge taking a dump. Each syllable had a deep, raspy whine followed by a series of loud grunts and high pitch wails, as if there were two voices struggling to exit his word hole, and the angry one, the barking one, was winning.

"AND I BELIEVE THAT BOTH BLACKS AND MEXICANS SHOULD BE TREATED WITH DIGNITY AND RESPECT!!!!!"

The audience stiffened. Their mouths popped opened, along with their eyes. Mark's sudden compassion was most unexpected, and it was causing a massive freak out.

Still, Mark's rabid followers had been trained to hoot and holler after every quantum of nonsense hurled out by their fearless leader, and tonight would be no different.

Without thinking, they began to clap.

And cheer.

And respond with a frothy enthusiasm normally reserved for football games or Nuremberg Rallies. They didn't hear a thing their false idol said. They only knew that he had stopped talking, and that was their cue to start screaming their blind support.

"BECAUSE IT DOESN'T MATTER IF YOU'RE BLACK OR MEXICAN OR RACIST…WE ALL HAVE THE SAME THING IN COMMON: WE'RE ALL GETTING SCREWED OVER BY THE SUPER RICH TROLLS WHO ARE FUNDING MY CAMPAIGN!!!"

George spilled his drink. "No, no, no…" he said, as he clawed out large chunks of his own hair.

"FOR THE PRICE OF ONE OF THEIR GILDED TOILETS, THEY COULD FEED AN ENTIRE VILLAGE, BUT THEY DON'T WANT US TO KNOW THAT, BECAUSE IF WE DID, WE MIGHT BAND TOGETHER, STAND UP — AND MAKE THIS WORLD A BETTER PLACE - FOR EVERYONE!"

Paul Hayes glared at his opponent in disbelief. Many a night he had prayed that his rival would see the light and agree with him, but now that it was actually happening, he didn't know what to do.

"THEY USE HATE AND FEAR TO DIVIDE US, TO CON US, TO CONTROL US — AND THAT'S HOW THEY GET US TO VOTE AGAINST OUR OWN ECONOMIC INTERESTS. THAT'S HOW THEY STEAL YOUR MONEY!"

***

By now, George was doubled over, lying in a fetal position. His phone was vibrating across the floor in front of him, like a runaway quarterback in one of those old, tabletop, electric football games. People were trying to reach him, with an endless cascade of horrified texts and panicked phone calls. George refused to answer. He couldn't. His brilliant mind had fled his skull, abandoning the man who had based his entire life on illusion and deceit, all of which were probably, most likely, over now. He might never work in this town again…or country…or planet.

Outside the green room, there was a clopping sound, almost like hooves or fancy penny loafers running down the hallway. This was followed by loud banging and many futile clicks of the door knob.

"Open up, George. We know you're in there!"

Thud. Thud. Thud. It may have been one fist or several or maybe even a forehead bashing against the door. Who knows? It didn't last long enough to discern, for soon the barrier was cracking open, propelled by kicking and punching and a litany of angry physical exertion. It sent furniture tumbling, especially the pieces George had carefully stacked against the entrance. Soon, the greenroom was redecorated to look like an overturned lumber truck, as several geriatric men in expensive suits rushed in, piled upon George, and shook him like a red-headed martini tumbler.

"Damn it! Get it together, man!!!" screamed J.J. Mercer.

"Our supporters are turning on us," added R.R. Murdoch.

"What the Hell is he doing out there?" barked $.$. Sinclair.

These men were rich and old, and they hadn't moved this fast in years. In fact, their doctors had warned them against such physical exertion. Still, right now, they weren't concerned about their health — just greed and illusion and the impending threat to both.

"Don't worry," George stammered. "I've got this."

He pushed his way past their knobby hands, straightened his clothes, and hurried out the door.

The geriatrics exchanged a concerned look, then...

They spotted George, through the open doorway, crossing their field of vision and going in the opposite direction, as if he were lost — because he was.

***

In the auditorium, Mark continued to growl.

"A HEALTHY TREE SHARES ITS NUTRIENTS - WHILE A DYING TREE STRANGLES ITS OWN ROOTS. SO, WHO ARE WE? A SOCIETY IN WHICH PEOPLE HELP ONE ANOTHER OR A SUICIDE CULT POSING AS A POLITICAL PARTY?"

The audience was a sea of nodding heads and thundering hand claps. Both parties, who minutes earlier were diametrically opposed, were now unified by Mark's words. Many people began to stand. Still more climbed onto their chairs and waved their arms in a show of wild support and manic enthusiasm, bordering on a psychotic episode.

Amidst all the tumult sat Jennifer Plum.

She was rigid.

Her eyes were intently focused. Right now, there was only one person who commanded her full attention, and it wasn't her husband. It was whatever had overtaken him.

True, Mark was capable of saying anything if it benefited him, but this seemed different. It was coherent and smart, as if somebody else's words were coming through his mouth, and he was just parroting them like some hopped up ventriloquist dummy. She didn't know what to do. She had no experience with such things, and for the first time in their long years of suffering, which some would call marriage, she found herself in a most confusing position: she agreed with her husband.

Eventually, by accident, George made his way to the wings of the stage.

"YOU CAN'T BE A GOOD PERSON IF YOU TREAT OTHERS BADLY. SO, WHO DO YOU WANT TO BE?"

Reverend Bobby Jimmy Bobbie pushed his way past the backstage riff-raff and slid up to George. He was an older gentleman with square glasses and a round paunch. On his neck, he wore a humble crucifix and a thousand-dollar tie.

"You've got to do something," Rev. Bobbie cried out, with an evangelical bombast normally reserved for informercials. "If he keeps talking like that, he'll destroy everything. He'll wreck the party!"

"I know," George replied. "But what do you want me to do? Until he comes off the stage...."

Rev. Bobbie didn't wait. He charged out onto the riser, pointing his crucifix like a weapon, like he was a Van Helsing, aiming it directly at Mark's forehead.

"Begone vile socialist!"

Mark pivoted toward his attacker. An inhuman howl erupted from his chest. It sounded like a witch being splashed with water or a hungry shopper on Black Friday.

"VOTE FOR ME! AAARRRRGHAAARRRGGH! VOTE FOR ME! AARRRRGHAAARRRGGH!"

Mark stuck out his tongue and waggled it while making guttural ululations.

"VOTE FOR ME! AAARRRRGHAAARRRGGH!"

George stood with his mouth agape. There was not a dry spot left on his clothing.

"NOOOOO!" he exclaimed. He had prayed for a classy way out of this, but the possibility of such a smooth departure was now dashed beyond repair, and all that remained was a litany of embarrassing solutions.

He chose one. He ran to the fuse box and flipped all the circuit breakers.

The auditorium plunged into darkness. A chorus of sharp cries filled the air along with Mark's raspy wail.

"VOTE FOR ME! AAARRRRGHAAARRRGGH!"

***

Satan was watching all of this on a small TV in his office.

At first, he thought one of the vacuum tubes had blown, but he quickly surmised the real trouble was in the live feed. The stage lights had gone out, and all that remained was the political analysis from the TV commentator....

"This might sway the election," the pundit calmly explained.

The Devil was at a loss for words, except two....

"Oh God."

The intercom buzzed.

"God's on line one," the receptionist hissed. "She wants to see you in her office."

"OH GOD!"

Satan dropped the phone and covered his mouth with both claws.

***

A FRIEND OF THE WORKING MAN

By the time Jenny pushed her way backstage, Mark was levitating.

His body was swooping, to and fro, like an angry piñata, dive bombing George and the geriatrics.

"FLOSS YOUR TEETH!!!! ARRRGHGHGHG!"

Rev. Bobbie leapt up and grabbed Mark's legs, but instead of pulling Mark down, Rev. Bobbie went up, floating into the air. He looked like a man trying to stop a runaway, giant balloon in a Thanksgiving Day parade, all the while refusing to let go.

Mark tried to shake him off, jerking his legs, like a fish whipping its tail, slamming Rev. Bobbie into a lamp, a snack table, a monitor. Soon, the pair were circling in wide swings, knocking over George and the geriatrics in the process. It was a wild scene, full of screams and loudness, displaying all the genteel dignity of a Benny Hill skit.

George turned to Jenny. "You're his wife. DO SOMETHING!"

He reached out and pushed Jenny, sending her forward.

"Honey. Can we talk?" she stammered quietly to Mark.

Too quietly. No one could hear her above the fracas.

"SPADE AND NEUTER YOUR PETS!!! ARRRRGGGHHH!"

"Mark, honey. It's me, Jenny. Your wife."

That caught his attention. Mark spun around to look at her. At least, his head did. It swiveled around 180 degrees, in a way that heads aren't supposed to swivel. The contortion sent George, Rev. Bobbie, and the geriatrics jumping back, aghast in a terror.

The horrific image scared Jenny, too, but she stood her ground. After all, she had made a promise, long ago, to always love him, in sickness and in levitation, in good times and revolting disgust.

"You're my wife?" Mark replied with a confused gurgle. His head swiveled back around, as his whole body turned to face her. The violent growling ceased as his voice relaxed into a caring tone.

"Poor Jenny. Such a beautiful creature," Mark said.

Jenny was stunned. It was something she never thought she'd hear from Mark - ever.

The others looked on with mild confusion and growing interest, especially George, who, for the first time, was seeing a possible way out of this political train wreck.

"Tell him 'Thank you,'" George whispered to Jenny. "And that 'You love him.'"

"Thank you," Jenny said to Mark. "I love you."

A strange look transformed Mark's face. Could it be compassion?

"And tell him…" George continued. "Tell him that 'If he really loves you….'"

"If you really love me…" Jenny repeated.

"He'll stop with all the hippie crap."

"What?" Jenny said, wrinkling her face.

"Yeah," Rev. Bobbie added. "Tell him to stop being such a goodie-goodie. He'll tank the ratings."

Jenny lowered her gaze. She couldn't look them in eye. Her hands were trembling, and it wasn't due to fear.

"Do it," George said, nudging her, again.

Jenny swallowed hard.

"Jenny," Mark said. "Please forgive me - for everything."

It was a few simple words, but they were powerful enough to shake Jenny to her inner truth.

"You deserve so much better than Mark Plum," Mark said.

The old men began to shout, but Jenny couldn't hear them. Their angry words became muffled and quiet, as they faded into the background, overpowered by the sound of Jenny's own beating heart, as it rumped and thumped and pumped in harmony with the rhythms drumming forth from Mark's own breast.

"No! Don't listen to him," George yelled.

The piercing shriek snapped Jenny out of her trance. She looked around and found herself encircled by a raging chorus of old, white guys. She turned to one, and then another, and then – she reached into her purse, grabbed some cash, and threw it into the air!

The angry chorus dove for it, jabbing and stabbing each other as they rumbled and tossed, snatching up Benjamins and wrenching them from each other's hands.

Jenny grabbed Mark's long tie and ran for the door. He bobbed along after her, still levitating like a kite. They banged down the hall, torpedoed through the exit and fled the building entirely. Once outside, they bounced to a stop.

Where were they? They were standing in the middle of a desolate landscape. The building was gone, and they were surrounded by a series of empty fields, bisected by a pair of crossroads worthy of Robert Johnson himself.

A pair of headlights danced along the horizon. As they approached, it became readily apparent that it was a golf cart adorned with the phrase "Deus Ex Machina." Eventually, it rolled to a stop directly in front of Jenny and Mark.

"Hello," said the driver. She was a middle-aged woman, and she looked like Gracie Allen, the old-time radio comedienne. Jenny didn't know anything about Gracie Allen or old-time radio, but she immediately liked the strange woman and her calming aura.

"I'm God," said the lady. "And this is Satan."

God motioned to her passenger, and sure enough, there was Satan, wrapped in a straitjacket.

"Doug..." God said, as she climbed out of the golf cart.

"Who's Doug?" Jenny asked.

"The demon inside your husband, silly."

God snapped her fingers. Mark dropped out of the sky and landed on his feet. God raised an arm toward him.

"Wait!" Jenny leapt between them, shielding her husband. "What are you doing?"

"Raising my arm."

"No. I mean, what are you going to do with it?"

"An exorcism."

"Stop! You can't!!!"

"Why?"

"Because, well...can't we just leave Mark alone? I mean, he's so much nicer when he's possessed by Satan."

"Leave me out of this," Satan interjected.

"Hey," Doug/Mark bellowed. "You're the one who wanted to outsource evil. What did you expect from the gig economy? ARRRGHGHRH!"

"Please. Let Doug stay," Jenny begged. "I mean, he brought everybody together. He'll be good."

"Good? If you take away someone's life, it's called murder. That doesn't sound like being good to me."

Jenny's brain misfired. God had given her the lowdown from on-high, and there was no way to dodge the Almighty's naked gospel once it had been laid bare. Jenny had wished ill upon her husband, and she immediately conceded her remorse.

God stepped in front of Doug/Mark and grabbed him by the lips. A strange glow emanated from God's fingertips, as Jenny stared in disbelief. This was it. End of the line. In a moment, Doug would be gone, and Mark, the real Mark, would be back in all of his nasty glory.

"Wait!" Jenny shouted. She grabbed Doug/Mark's shoulder. "Before you go, could you do me a favor? Could you tell me that you love me?"

"What!?!" Doug/Mark replied through pinched lips. "Why would I do that? I'm a demon."

"Yes, I know. And you're all about pain and suffering. But think about it. What could be more painful than to be shown the possibility of love, even for a second, and then have it taken away?"

Doug/Mark glared at her. For the first time in his sick existence, he felt a strange kind of terror. It was called fear, and it was something that often happens when people talk about "love."

"Please," Jenny begged. "Leave me with at least that illusion."

God released Doug/Mark's lips. The demon turned toward Jenny. He studied her face, her temporal nature, her frail body, her yearning eyes.

"I love you, Jenny Plum."

It was a lie, of course, and they both knew it, but for one glorious moment, Doug/Mark pulled Jenny close and gave her a passionate kiss, full of hey-hey and ah-cha-cha-cha.

Doug/Mark stepped back, leaving Jenny a weak-kneed, wobbly mess.

Once more, God grabbed Doug/Mark by the lips and gave him a mighty tug. Doug's demonic form soon crowned and passed through Mark's mouth, until the beast was out and lying in a pool of ick.

God stooped down and grabbed Doug by the ear. "Time to go."

"Ow! Ow! Ow!" Doug yelled as he was yanked up and thrown into the back of the golf cart. God circled around to the driver's side and climbed in.

"Listen, Jenny," God said. "I'm sorry I have to take Doug away, but I am leaving you with one gift. Use it wisely. Oh. And remember this. This is very important: blessed are the humble — GOD HAS SPOKEN!!!! SING PRAISE UNTO ME!!!!!"

A crash of lightning sliced across the black sky, as God turned to the Dark One and smiled, "Say, 'Goodnight,' Satan."

Satan rolled his eyes, like a jaded teenager annoyed by a corny parent. God nudged Satan once, then twice, until finally Satan relented and said....

"Goodnight, Satan."

"BWHAHHAHAHAHAHA!" The omnipotent being with Gracie Allen's face burst into laughter, as she threw the vehicle into gear and drove off down the dark, country road.

By now, Mark, the original Mark, was moaning and coming to. Jenny tried to help him up, but her husband met her caring hand with a shove.

"Don't touch my hair."

A FRIEND OF THE WORKING MAN

Jenny complied, like she always complied. She stepped back and turned toward the crossroads, looking off into the distance, as she tried to make sense of all this madness and sorrow.

What gift was God talking about? What would become of Mark's campaign? Would the public stay united or would Mark divide them, once again, with his selfish hate and fear and rage?

Jenny didn't know the answer to any of these things — and she didn't know what would happen on Super Tuesday. But she did know one thing.

There would be tacos. She'd make damn sure of it.

THE GREATEST SHOW ON EARTH

by Lena Ng

After the lights were dimmed and the popcorn swept up, beneath the striped canvas of the Big Top, circus ring leader Barnum, wearing his white jacket and dapper, red bow tie, led the debriefing.

"Alright, everyone, I'd like to commend all of you for your tremendous work in tonight's show." His audience—the whip-carrying animal tamers, the mustachioed and bearded ladies, the lithe contortionists, the bulging strong men, and the clowns in polka-dotted costumes—cheered.

Gesturing for silence, Barnum raised a dramatic hand. "Let us rest not upon our—" he glanced at the chunky clown, Marshmallow, "—ample laurels. As we strive for entertainment perfection, here are some things we can improve upon."

First he addressed the lion tamers. "Come on, guys, let's give the audience what they paid for. Thrills and chills! More pawing, more growling, more roaring."

Next he addressed the trapeze artists, simply saying, "Higher, higher, higher," as he swept his hands upwards.

Then he addressed the contortionists. "Bums on heads, ladies. Beautiful bums on heads."

by Lena Ng

To each section in turn, the Ring Leader gave advice: the fire-eaters, the freaks (as they proudly called themselves), the elephant minders, the jugglers, and the sword-swallowers.

Finally, Barnum addressed the clowns. "Good job," he started, "very funny. Lots of laughs." He scanned the wacky crowd. "But I think we can be bigger. We can be funnier. Instead of ten clowns jammed into a car," he paused dramatically, "I think we can have twenty."

First there was silence. Then there was shouting.

"Are you kiddin' me? Stinky hasn't showered in three weeks!"

"Four," yelled Stinky. "Marshmallow needs to go on a diet!"

"Hey," Marshmallow cried, his bowl full of jelly jiggling, "skinny clowns ain't funny."

"What?" yelled Pencil, kicking up his long legs.

Then indignation turned into grumbling. "What does Barnum know about clowns?" one jug-eared clown asked. "He's not a clown."

"Yes," another agreed. "Our act ain't broke. Why's he tryin' to fix it?" He crossed his arms. "'Barnum's not fit to lead us. Only clowns know the plight of clowns." He cupped his hands around his mouth. "We need a clown to lead clowns."

The other clowns joined in. "Clowns lead clowns! Clowns lead clowns!"

As the shouting grew louder, Barnum grew paler than his waiter's jacket. The ring leader dared not face the wrath of clowns. He knew that, for clowns, the fountain of humour was replenished by the deep well of anger. They would think it funny if Barnum were trampled beneath a dancing elephant or accidently locked in Shere Khan's cage.

Barnum brought his hands down in an appeasing motion. "Clowns, gentle, beloved clowns, if this is what you truly want, this is what you will have. Choose amongst yourselves a leader who will decide your act."

The audience wiggled and squirmed. Ring Leader Barnum and all his talk was holding up the obligatory all-night party and the usual libations and debauchery.

As the corks popped and the calliope music blared, only Pagliacci, the melancholy clown with cosmetic tears drawn onto his face, seemed to have any concerns. Turning to Bom Bom, who specialized in mime, Pagliacci asked, "Would you want him to elect the leader of the greatest show on earth?" He pointed to Loopy, a drunken clown who was sprawled over the stands with his pants undone. Bom Bom turned up his palms and shrugged his shoulders.

The next day, the clowns, still nursing fierce hangovers, gathered under the Big Top. Colourful costumes like lively, exuberant flowers filled the ring.

"I'm scared," said Sweet Cheeks, in a tiny, high-pitched voice. "How are we going to choose?"

Winks, an oddly dignified clown, stepped forward. He was their oldest working clown, rising up from the lowly rank of pratfalls to the esteemed rank of impersonations. He had clowning in his blood. His mother was a clown, and possibly his father (if he wasn't one of the trapeze artists). "We must hold elections."

"Will you run?" asked Barnacle, the juggling clown.

Wink's big, rubber nose shook from side-to-side. "Politicking is a young clown's game." He called out into the brightly costumed crowd. "Who here would like to be a candidate?"

Boffo, a penguin of a clown who had spent most of last night's show on the sidelines, sprang up. "I'll run." He turned to his electorate. "With me as your president, there will be no more lack of show-time. There will be no more lack of applause. I promise you, my fellow comedic artists, all clowns will have equal time in the spotlight."

Hugs, the reigning clown star with floppy orange hair and a matching bright orange face, crossed his arms. Equal time in the spotlight meant a lot less time for himself. He heaved himself to his feet. "I'm running, too." Hugs then turned to the audience. "I promise you, my fellow clowns, with me as your president, I'll lead you to stardom."

When Barnum inspected his exhibits—the lions were locked up, the elephants neatly put away—he was surprised at how seriously the clowns were taking their election. All around the circus, garishly coloured signs had popped up, some for Hugs, some for Boffo.

The pro-Hugs signs read: "A star among clowns." "Funny days have returned." "Make clowning great again."

The pro-Boffo signs read: "Everyone's a star." "It's your time to shine." "All for clowns and clowning for all."

Conversely, the anti-Hugs signs read: "Spot-light stealer." "Crook." "Capitalist pig." And the worst, "Not funny."

While the anti-Boffo signs read: "Stifles innovation." "Squashes success." "Communist." And the worst, "Not funny."

Barnum ran into Pagliacci who was closely examining each sign. "Looks like a lot of fun going on. Have you decided who you will vote for?"

THE GREATEST SHOW ON EARTH

Pagliacci gave a droopy-shouldered shrug. "The candidates are holding rallies tonight. I'm going to learn about their positions and make an informed choice."

That night, from the cheers coming from Boffo's tent, Pagliacci could tell the rally was a rousing success. He seated himself at the top of the grandstand.

Boffo pin-wheeled his arms. He pointed to Marshmallow. "You! What position are you in our clown pyramid, the Burj Kha-Laffa?"

Marshmallow stood, his triple chins trembling. "The bottom!"

Boffo nodded sagely. "You will always be at the bottom. And your son will always be at the bottom."

Boffo spun around. This time his oversized, purple-gloved clown finger pointed at Barnacle. "And you! Where are you in the clown car?"

"The trunk."

"Have you ever been in the driver's seat?"

"Never."

Again, Boffo nodded sagely. "And your son will never be, and your son's son will never be." He puffed out his chest, his floppy bow tie looking bigger and floppier than ever. "My friends, tell me, if you are on the bottom of the pyramid, who is on the top?"

"Hugs!"

"Now tell me, friends, who is always in the driver's seat?"

Again the crowd cried, "Hugs!"

"Yes, Hugs is always in the driver's seat. He's always on the top of the pyramid. He climbs your back, he puts his orange shoe in your face to get there. And he stays there. And his son will stay there, and his son will stay there."

Boffo raised his hands to the rafters. "Hugs breaks your back so he can be a star. His empire is founded on our spindly spines. We all deserve our time in the spotlight. We're all entitled to our fifteen minutes."

"Boffo, Boffo," the crowd chanted, and Pagliacci wandered off to attend Hugs's rally.

From the cheers emerging from the opponent's tent, Pagliacci could tell Hugs's rally was also a rousing success.

"Dear, sweet Sweet Cheeks," Hugs was saying, "what about your act? It runs for twenty minutes." He shook his head sadly. "Won't have time for it any more if everyone were equal."

"What is the meaning of success?" Hugs put an orange-gloved hand to his ear. "To be better than others!" He waved to the music of bellowing cheers. "How can the cream rise if we're homogenized milk? If everyone were equal, how can we strive for excellence?" Hugs thundered out. "Boffo squashes innovation! Boffo squashes success!"

"Hugs, Hugs," the crowd chanted. Pagliacci went home and thought long into the night.

The day before the election, Winks stopped by Pagliacci's trailer for milkshakes. The old clown put down his banana-berry shake. "Have you decided who you are voting for?"

"I don't know," the sad clown replied. "They both have good points. I might not vote."

"Not vote?" exclaimed Winks. "Not vote? Come now, you must do your comedic duty." He tapped his rubber nose. "I know what will help you decide. A debate. Tonight. Then you can compare them."

With such short notice, each camp was in a flurry of activity. There was hair and makeup and costumes and stretching. As they were wrapping up, Hugs whispered in Loopy's bourbon-bright ear, "I don't trust that Boffo. He's stirring up his followers. Forewarned is forearmed which is exactly what we need to do—arm ourselves. You know, strictly for self-defence." Loopy staggered off to find munitions.

In Boffo's tent, things were in a tizzy as well. There was bow-tying and shoe-spraying and pomade-wearing. As they were wrapping up, Boffo whispered into Marshmallow's corpulent ear, "I don't trust that Hugs. He's stirring up his followers. I saw Loopy staggering about when he should've been sleeping." He whispered instructions to Marshmallow who lumbered off in search of munitions.

An hour later, under the Big Top, Winks banged down his giant rubber mallet. "Who will be the president of the greatest show on earth?" The clown audience bobbed their signs and cheered.

Again, down came the rubber mallet. Winks addressed the short, round clown. "Boffo, what have you to say about the charges that you stifle success?"

Boffo cleared his throat. "My dear Winks and fellow clowns, I believe every clown should get a chance. I believe every clown deserves to shine."

"Thank-you, Boffo." Winks turned to the orange-haired opponent. "Now Hugs, what do you say about the charges that you're a crook who steals the spotlight?"

Hugs grew red under his orange make-up. "What do you know about clowning, old clown? You think water-squirting flowers are funny."

Winks removed the soggy pansy from his lapel.

Hugs's voice filled the Big Top. "Furthermore, my esteemed opponent is so stupid, he should shove a pie in his pie-hole."

Boffo grew red under his purple make-up. "Well, my opponent is so stupid, he would shove a pie in his cornhole."

In comedy, timing is everything. Hugs, seasoned clown as he was and apoplectic beyond speech, knew now was the time. He reached beneath the podium into his secret arsenal. He pulled out a weapon. With a practiced movement, he brought his arm back and flung the weapon directly at Boffo's face.

The missile hit its target with a climactic splat. Boffo, wiping whipped cream off of his face screamed, "See that! See that! I will rise above!" as he reached into his costume and flung his own baked armament.

Hugs wiped the dripping pie from his face. He stepped out from behind the podium, slipped on a patch of whipped cream, and landed ass over kettle. His orange toupee flew off, revealing an orange bald spot. He crawled over the floor until he reached his stockpile. He whipped another pie at Boffo then another and another. Boffo gave back as good as he got.

As the clown politicians debated by flinging coconut cream pies, the clown audience members peed their pants laughing.

Pagliacci laughed the loudest of them all. He laughed until real tears streamed down his face, overlaying and smearing the make-up tears. Another clown might have mistaken him for weeping. For Pagliacci alone seemed to understand the bigger joke, the real joke—that they were electing one of these clowns.

A ridiculous clown who would, one day, control their destiny.

A HISTORY LESSON

by Ben Boegehold

Large eyed hunger remade the city
in the last years of the monarchy.
The peasants had no food, no bread.
So the royal physician planted

"apples of the earth" outside the palace gate,
and paid the guards to look the other way.
In the summer heat, the sprawling nightshade
leafed out in the sunshine. Starving, unafraid

of night, the skeletal peasants stole the harvest,
while the fat, starchy nobles celebrated their latest
swindle, weaving crowns of the purple vines,
swallowing mouthfuls of cake. But history often rhymes.

When the nobles lost their heads to the slaves,
potatoes blossomed on their unmarked graves.

DEAR MR. PRESIDENT
by Jim Courter

Charlie Sykes took the sheet of paper from the printer, added his signature with a pen, and laid it aside. Using the same pen, he addressed a business-sized envelope:

> President of the United States
> The White House
> 1600 Pennsylvania Avenue
> Washington, D.C. 20500

He affixed a first-class stamp in the upper right corner, then a label with his name and address in the upper left corner. Taking up the sheet, he looked once more at what he had written:

> *Dear Mr. President:*
> *You will die.*
> *[signed] Charlie Sykes*

Printed below that were Charlie's home and email addresses and phone number. He folded the sheet into thirds, slipped it into the envelope, licked and sealed the flap. Lest he succumb to doubt, he went out, got in his car, and drove straight to the nearest mailbox and dropped it in.

He returned home to begin his wait, curious about whether the Secret Service would show up at his front door, and if so, how long it would take. His curiosity was satisfied eight days later when he had just finished breakfast and the doorbell rang.

Charlie opened the door to find two men on his front porch. They wore dark suits and white shirts. The only difference was their ties; one was blue and one was red. The taller of the two, the one with the red tie, was blond, his medium-length hair parted on the side. The other had black hair slicked straight back. Charlie expected them to be wearing sunglasses and to look deadly serious, but neither was the case. The blond-haired one wore rimless spectacles, the other none. Both had the neutral expression of someone who had come to the door to ask for directions. They introduced themselves—the taller one was named Hoffmann, the other one McKenzie—and opened wallets to show Charlie their badges and Secret Service IDs.

"Gentlemen," Charlie said with a welcoming smile. "Come in. I've been expecting you."

They stepped through the front door and into the living room.

"Please have a seat," Charlie said, gesturing to a matching set of chairs on the other side of a coffee table from a leather couch. When they sat Charlie excused himself and went into the kitchen. Moments later he returned with a tray bearing a carafe of coffee and three cups on saucers, along with cream and sugar and some spoons. He set the tray on the table and went to the couch, smiled warmly at them and said, "Coffee?"

Hoffmann spoke for both of them: "No thanks."

Charlie laughed. "Trust me, it's not poisoned," he said as he poured some for himself. He set the carafe down and said, "Perhaps you'd prefer to dispense with pleasantries and get right down to business."

"Yes, I believe we should," Hoffmann said. "First some preliminaries. You are Charlie Sykes?"

Charlie nodded in the affirmative.

"You never married, were honorably discharged from the Marines, and are a retired political science professor."

"You've done your homework," Charlie said, then smiled and added, "But of course you have resources."

Hoffmann pulled an envelope from an inside pocket of his suit coat, pulled a folded sheet of paper out of it, unfolded it, held it out for Charlie to see and said, "Did you write and send this?"

Charlie leaned forward from his seated position and looked at the sheet. He beamed as if proud and said, "Yes, I did. To be honest, I'm surprised. I can imagine that this President gets a ton of mail just about every day from his adoring fans, and I had trouble envisioning my little letter in such a big pile attracting any notice."

Hoffmann set the letter on the coffee table. "Well it did," he said, "and as you can guess, that's why we're here."

Charlie brightened. "Has the President seen it?"

"No," Hoffmann said.

"Darn," Charlie said, looking disappointed.

"Care to tell us why you sent it?" Hoffmann said.

"Sure," Charlie said. "Goodness, where to start. I might point out that this President—the youngest ever by three months at his swearing in, as I'm sure you know—is a preening peacock, or that he lacks the gravitas required for the job, or that he is supercilious, vacuous and self-absorbed. But all that is strictly my opinion. Did you see him on MTV a while back? I confess I didn't, but I heard about it. Same for his appearance on Saturday Night Live, and numerous late-night talk shows. He's the absolute darling of the Hollywood crowd." He picked up a remote from the coffee table. "Let me show you footage of a news conference I recorded in which the President comes off like he's auditioning for Comedy Central."

Hoffmann held up a hand and said, "That won't be necessary."

"Suit yourself," Charlie said. "Back to your question. This President speaks and behaves as if he has no awareness of his own mortality. I sent that letter"—he waggled a finger at it on the coffee table—"by way of providing him with some perspective. I considered adding that from dust he came and to dust he shall return, but I wanted to keep it simple."

"I hope you realize," Hoffmann said, "that threatening the life of the President of the United States is a serious offense."

"Yes I do," Charlie said with a smile and an earnest nod.

"And yet you not only sent this but made sure that we could find you."

"Why not?" Charlie said. "The letter contains no threat. Strictly speaking, I have done nothing more than state a fact, the incontrovertibility of which is . . ."

"Whoa!" Hoffman said. "Incontrovertibility?"

Charlie smiled. "Yup. The incontrovertibility of which is demonstrated in a classic syllogism. Would you like to hear it?"

Hoffmann folded his arms over his chest and didn't answer. McKenzie, who so far hadn't spoken except to introduce himself, said, "I would."

"It goes like this," Charlie said. "All men are mortal. Socrates is a man. Therefore, Socrates is mortal. Now tell me, do you acknowledge the truth of the major and minor premises in that syllogism?"

They didn't answer, but McKenzie looked bemused, as if curious to see how this would play out.

"I take from your silence that you do," Charlie said. "Then I trust that you grant the validity of the conclusion, that Socrates is mortal, in other words that he will die."

Again silence.

"Very good. Now, I assume you'll agree with me that it's reasonable to substitute the President's name for that of Socrates. After all, the President is a man, which is to say human, one of that group, 'all men,' referred to in the major premise." He waited, then said, "Again, I take your silence for agreement. It follows then, that the President of the United States will die." He waved a hand. "Of course we don't need an exercise in formal logic to know that. It's something we learn when we grow from children into adults, which this President seems never to have done. At the risk of stating what ought to be obvious, allow me to point out that nowhere does it say in the letter when he will die, or by what means, or that he will die unnaturally, or at my hands or the hands of anyone else with murderous intentions. Tell me, then," Charlie said, "in light of all that, where is the threat?"

McKenzie looked intrigued. Hoffmann sat in silence, looking annoyed and frustrated. He drummed his fingers on the top of his thigh and seemed to be searching for an answer to Charlie's question and not finding one.

"I wish I could haul you in for wasting our time," Hoffmann finally said with a sour look on his face.

by Jim Courter

"Then stay a while and have some coffee," Charlie said. "I have cookies in the kitchen. Chocolate chip. Made them myself. We could enjoy them while we watch that news conference I recorded. I hate admitting it, but there's some entertainment value in watching the President of the United States make a fool of himself."

Hoffmann rose. So did McKenzie.

"I must warn you, Mr. Sykes," Hoffmann said, "that if you persist in this and it's determined that you're a threat to the President, your logic will prove to be a flimsy defense."

As he spoke, McKenzie, from behind his partner, gave Charlie a smile and a look of appreciation.

Charlie accompanied them to the front door and showed them out, wishing them a good day and safe travel. As they went down the sidewalk, Charlie stood in the doorway and said, "By the way, agent Hoffmann, in case it hasn't occurred to you, you too are mortal, you too will someday die."

Hoffmann stopped, turned, and with a bitter look on his face said, "And so will you, pal."

"Brilliant riposte!" Charlie said. He smiled, waved, and said, "See you in hell."

THE ELECTION-YEAR GENIE
by Richard Lau

Marilyn Holbrook tried not to look reluctant as Sarah, her campaign manager, dragged her into the antique store. She knew next to nothing about antiques and wasn't the type of person to collect useless knickknacks or invest in older memorabilia for the future.

Still, she smiled and waved to the gathered reporters.

"Remember," shouted Sarah. "Marilyn supports small business, and small business supports her!"

While Sarah and the shop's owner spoke to the press outside, Marilyn sucked in her gut as she negotiated the narrow walkway between towering topsy-turvy cliffs of furniture, clothing, and outdated decorations from another time.

"How about buying something?" called a photographer who had somehow gained entry.

Marilyn understood. He was challenging her about whether this was just a photo opportunity or was she really going to support the business.

The candidate would not disappoint. She looked around her immediate area, and her gaze fell on a tall bottle of green glass. She picked it up and under closer examination, she could see and feel a pattern of intricate swirls raised all over the opaque surface, like letters from a foreign alphabet. A screw top resembling a tangerine-sized faceted gem capped off the bottle's three-inch neck. The remaining section of the foot-long bottle was its cantaloupe-shaped body. But best of all was the price tag on the base. Ten dollars. It would be a good gift for Sarah since this stop was her idea.

"Why, I'd like to purchase this bottle," she told the clerk at the register and the photographer. And she smiled for both.

***

An hour later, Marilyn was having a quiet moment to herself in the dressing room of an auditorium before addressing a standing-room-only crowd. She realized she was still carrying around the gift bag containing the bottle from the antique shop. She pulled out the bottle, undid the protective giftwrapping, and unscrewed the top.

"Anyone in there?" she asked jokingly, rubbing the side of the bottle.

To her surprise, a stream of smoke bubbled up from the bottle's mouth and condensed to one side of the room, taking the form of a six-foot-tall man dressed in a blue power suit. His appearance and posture reminded Marilyn of a television news anchor.

"Hello there!" he said in a polished, honey-smooth baritone. "You are Marilyn Holbrook, future President of the United States!"

"Well, that's very nice of you to say," replied Marilyn. "But currently, I'm just one candidate out of many. I don't even have my party's nomination yet." She paused, blinking, not believing her eyes or the conversation. "And you are?"

THE ELECTION-YEAR GENIE

The man's white, toothy smile was blinding, almost like staring into the sun. "I am...an Election-Year Genie!"

Seeing Marilyn's expression of nonrecognition, the genie explained further. "If you had rubbed my bottle in any other year, and many people have, nothing would have happened. I only appear during an election year."

Marilyn had prepared for a lot of contingencies before deciding to run for the highest office in the land. This wasn't one of them. "Are you really a genie? Or am I just tired and overworked?"

"Yes, I'm a genie," answered the smiling man. "And if you're tired and overworked, I can fix that."

"Ah yes," said Marilyn, catching on. "The three-wishes deal."

"Three wishes?" the man laughed. "That's for ordinary genies! I'm an election-year genie! Have as many wishes as you want!"

"Really? You mean I can wish for more wishes?"

"Only if you want to. Or you can just keep wishing. My only limits are that all your wishes must be done in this one session, and you can only summon me one more time. After that, I am free!"

Marilyn asked about the thing that was foremost on her mind. "Are you certain I will become President?"

The man nodded. "It is in my nature to see the future."

"So, I don't need to wish for that?"

"Again, you can, if you want to. But it would be redundant. I suppose you have more important, unfated things to wish for."

Marilyn thought of all of her predecessors and their battles with an uncooperative Congress. "I wish to have a cooperative Congress when I become President."

The man nodded. "It will be so on your first day as President. But may I politely point out that you are thinking small."

"Am I?"

"You want a cooperative Congress to get something done. Why not just simply wish for the thing to be done?"

"You mean like wishing for affordable health care for all my countrymen?"

The genie prompted her some more. "Ah, for all of the ages, humans have always only looked at the tiny fingertip of possibilities! Why affordable? Why any healthcare at all? And why just for your countrymen?"

Marilyn got the point and changed her focus. "I wish for good health for people all over the world."

The man's smile got broader and brighter, if such a thing was possible. "On your first day of Presidency, it shall be so."

Now Marilyn was on a roll. "I want an end to world hunger. I want an end to poverty. I want pollution to be cleaned up and environmental damage to be repaired."

"It shall be so. It shall be so. It shall be so." the genie chanted, never wavering his smile or tone.

Marilyn had just listed "true justice" and "a viable space program to colonize other planets" when a knock came at the door.

"Marilyn?" Sarah's voice came through the closed door. "Five minutes 'til stage time. Is there somebody in there with you?"

THE ELECTION-YEAR GENIE

Marilyn was quickly returned from her future fantasies to the harsh reality of a female candidate being caught with a strange man in her room. "Thanks, Sarah! I'm just going over my speech, and I guess I was projecting too much. I'll be right out!"

Acknowledging her silent gesture, the election-year genie returned to his bottle.

***

Marilyn campaigned with a confidence that had not been demonstrated for a long time. She promised specific, absolute improvements with no weaselly words, no half-truths, and no vague statements.

Her critics pointed out she couldn't possibly achieve all that she promised, but the tide of true-believing voters, long-starved for a sincere candidate washed over those same critics like a tsunami over low tidepools.

The secret of Marilyn's positivity was that she knew what the future held. She didn't need to rely on polls, the press, money donors, the endorsement of politicians, or even the good will of the people. She had genie magic.

***

"Genie!" The word rang like a shotgun blast within the hallowed walls of the Oval Office.

The call was a demand not a request. A gush of smoke, and the same smiling man appeared, this time dressed in a tropical floral print shirt, wicker hat, Bermuda shorts, and flip-flops. The same bright smile flashed below a pair of dark glasses and sun-screened nose. "Yes, Madam President?"

by Richard Lau

Marilyn was not happy. "At least you know whom you are addressing." Then she asked sharply, "Do you have any idea what day it is?"

"Uh, Friday?"

"Yes, Friday. Three days after my swearing in as President of the United States."

"Congratulations."

"Not really. On the first day of my presidency, no less than seven drilling platforms and twenty-three tankers leaked a vast amount of oil into the ocean. Since that time, a contagious virus has swept across several countries, including the U.S. Companies and investors have panicked. Wall Street crashed. People are unemployed. Congress is blocking all of my emergency proposals while refusing to do anything. I can't even rely on members of my own party for support! On the second day of my presidency, World War Three broke out."

"The situation sounds dire." The man was still smiling but sadly. "In my considerable lifetime throughout the centuries, I've noted such events are all too common in this world."

"Yes, maybe things would be better on another world. But we have no chance of getting there. Today, Congress canceled all funding for NASA and other space projects. And as I mentioned, private industry is in turmoil. We're no longer even close to a viable space program, not to mention true justice, perpetual happiness, and global education for the world's citizens."

"Thanks for bringing me up to date. I'll have to check for pollution, war, and disease at my destination before going there. With the budget cancellations, good thing I'm flying by carpet, not space shuttle." The genie pulled out a brochure about the beaches of Tahiti. "I guess I'll be off now."

"No, you won't," Marilyn countered. The toe of her shoe edged closer to the concealed alarm button underneath the carpeted presidential seal, but she wasn't sure what the Secret Service could do against a magical being. "Not before explaining something and fixing what hopefully are just temporary delays and setbacks."

"Delays and setbacks?"

The President growled uncharacteristically. How could someone as old as the genie be so obtuse? "What happened to my wishes?"

"Oh, those." The genie was nonchalant. It was as if he had already turned to vapor and was fading. "I guess they didn't come true."

"Is that all you have to say?"

"Is there more?"

The most powerful person in the world leaned across her desk, feeling incredibly frustrated and powerless. "You said my wishes would come true! They haven't! I haven't been able to keep any of my campaign promises!"

"So. what's the big deal? I never keep my promises, either!"

Marilyn was shocked. "You don't?"

"Of course, not! Remember the first day we met? I told you what I was...an Election-Year Genie!"

THE MASQUE OF THE 19
by E. E. King

19 had devastated the country. No plague had ever been so enormous, or so unexpected. It crept stealthily through the night. There was nausea, and sudden fever, food lost its flavor, the scents of the world vanished, and the body was wrenched with a violent, empty cough. If seen, the scarlet rash on the toes of the victim, might shut her away from the world for days, or weeks, or for forever, depending upon the whimsy of fate.

But the Leader was pugnacious and undaunted and ignorant. When the unchecked infection rate of his people far exceeded other regions, when hundreds of thousands died, he signed a bill to cut health care and called to his chambers one hundred rich, fat, white minions from among his government, and with these he withdrew to the subterranean refuge of one of his shelters.

This was a large and extravagant construction, the conception of the Leader's own gaudy and overdone taste. A large and lofty wall surrounded it. The Leaded loved walls with a passion he rarely had for his wives after the first week or so. The seven-day itch, he called it.

This wall had doors of titanium locked with the latest, and most advanced super-duper high-security bolt.

by E. E. King

The administrators took small slips of paper from their briefcases, not unlike to the size and shape of a fortune cookie. Each had a cypher printed on it. They punched in the lock's code. It took ten of then inputting data at the same time to secure it. Then they ate the paper. It was good. They needed roughage. Besides, they had determined to leave method neither of entrance or egress to the impulsive urges of depression or of fever.

The shelter was plentifully provisioned. With such protections the administrators could afford to be impertinent and forget infection. The outside domain could take care of itself. In the interim, it was irrational to grieve, or to look inward.

The Leader had afforded all the equipment of indulgence. There was an indoor putting green, there were fast-food trucks, there were topless dancers, there musician, or one at least one. Well, actually only Kid Rock. There was Beauty, there was wine, there were underaged girls, and a few endangered species caged for the sons of The Leader to slaughter. All these and sanctuary were underground. Without was the 19.

It was near the end of the sixth or seventh month of his isolation, and while the epidemic erupted most heatedly at home and slowed abroad, that the Leader entertained his hundred minions at a masked ball of the most uncommon splendor.

"I, who have always refused to wear a mask, will now have a masked ball," he chortled.

It was a spectacular scene, that underground masquerade. Let me tell of the chambers in which it was held.

In most shelters, such suites are long and straight, so that the view of the entire shelter is barely obstructed. Here the situation was very different, as might have been predictable from the Leader's love of backstage dressing rooms.

There was a sharp turn every thirty yards or so, and in the center of each corridor was lit by a tall and narrow Gothic window. The corridor and the walls both inside and out was of gold-covered - lead leaf, but the windows were of stained glass.

The westernmost room had vibrant blue windows. The second room had purple. The third, green. The fourth, yellow. The fifth, white. And the sixth, violet.

The seventh was the only place not gold, but rather meticulously veiled in black velvet. And the glass in that room was the color of blood.

The seven rooms were without lamp, lantern, or candle. But in the passageways, there stood across from each window, a metal easel, whose flat top held a tiny fire, that cast its rays through the tinted glass and so illumined the rooms.

This made each face and every shadow seem a flickering grotesque manifestation. But in seventh, the black velvet room, the effect of the fire through the blood-tinted glass, was gruesome, and created so grisly an aspect, few were bold enough to set foot within its confines.

It was in this room, also, that there stood an enormous ebony clock. Its pendulum swayed to and fro with a leaden, heavy, repetitious knell; and when the hour was struck, there came from the deep chest of the clock, a tone which though rich, clear and exceptionally harmonious, lingered so strangely, that every hour, the musicians, that is, Kid Rock, was forced to stop his performance and listen. And also, the topless dancers ceased their gyrations; and while the bells of the clock hung in the air, the silliest grew still, and the aged breathed slowly and deeply as if in profound meditation. As soon as the echoes died, before one could even notice the silence, bright laugh permeated the gathering; all grinned at their uneasiness and swore that the next striking of the clock would create no such reaction.

But, despite this, it was a golden celebration. Though The Leader had never lifted a hand, except to test the smoothness of the putting green, or to grab a pussy, his own garish taste had specified the atmosphere. He had no eye for color and effect. He ignored the harmony of simplicity, for the stuffed carcasses of wild beasts and golden ornaments. There was much glare and glitter. There were half-naked women with unnaturally large breasts. There were girls just teetering off the brink of childhood. This party would give them a push. There was much of the beautiful, much of the wanton, and not a little of the repugnant.

There were some who thought The Leader senile, or demented. But his followers believed in him blindly, and deafly and without reason, for such is the way of things.

His people had paid for all the trappings of the seven rooms, the babes and the beasts, the girls and the glitter. Only Kid Rock had volunteered.

***

The ebony clock which stands in the hall of black velvet, strikes. For a second, the partiers are motionless and still. But as sound fades into the perfumed air, muted laughter chases the last resonance away. The music swells. Kid Rock is getting a workout. The partiers dance more gleefully than ever, shaded by the shifting firelight flowing through the stained windows. Still, no one ventures into the black velvet room with the blood-colored panes; for they have abandon science and are deeply superstitious.

***

The party whirled on until midnight. When again, all are stilled by the ebony clock. Before the last peal had sunk into silence, many became aware of a masked figure, no one had noticed.

Now the license of this night and its celebrants was nearly unlimited. No costume was too garish. No make-up too black. All the assembled had reached deeply into the pockets of the people for their splendor, with never a thought for anyone but themselves. In a congress of such masked, and exalted celebrants, no ordinary appearance would have provoked such a fuss.

But the figure in question had gone beyond the bounds of even this parties' inappropriate sense of the appropriate. There are harmonies even in the souls of the most inattentive.

Upon seeing the stranger there rose from the whole company a murmur of surprise, and disapproval and revulsion.

For the figure was swathed from head to foot in a shroud. The mask which concealed the face was painted like a skeleton, with bones so detailed even the closest scrutiny must have had difficulty in recognizing the façade.

Even this might have been tolerated by the heartless assembly. But the masked woman, for the figure was small and slight, had gone so far as to assume the look of those felled by 19. Her shirt was splattered with blood. And her bare toes had been decorated with a red rash, so excellent in detail it made every guest rub their toes uncomfortably against the sides of their velvet slippers.

When the eyes of Leader fell upon this unearthly image (which with a measured and grave step, as if more fully to maintain its character, stalked to and fro among the dancers, pausing only to cough) his orange forehead reddened.

"Who dares?" he demanded nasally of the administrators who stood nearest — "who dares mock me with this offensive sarcasm? Seize her, and don't be gentle. Unmask her — that I see who I am locking up!"

The leader was in the blue room as he spoke these words. But they sounded through the seven chambers loudly and clearly — for the Leader had a microphone that he carried always with him, and the music quieted at the sound of his baying.

"Lock her up!" the partiers echoed enthusiastically, lurching toward the intruder. Several pulled out guns, even though the shelter was crowded with security.

The security stood against the walls by folds in the drapery. They avoided the sparkling stained light pouring through each window. Such large men, it was amazing how unobtrusive they were, appearing like dark statues against a gold wall. Like pillars of men.

But though guns had been drawn, no one fired, they remained motionless, frozen ice sculptures trapped in the moment of drawing a gun. They were so still, because their Leader was approaching the stranger. It was so unlike him, to approach or even to be aware of danger.

No one had tried to detain her. Unimpeded, she passed within a yard of the Leader's person; and, while the vast assembly, as if with one impulse, shrank from the centers of the rooms to the walls, she made her way through the blue chamber to the purple — through the purple to the green — through the green to the orange — through orange to the white — and to the violet, ere a decided movement had been made to arrest her.

Then the leader, madded with rage lumbered after her as quickly as his corpulent, ancient body could shuffle. None followed him, a deadly terror detained them all.

He approached, to within three or four feet of the retreating figure, when the latter, having reached the end of the velvet apartment, turned suddenly and confronted her pursuer. There was a sharp cry, the Leader toppled to the floor in death.

Then, summoning the wild courage of despair, the crowd threw themselves into the black apartment, and, seizing the masked visitor whose small, erect figure stood motionless within the shade of the ebony clock, gasped in terror and revulsion at finding the shroud and corpse-like mask empty of any tangible being.

"Darkness and Decay and the 19-hold illimitable dominion over all," cried a voice.

Then the emptiness behind the mask spoke.

"Actually, I'm not the 19, I'm much, much older. We still get mistaken for sisters, though," the emptiness gave a hollow laugh.

"My roots stretch back to the first humans' who crossed the Bering land bridge 13,000 years ago destroying giant ground sloths, woolly mammoths, saber-toothed cats, and all the glorious megafauna that once roamed this planet.

"Even your idea of paradise, your Garden of Eden was born from the destruction of the Middle East's lush woodland. I can still hear the rustling of trees and the calling of huge river birds over the marshes at twilight.

"The Epic of Gilgamesh, which you proudly claim as your earliest surviving great work of literature tells of the vast cedar wildernesses that carpeted southern Iraq.

The emptiness sighed. "I can still smell the fresh sweetness of their shade. But by 2100 BCE the Sumerians had turned forest into desert.

"According to The Epic, Gilgamesh defied the gods by cutting down the trees. In return the gods cursed the land with fire and drought, so perhaps it was a prediction. Humans are not very difficult to predict. Always the same story. And lately you have been speeding up the process."

It was Environmental Devastation; she had come like a thief in the night when another had been expected. And one by one all the president's men dropped in the blood and jeweled halls of their shelter and died each in the miserable pose of his collapse. The ebony clock rang once and was silent. And the fires on the easels expired. And Darkness and Decay and Environmental Devastation held illimitable dominion overall.

HOSTAGE AT THE HILTON
by Teresa Milbrodt

Our economic plan was simple: meet the delegation at the airport, offer them kind smiles, and promise pastries and coffee as soon as we arrived at the hotel. Upon reaching the hotel and grand ballroom, provide aforementioned pastries and coffee, and explain to delegation that they had been taken hostage. Send ransom notes, and let captives know where they could find a bathroom.

We knew negotiations and bank transfers might take a while, which is why we'd chosen to hold them captive at the Hilton, while making it clear that they had to pay their own expenses. In cash. They bellyached but had adequate resources on hand, and they knew things could be worse. We could have taken them to some smelly half-star motel with water stains on the ceiling, forty-year-old carpet, and a vibrating bed that required quarters. They weren't going to argue with a four-star restaurant and spa on the premises, so why would they want to leave? Of course there was a larger city beyond the hotel, but in places it was rather dirty and disgusting, while the Hilton had very polite waiters, a housekeeping staff, and masseuses who thought our guests' accents were quite charming.

We weren't crude, just hard up for cash to fund our social programs and debts to other countries. Everyone knew that—their president and ours—and it wasn't our current president's fault that our previous president had used the country as his personal bank account, rendering this hostage-taking an economic necessity. We realized negotiations could last a few years, depending on how badly the families of said delegates wanted them back, but we could tell our creditors that their money was coming as soon as we finalized negotiations. The creditors grumbled a few times between sips of their triple mochas, but we could now boast of a financial recovery plan that was far more secure than most of the fiscally-ravaged countries in our region.

We were not surprised when the president's family was first to pay our requested fee for his safe return, and we had a very nice wine and cheese reception before he left. Three more hostages from the party of twenty departed shortly afterward, but we were rather surprised when the president returned two weeks later in a private jet and asked to exchange himself for three more hostages who had lower return fees. While confused we were quick to agree, since we are not unreasonable people. At that point we were also curious as all hell.

At the press conference prior to the wine and cheese reception to welcome the president back to captivity at the Hilton, he explained that this was the right and patriotic thing to do for his country, that other members of the diplomatic party needed to be released to their families, and this and that and the other thing.

Because we work for the government we are quite astute at reading between the lines and noting facial expressions, so we were keen on the wrinkles in his forehead and the tension in his jaw. He didn't have to tell us that he was escaping. The problems at home had become too overwhelming—we read all their tabloids—and amid various fiscal and sexual scandals among higher-ups in his administration, the president found it easier to abdicate his country and call himself socially-minded.

He didn't exactly ask for political asylum, but inquired if the Hilton had a monthly rate. Clearly he wanted to pay his bill, not a ransom. We were rather disgusted, because we had never intended to be used as a scapegoat. As an elected official it was his duty to return to his country and sort out these difficulties. We did not appreciate the image he was trying to project, a noble ruler who found himself in chains, while he was sitting on a queen-sized bed, flipping through cable channels, and expecting his vice president to take care of the messiness.

When we cut off his room service and stopped restocking the mini-bar, he realized we were serious. He yelled at a few members of the housekeeping staff about the lack of sparkling water and tiny bottles of Jim Beam, but they only looked at him quizzically and chattered to each other that his accent was adorable. After cussing out the front desk several times over the phone and only receiving another set of clean towels in return, he asked for a private meeting in one of the conference rooms.

"You know how it is," he said as we sat across from him with our arms crossed. "When you're elected to office you have all kinds of goals and dreams, and you imagine how easy it will be to accomplish your agenda once your policies are in place, but then you find it's much more difficult than you ever dreamed. No one can even agree on what kind of sandwiches to order for lunch. All you really win are a few paltry victories and gray hairs." He gave us a smile, pleading for sympathy.

by Teresa Milbrodt

We talked in low voices after he'd been escorted back to his room. Of course we were sympathetic as we knew the task of governing was not easy, but we needed the money. The solution we devised was quite simple. Have him pay us a ransom to stay.

"My hotel bill isn't enough?" he said. His face turned from pink to deep fuchsia to red to an interesting shade of violet before we gave him a response. We calmly explained that the bill covered his expenses to stay at the Hilton, not the monthly cost of maintaining his visa to stay in our country as a foreign dignitary. We don't know who was at fault for the lack of communication between him and other members of his government, because they unceremoniously decided to shoot a few missiles at us the following day, which we did not appreciate. We stood in his hotel room, arms crossed, while he placed a call to let them know he was just fine, negotiations were continuing apace, and to please knock off the bombing.

It took four more days to declare a formal cease-fire, but he knew the consequences of failing to find an accord—we were already threatening to send him back to his home country, ransom or not, an idea that he did not relish. But we weren't exactly sure what to do with him, cooped up as he was in the Hilton all day, until several television executives approached us with a novel plan. They needed a host for a kids' television game show—the last host had been dismissed in a scandal which they did not want to discuss— and perhaps our foreign dignitary would be able to fill the post since he already had a wardrobe of expensive suits. We thought it was a fine idea since the TV executives were willing to pay us for the loan of our hostage, and he did a reasonable job of reading the quiz questions as long as they were printed in capital letters on the little cards.

HOSTAGE AT THE HILTON

We still had to deal with his outbursts, such as the tantrum he threw when the vending machine ran out of peanut butter cups, leading him to rip all the leaves off a plastic potted plant in the hallway (which we billed him for later). Even more fabulous was his screaming fit when members of his own party proposed holding new elections, since the country had stopped negotiating for his release (though his estate was still paying the monthly foreign visa fee). Apparently some in the government had intuited that he wanted to be removed from his post, which was true, yet he was also riled that his countrymen no longer wanted him in charge.

"After all I've done for them," he screeched while watching the evening news in his bedroom and shredding three pillowcases with the help of a complimentary pen. We were terribly glad that we had the forethought to install video cameras in his room, since all of his performances were broadcast on the evening news. The public was delighted. We assumed his theatrics were a fairly normal reaction to a political ouster, though we took pains not to bring up that he'd ousted himself, or that his countrymen were likely deriving much enjoyment from his nightly performances on the kids' quiz show. But the television executives were tickled by his ratings, which allowed us to charge a higher rental fee, and he was pacified when we resumed stocking his mini-bar and snacks. We cordially patted ourselves on the back, and started budgeting for the next fiscal quarter.

THE WENDIGO
by Andrea Goyan

When the Wendigo announced his candidacy for president, I thought it was a joke.

"No one's going to vote for him," I said. "He's the Wendigo."

I fixated on a screenshot of him from his *Elect The Wendigo* website. Except for a pair of dark sunglasses which masked his very human, although abnormally bloodshot eyes, he'd done nothing to hide his frightening visage. His skin pulled taut against a Cervidae shaped head, and an unkempt brown mane stuck out from his jacket collar. Long bony fingers with tiger length claws protruded from his sleeves. He was a monster in a three-piece suit.

Ten years earlier, he'd hired me to be the ghostwriter for his memoir. I'd spent eighteen months in his orbit, and he'd opened his inner sanctum to me. As a result, I knew more about him than his first three wives combined. I'd watched him at work, seen his voracious appetite and inexhaustible need to dominate everyone and everything around him. I'd met the abyss, and it was the Wendigo. No amount of power or material wealth could fill his void.

I would have quit after the first week if I hadn't already spent the advance. Instead, I soldiered on despite breaking out in daily hives (I may have been allergic to his fur). I struggled to maintain my sanity as his mercurial moods kept me on edge. His rages were legendary, as was his undeniable, curious allure with gorgeous women. Rumors around the Wendigo's sexual prowess and, of course, his extreme wealth meant that he always had some beautiful dame or two dangling from his arms—and don't even get me started about what dangling meant; you've seen his nails. When the women aged out at 30 or the Wendigo became bored, they disappeared. His publicity firm insisted they'd been paid off with NDAs, but I'd seen enough of the creature to believe that many of those women met violent ends. Unfortunately, without bodies or evidence, no one paid attention to my gut feelings.

So, the day he stood before the press to say he wanted to be our next president, I laughed out loud.

I turned to my husband and said, "Wendigos don't change for the better."

My husband Peter shushed me to watch the announcement, and then he said, "Liam, the Wendigo has charisma and a certain *je ne sais quois*. I wouldn't rule him out."

"He'll never win."

But something about the creature captured people's imagination, and he gathered momentum.

During the debates, he stood a head taller than the other ten candidates. His massive shaggy visage stood in contrast to the rest of the clean-cut contenders. He'd painted his antlers red, white, and blue, and soon, the campaign began distributing headbands to match. Of course, not to be outdone, the Wendigo insisted the fake racks have only 8-points whereas the one growing from his skull boasted a spectacular 47-points.

THE WENDIGO

At his rallies, he started calling his followers his *Little Deer* and ran his campaign on a few key points:

"Prime steaks for all."

"Vegetarians are anarchists."

"Public land is good grazing land."

His *Little Deer* ate it up. The Wendigo's cattle operations soared. Cardiac arrests increased, and his followers gained an average of twenty pounds each. They weren't such Little Deer anymore.

I pointed at the screen, calling Peter over from where he was grilling steaks on our patio. "He's on. Hurry. You'll see. No teeth."

The Wendigo strode onto stage and waved to the cheering crowd.

I'd noticed that during all his public appearances, the Wendigo never showed his teeth when he smiled, and I knew exactly why; I'd seen what he kept hidden behind his furry lips. He may have hypnotized parts of the nation into believing he was something akin to a deer, but he wasn't. His teeth belonged to a predator. As did his long, sharp nails. During my early days shadowing him, he'd taken me into his self-care room.

"This is a very special place, Liam," he said, opening the door. "It's where I am my true self. Few men have seen it and lived to tell anyone."

I must have blanched because he slapped me on the back, nearly knocking me over.

"Kidding," he said. "One thing you'll learn about me, I'm a kidder. I have the best sense of humor you'll ever come across."

I nodded and said something like, "Of course, sir."

by Andrea Goyan

But I don't remember for certain because I was gobsmacked at the room itself. It had to be 1000 square feet. It was cave-dark, the only light coming from televisions mounted throughout. Three different shows screamed from the screens: investment, BBQ cooking, and porn. He'd focus on one show for about ten seconds before moving to the next.

"I do my best thinking here," he said.

After ten minutes, he seemed to lose interest. That was when he sidled up to a wall on the other side of the room. I followed. It was covered in dark wood that looked severely damaged. Long deep gouges ran vertically to the floor. As I drew near, I stepped on bits of shredded wood.

The Wendigo sniffed the wall, then reached up to sharpen his nails. It was like watching a gigantic cat scratching a post. I still remember the sound like wood screaming. When he urinated on the wall, I almost lost my breakfast.

He turned to me and laughed.

"But this…" he flipped a switch, and the room was flooded with light. "This is why I brought you here."

The entire room was an industrial-sized kitchen. Commercial prep and worktables lined the walls. Stainless steel hooks hung from the ceiling over two of the largest sinks I'd ever seen. A hose dangled from a metal butler on the wall, and taking a quick glance at the floor, I saw it sloped down to the center of the room where there was a big drain. Someone could wash away a whole lot of evidence. But it was also what was missing from the room that told me something was wrong.

"You don't have an oven or refrigerator," I said.

THE WENDIGO

"You know what I am, Liam. I've been transparent with you."

He reached up and caressed one of the hooks. "This is where I feast. Of course, I've never eaten anyone who didn't want me to."

He looked right into my eyes, which he rarely did, and licked his lips.

I cleared my throat. "Well, I certainly don't want you to consume me."

He laughed and thumped me on the back again. This time one of his nails raked my arm and drew blood.

"Consume. Big words. That's why I need you to write the book. You're safe. You're safe."

He sniffed the air, and I knew he'd smelled my blood. He leaned in until his head, which was the size of a grizzly bear's, stopped inches from my face. Then he opened his mouth; I smelled his foul breath, and his razor-sharp teeth were close enough I could've counted them. His tongue slowly emerged, it had to be over a foot long, and the tip delicately lapped away my blood.

I shivered.

"There now," he said. "When we get upstairs, my assistant will bandage it for you."

***

The crowd roared as the Wendigo tossed some fake horns out to them, and the moderators struggled to get him to take his position on stage.

Peter hurried in from our patio, still holding the BBQ tongs, and gazed at the television.

"There he is. Look at him strut." Peter snapped the fingers of his free hand. "Bring it. He's the Man."

"Wendigo."

He shook the tongs at me and sang, "You say potato, I say *potahto.*"

The Wendigo stalked across the stage to his podium. His closed lips were turned up in what I'd call more of a sneer than a smile.

I pointed at the television. "What did I tell you?"

Peter flashed me the identical smirk. "It's just how some people smile, Liam. You read too much into everything." He patted my thigh. "Make room."

"You still have..." I pointed to the tongs.

"I gotta flip the steaks soon."

I slid over on the couch, and he sat beside me to watch the dog and pony debate.

When asked about peace in the Middle East, the Wendigo said, "I believe that all red-blooded Americans deserve quality meat."

I looked at Peter in disbelief and noticed his eyes dilate. "He's such a patriot. He cares about all of us. And speaking of caring, I have to tend to dinner."

The Wendigo paced the stage like a caged animal. The debate officials gave up trying to control him; their ratings had never been so high. Over steak dinners, Peter and I watched all eight of the primary debates. The Wendigo destroyed his opponents one-by-one, leaving each man quivering at their podiums. They dropped out in record time, until only one opponent was left; the Governor of Texas.

It was the final debate. After a contentious back-and-forth between the Wendigo and the Governor, the

THE WENDIGO

Wendigo lunged and bit the Governor in half. Then he devoured him.

His fans in the audience cheered.

I leaped to my feet. "Oh, my God! He just—"

Peter wagged a finger at me. "He doesn't know his own strength."

All the *not so Little Deer* interviewed on the street gave pat responses like:

"It was an accident."

"He didn't mean to hurt him."

"It's a joke."

They seemed to forget that the Wendigo hadn't simply killed the Governor, he'd eaten him on live television for the world to see. That clip was viewed more than any other in history.

I wasn't crowing about the Governor's death, but I was relieved because I thought the Wendigo had finally overstepped. Governing officials or the justice department would step in and put the Wendigo away.

And then, they didn't; the Wendigo became the party's nominee. The country was a train wreck, and all I could do was watch it burn. The people saw what he was, what he was capable of, and rather than disgust them, it thrilled them even more.

I'd seen the abyss, and we'd all joined the Wendigo inside of it.

But I held on to the hope that the other party would win the White House in November. Or, that even if the Wendigo won, my own life wouldn't really change.

I never understood how the Wendigo turned Peter. I knew Peter loved the drama and showmanship that followed in the Wendigo's wake, but I never expected him to become an actual believer. The day Peter came home with an 8-point rack on his head, I moved out.

"It's my patriotic duty," he said.

I put the last of my things into my car and slammed the trunk shut. I turned and gave him a sad, closed-lip smile. "And leaving is mine."

In the solitude of my morning showers, I'd touch the ring of white skin once encircled by my wedding band. I recalled Peter's dark eyes, and I'd think about the way he'd rest a hand on my stomach every morning when he woke. His touch was gentle yet masculine at the same time. His laugh could lift me out of the darkest moments.

I wished for that laugh, wished for it every day. It never returned.

***

After the Wendigo won the election, I wrote an Op-Ed entitled, "The Cannibal in the White House." I included a definition of Wendigo: *A cannibalistic giant. A human turned into a monster after the consumption of human flesh. Other hallmarks include insatiable greed and environmental destruction.*

People who didn't like him were angry at me. "Where were you before the election?" they asked. "You're too late." People who loved him hated me. The Wendigo's Press Secretary said, "Is it really cannibalism if you're not one-hundred-percent human?" And the Wendigo stood by his long-time lie. "I never eat anyone who doesn't want to be eaten."

Near the end of his first term, he converted the acres of federal land he'd stolen for his cattle into detention centers.

THE WENDIGO

He said it would help manage the country's immigration problem, but really, it was a dumping ground for dissenters.

I dug out the letter I'd received after the publication of my opinion piece. The presidential seal was at the top of the paper. The note simply said, "You betrayed me." The Wendigo had signed it with a large felt pen, his signature a scribble that resembled an EKG.

I went into hiding.

My sister was married to a Canuck, so I slipped into Canada days before the Wendigo closed all the borders.

When folks in town discovered I was American, they'd stop me on the street.

"What were you all thinking? I mean, he's the Wendigo," they'd say.

Closing my eyes, I'd first nod and then shake my head, because it was too painful to answer. The person who'd questioned me would wait a minute or two for a verbal response before finally walking away. Sometimes, they'd mumble that I was *another crazy American*. Maybe they were right because I'd stand there, with my eyes shut and say a silent prayer for my country. I'd remain still for as long as it took to quell the tears that always came as I remembered my life before the Wendigo.

COPYRIGHT AND AUTHOR INFORMATION

"A Feast Tale" by Cathy Adams. Copyright © 2020 by Cathy Adams.

Cathy Adams' latest novel, *A Body's Just as Dead*, was published by SFK Press. Her writing has been nominated twice for a Pushcart Prize. She is a short story writer with publications in The *Saturday Evening Post, Utne, AE: The Canadian Science Fiction Review, Barely South, Five on the Fifth, Southern Pacific Review*, and 46 other journals from around the world. She earned her M.F.A. at Rainier Writing Workshop, Pacific Lutheran University, Washington. Due to Covid-19, she is residing temporarily in Kansas, but her home is in Liaoning, China, with her husband, photographer, Julian Jackson.

https://www.facebook.com/caawriter/?modal=admin_todo_tour
https://cathyadamsauthor.com/

***

"Six Views of the Wall" by Daniel Ausema. Copyright © 2020 by Daniel Ausema.

Daniel Ausema's fiction and poetry have appeared in many publications, including *Strange Horizons, Daily Science Fiction*, and *Diabolical Plots*. His novel *The Silk Betrayal* is published by Guardbridge Books, and he is the creator of the steampunk-fantasy Spire City series. He lives with his wife and children, masked and isolated, in Colorado at the foot of the Rockies and can be found online at https://danielausema.com.

***

"Rogue Scholars" by Eric Avedissian. Copyright © 2020 by Eric Avedissian.

Eric Avedissian is an author and award-winning journalist whose work includes the YA novella *Gargoyles & Absinthe*, published by Aurelia Leo, and the science fiction/pulp role-playing game *Ravaged Earth*. His short fiction appears in *Outposts of Beyond, Aphotic Realm*, and the alternative Beatles-themed anthology *Across the Universe*. He is a member of the Science Fiction and Fantasy Writers of America (SFWA) and has an M.A. in Writing from Rowan University. He lives in New Jersey where his hobbies include reading, hiking the pinelands, and battling writer's block. You can follow him on Twitter @angryreporter.

***

"Heredity" by Paul L. Bates. Copyright © 2020 by Paul L. Bates.

Paul L. Bates is retired from a career in construction management. He lives with his two lady loves (one of whom is a cat) on the shore of a small lake in western Massachusetts, writes when the muse comes to call. Writing credits include the novels *IMPRINT* and *DREAMER*, short fictions in periodicals and anthologies including: *Vastarien: A Literary Journal*, issues 1.1 & 2.2, *Dim Shores Presents*, vol. 1, *For When the Veil Drops, Arcane*, and *Darker Than Noir*.

***

"Florence" by Jane Blanchard. Copyright © 2020 by Jane Blanchard.

Jane Blanchard lives and writes in Georgia (USA). Her poetry has been published around the world as well as posted online. Her fourth collection with Kelsay Books is *In or Out of Season* (2020).

***

"A History Lesson" by Ben Boegehold. Copyright © 2020 by Ben Boegehold.

Ben Boegehold is a writer, MFA student, and teacher living in Portland, Maine. His work has appeared in the online literary journal, *Rue Scribe*, and will also be appearing in the forthcoming anthology, *Paul Bunyan Wears a Facemask*. When he isn't discussing books with his students or writing poems, he can be found walking his dog, weeding his garden, or exploring Casco Bay in a kayak. http://www.benboegehold.com/

***

"Idea Dolly Boss" by Warren Brown. Copyright © 2020 by Warren Brown.

Warren lives and writes poetry and fiction in Tulsa, Oklahoma. He has published poetry and science fiction stories in various periodicals, and has a poem upcoming in *Speculative North*. His novel, *What Happened in Fool the Eye,* is available on Amazon, Barnes and Noble, and Smashwords sites. His web page is http://warrenbrown.synthasite.com/.

***

"Dear Mr. President" by Jim Courter. Copyright © 2020 by Jim Courter.

Jim Courter's short stories have appeared in the United States, Canada, and England. He is a Pushcart Prize nominee and has won an Illinois Arts Council award for short fiction. His essays have appeared in *The Chronicle of Higher Education, Smithsonian*, and on the op-ed pages of the *Chicago Tribune* and *The Wall Street Journal*. His mystery novel, *Rhymes with Fool,* was published in 2018 by Peasantry Press. Its sequel is forthcoming. *First Things First: Ephemera and Offscourings of a Distracted Writer*, a collection of essays, humor, and short stories, was published in 2019. He can be reached through his web site: Jimcourter.com.

***

"Freedom over Good" by Devo Cutler. Copyright © 2020 by Devorah Cutler-Rubenstein.

Devo Cutler graduated USC in 2015 with a Masters in Professional Writing after a long stint as a writer-director-producer-studio exec as President of Noble House Entertainment. Aside from Executive Producing a movie franchise, she is a lover of words and won her first contest at 13 for a psychological horror short story, THE MONARCH BUTTERFLY. Since then, her fascination with the duality of oppression and freedom has led her to write poetry and short stories; she co-wrote the award-winning short film, *Not Afraid to Laugh*, about using humor to heal, now archived in the museum of broadcasting for social significance and cultural excellence. She has been teaching producing and writing at USC and UCLA Extension for many years, and as a consultant she helps inspire writers through her new company "*YOUR WRITE COACH*," a division of The Script Broker ®. Now residing in Newport Beach, CA she writes near wildlife and strolls the sand for shells and inspiration. Her book *DATING YOUR CHARACTER* ... a sexy guide to writing for film and TV was published by Stairway Press, and she is a contributor to several anthologies, including *NOW WRITE!* Science Fiction, Fantasy & Horror (Tarcher/Penguin).

***

"The Scourge" by Derek Des Anges. Copyright © 2020 by Derek Des Anges.

Derek Des Anges has been writing for over twenty years and has yet to be stopped; his most recent novel is called *A Tourist's Guide To The Ideal London.*

***

"Minutes" by Buzz Dixon. Copyright © 2020 by Buzz Dixon.

Buzz Dixon writes oddball TV / movies / games / comics / novels, putting words in the mouths of Superman, Batman, Conan, The Terminator, Optimus Prime, The Teenage Mutant Ninja Turtles, Mork & Mindy, Scrooge McDuck, Bugs Bunny, Yosemite Sam, plus more G.I. Joes and My Little Ponies than you can shake a stick at. His short fiction appears in Mike Shayne's Mystery Magazine, the Pan Book Of Horror Stories, National Lampoon, Analog, and numerous original and "best of" anthologies, and he regularly makes a pest of himself at www.BuzzDixon.com.

***

"The Dictator's Dream about Painting" by Katrina Dybzynska. Copyright © 2020 by Katrina Dybzynska.

Katrina Dybzynska is a nomadic writer with texts published in the US, Ireland, Australia, Germany, and Poland. She's been awarded second prize at the Red Line Book Festival Poetry Competition in Dublin. Her debut concept poetry book received Grand Prix at the 2017 Rozewicz Open Competition. Recently featured in anthologies: *"Beautifullest"*, *"POETRY in the TIME of CORONAVIRUS"* and The London Reader's issue on stories from the lockdown. Dybzynska lives in a campervan.

***

"Female God" by Mike Ekunno. Copyright © 2020 by Mike Ekunno.

Within the Lockdown, Mike has had works published in *Mysterion, The Blue Nib, Oddball Magazine* and *Written Tales* with pending anthology publications in *Essential Anthology of* Underground Writers Association of Portland, Maine, and *Omens Anthology* of Antimony and Elder Lace Press. He is a freelance book editor, ghost biographer and author of *Cowboy Lamido*, a children's book approved as school text across Nigeria. Mike venerates the late Mohammed Ali and is a massive fan of the defunct ABBA which doesn't make him New School by any means.

***

"Baba Yaga's Apprentice" by Louis Evans. Copyright © 2020 by Louis Evans.

Louis Evans is an NYC-based writer with work in Analog, Interzone, Escape Pod and more. He's a member of SFWA and of the Clarion West class of the plague year. Louis would never sign a deal with a magical entity without having an attorney review the contract. Or vice-versa. You're welcome.

***

"Superlative" by Robert Morgan Fisher. Copyright © 2020 by Robert Morgan Fisher.

Robert Morgan Fisher won the 2018 Chester Himes Fiction Prize and was shortlisted for the 2019 John Steinbeck Award. His fiction and essays have appeared in numerous anthologies and literary journals including *Upstreet, Pleiades, Cowboy Jamboree Magazine, Storyscape Journal, Teach. Write., The Wild Word, The Arkansas Review, Red Wheelbarrow, The Missouri Review Soundbooth Podcast, Dime Show Review, 0-Dark-Thirty, Psychopomp, The Seattle Review, The Spry Literary Journal, 34th Parallel, The Journal of Microliterature, Spindrift, The Rumpus, Bluerailroad* and many other publications. He's written for TV, radio and film. Robert holds an MFA in Creative Writing from Antioch University Los Angeles and is currently on the teaching faculty of Antioch University in several capacities. Since 2016, Robert has led the UCLA Wordcommandos, an acclaimed twice-weekly writing workshop for veterans with PTSD. He often writes companion songs to his short stories. Both his music and fiction have won many awards. Robert also voices audiobooks. (www.robertmorganfisher.com)

***

"The Wendigo" by Andrea Goyan. Copyright © 2020 by Andrea Goyan.

Andrea Goyan lives a pretty ~~boring~~ *normal* life. Through storytelling, she spices things up by exploring the crazy characters who lurk within her mind. She credits her years as an actress for teaching her how to find humanity in even the most despicable villains (except, the Wendigo), and she believes that a lot of fears are driven by simple misunder-standings. Her stories have appeared in *Luna Station Quarterly, The Dark Sire, 101 Words, Sirens Call Publications, On Loss: An Anthology, Dirty Girls Magazine, Newfound Journal, Halloween Party 2019*, and

What Sort of Fuckery is This? She's an accomplished playwright. Her monologue "*Goodbye*" appeared in the Lockdown Monologue Festival 2020 at www.suki.tv. Many of her plays have been produced in Los Angeles where she lives with her husband, a dog, and two cats. More at Facebook: Andrea Goyan Storyteller, andreagoyan.com, Instagram: @andreagoyan

***

"The Elves' Rebellion" by N.E. Griffin. Copyright © 2020 by N.E. Griffin.

N.E. Griffin lives in Arlington, VA and works for the federal government. She holds a B.S. in Biology and a B.S. in Finance from Arizona State University and an M.A. in International Affairs from George Washington University. She is a lifelong writer who dabbles in fiction, poetry, and occasionally creative non-fiction. Her work recently appeared in the *Constellate Literary Journal.* You can follow her on Instagram (@n_e_griffin), where she mostly shares pictures of her travels and her dog and cat, or Twitter (same) where she tries to avoid commenting too much on politics.

***

"Team Building and Other Horrors" by Jill Hand. Copyright © 2020 by Jill Hand.

Jill Hand is a former newspaper reporter and a member of International Thriller Writers. Her novel, *White Oaks*, about a family battling each other while trying to prevent the end of the world, is available from Black Rose Writing. A sequel, *Black Willows*, will be released on Oct. 22, 2020.

***

"Dear Joyce" by Langley Hyde. Copyright © 2020 by Langley Hyde.

Langley Hyde's has upcoming fiction in *Hybrid Fiction and Escape Pod*. Her short stories have appeared in *If This Goes On, Unidentified Funny Objects (vol. 6 &7), Podcastle, Terraform*, and her debut novel, *Highfell Grimoires*, was named a *Best Book of 2014 in SF/Fantasy/Horror* by Publishers Weekly. Currently, Langley Hyde lives in the Pacific Northwest along with her partners and her two children. You can visit her at http://langleyhyde.com/ or find her on Twitter @langleyhyde.

***

"Damage Control" by Will Isenberg. Copyright © 2020 by Will Isenberg.

Will Isenberg graduated from a fancy Ivy League school that taught him absolutely nothing about the real world. He performs stand-up comedy in Madison, Wisconsin, and writes short stories at https://icebergking.com. His work has appeared in *Literally Stories* and in *House of Zolo Journal*. In his spare time, he works a riveting 9-5 desk job where he turns unorganized data into slightly less unorganized data. He can be followed on Twitter at @isentrigger or reached at willisenberg2@gmail.com.

***

"CORVID-19: The Crows! The Crows!" by Andrew Jensen. Copyright © 2020 by Andrew Jensen.

Andrew Jensen lives in Braeside, Ontario with his family and too many dogs and cats. He is the minister at Knox United Church, Nepean. Almost twenty of his speculative short stories have appeared in magazines, anthologies and podcasts, including a cover story for *Dreamforge Magazine* and a special Christmas story for *Abyss & Apex*. Andrew is also the author of a book of Church humour called *God: The Greatest User of Capital Letters*, published by Wood Lake Books. When not writing or ministering or walking dogs, Andrew plays trumpet, impersonates Kermit the Frog, and performs in musical theatre. You should have seen him as Henry Higgins . . .

***

"Charisma" by Dan M. Kalin. Previously published in "Chasing Eleven" by Feral Cat Publishers April 2020, Copyright © 2020 by Dan M. Kalin.

Award-winning author, recovering engineer/Mensan, inventor, and occasionally-retired management consultant living large in Melbourne, FL under the seemingly constant direction of two herding canines, Annie and Stella. He can be contacted through https://dmkalin.com/. His award-winning novel "Martyrs al-Sabra" was published in 2019 and his next "Pandora's Children" will be released in the first quarter of 2021.

***

"Conrad's Moustache" by John H. Kalin. Copyright © 2020 by John H. Kalin.

John Kalin resides in Maryland, where he lives in constant fear that his dachshund's voracious appetite will one day consume us all. In the meantime, John distracts himself from the impending shin-high apocalypse by writing historical fiction, which allows him the freedom to work in humor while still managing to defame beloved historical figures… his two true passions.

***

"The Mug Lied" by Sarah M. Kalin. Copyright © 2020 by Sarah M. Kalin.

Sarah Kalin lives in Denver, Colorado with a rigorously-guarded, dragon-sized hoard of books. In addition to writing, she operates Dreamlined LLC – an editing business specializing in services for self-publishing authors. (www.dreamlined.com)

***

"A Friend of the Working Man" by J.J.J. Kearns. Copyright © 2020 by John Donald Kearns.

J.J.J. Kearns has written material for Jerry Lewis, Adam Corrolla, Ralph Garman, and Rodney Lee Conover. In the field of animation, he has penned scripts for Walt Disney, Warner Brothers, BBC America, and Mondo Media. Additionally, he wrote for two seasons on the series *"Pucca"* and *"Kid vs Kat."* His original radio show, *"Danger Cow"*, was syndicated nationally by the Premiere Radio Networks, and it is part of the Paley Center for Media's permanent collection. He has made numerous short videos, including *"The Ascent and Destruction of Doobie the Dog"*, which was nominated for a Student Emmy in 1990, *"The Expensive Guy"*, which was screened at the Mill Valley Film Festival in 1992, and *"Speed Racer Goes Crazy"*, which currently has over 930,000 views on YouTube. Mr. Kearns currently lives in Burbank, CA, and this is his first published short story.

***

"The Faithless Angel" by E. E. King. Copyright © 2020 by E. E. King.

"A Morality Tail " by E. E. King. Copyright © 2020 by E. E. King.

"The Masque of the 19", by E. E. King. Copyright © 2020 by E. E. King.

E.E. King is a painter, performer, writer, and biologist - She'll do anything that won't pay the bills, especially if it involves animals. She's worked with children in Bosnia, crocodiles in Mexico, frogs in Puerto Rico, egrets in Bali, mushrooms in Montana, archaeologists in Spain, butterflies in South Central Los Angeles, lectured on island evolution and marine biology on cruise ships in the South Pacific and the Caribbean, painted murals in Los Angeles and Spain and has been published widely. Check out paintings writing and musings at www.elizabetheveking.com.

Ray Bradbury calls her stories "marvelously inventive, wildly funny and deeply thought-provoking. I cannot recommend them highly enough."

Her books include *Dirk Quigby's Guide to the Afterlife, Electric Detective, Pandora's Card Game, The Truth of Fiction* and *Blood Prism*.

***

"Catmander-in-Chief" by Richard Lau. Copyright © 2020 by Richard Lau.

"The Election-Year Genie" by Richard Lau. Copyright © 2020 by Richard Lau.

Richard Lau is an award-winning writer who has been published in newspapers, magazines, anthologies, and the high-tech industry. He has had several of his plays produced and performed as readings. He does not maintain an online presence but may be reached at readers2rlau@gmail.com. He wishes to thank his "Dear Reader" Barbara for her support and guidance.

***

"Hindsight 2020: The Devolution and History of The New Breed" by Kate Maxwell. Copyright © 2020 by Kate Maxwell.

Kate Maxwell has been a school teacher for possibly too many years. She has been published in Australian and International literary magazines such as The Blue Nib, The Chopping Blog, Hecate, Linq, Verandah, Lightbox Originals, The New England Review, Tirra Lirra, Social Alternatives and Swyntax. Writing has always been her therapeutic and creative outlet. Kate's interests include film, wine and sleeping.

***

"Hostage at the Hilton" by Teresa Milbrodt. Copyright © 2020 by Teresa Milbrodt.

Teresa Milbrodt is the author of three short story collections: *Instances of Head-Switching*, *Bearded Women: Stories*, and *Work Opportunities*. She has also published a novel, *The Patron Saint of Unattractive People*, and a flash fiction collection, *Larissa Takes Flight: Stories*. Her fiction, creative nonfiction, and poetry have appeared in numerous literary magazines. Currently she teaches at Roanoke College in Salem, Virginia. She believes in coffee, long walks with her MP3 player, real-time conversation, and writing the occasional haiku. Read more of her work at: http://teresamilbrodt.com/homepage/

***

"The Greatest Show on Earth" by Lena Ng. Copyright © 2017, 2020 by Lena Ng (originally published in Gathering Storm Magazine, Vol 1, No.2, 2017).

Lena Ng skulks around Toronto, Ontario, and is a zombie member of the Horror Writers Association. She has short stories in four dozen publications including Amazing Stories, in venues from Australia, Canada, the United States, and the United Kingdom. *"Under an Autumn Moon"* is her short story collection. She is currently seeking a publisher for her novel, *Darkness Beckons*, a Gothic romance.

***

"A Great Goat" by Peter Ntephe. Copyright © 2020 by Peter Ntephe.

Peter Ntephe has several degrees, including from Oxford University and a PhD from the University of London. He has won international writing prizes for non-fiction, including the AMEX Bank Review Awards (Special Merit) and the Shell-Economist Writing Prize (Bronze). He lives in Houston from where he publishes the online literary magazine, *Akikiro* (www.akikiro.com). He is currently working on a collection of short stories with an African flavor but universal themes

***

"Revolt of the Tubas" by Mark Nutter. Copyright © 2020 by Mark Nutter.

MARK NUTTER grew up in a motel near Joliet, Illinois, which is not as glamorous as it sounds. He's the author of *Sunset Cruise on the River Styx: Dark, Absurd Tales*. Mark has also written for the stage (*ReAnimator: The Musical*), television (SNL, 3rd Rock from the Sun), and film (Almost Heroes). www.marknutter.com.

***

"An Office Party" by Nicole M. Pyles. Copyright © 2020 by Nicole M. Pyles.

Nicole M. Pyles is a writer living in Oregon. She currently works as a Blog Tour Manager for WOW! Women on Writing. Her writing has been featured in WOW! Women on Writing, Sky Island Journal, Ripley's Believe it or Not, and Restless Magazine. Say hi to her on Twitter @BeingTheWriter.

***

"An Honest Politician" by Jim Robb. Copyright © 2020 by Jim Robb.

By day, Jim Robb is a professional accountant working as the group controller of a multinational fashion jewelry company. He lives in southern Saskatchewan, Canada with his wife Donna and their canine and feline associates. This is the third outing for the Pink Chameleon, who first tried to take over Canada in the Canadian online science fiction magazine AE, and then Ireland in the children's anthology "*C is for Cabbage*". Jim's stories have also appeared in Sherlock Holmes Mystery Magazine and Space Force: Building the Legacy.

***

"The Z Word" by Jeff Seeman. Copyright © 2020 by Jeff Seeman (originally published in Red Planet Magazine, July 2020)

Jeff Seeman is the author of two novels, *Political Science* and *Guns and Butter*, and a tribute to Edgar Allan Poe, *The Scythe of Time: An Essay and Homage*. His stories have been featured in a variety of literary magazines as well as the anthologies What Monsters Do For Love, Horror USA: California, Tales For the Camp Fire, 18 Wheels of Science Fiction, 18 Wheels of Horror, and the Bram Stoker Award-nominated Hell Comes to Hollywood. His most recent story "*A Purple Heart*" appears in the collection Bloodlet: An Anthology of Violent Fiction (CultureCult Press). For more information, go to www.amazon.com/author/jeffseeman.

"The Curious Cat of Culpepper County" by Margaret S. E. Smith. Copyright © 2020 by Margaret S. E. Smith.

"A Night of Rapture" by Margaret S. E. Smith. Copyright © 2020 by Margaret S. E. Smith.

Maggie is a writer, artist, editor, and creative life coach who has spent over thirty years helping others find empowerment and healing through positive communication and the expressive arts. She has had several award-winning screenplays, short stories, and poetry in publication and production throughout the years, and her original artwork has been chosen twice for the University of Florida's Survivor's Exhibit. As a survivor of childhood trauma who eventually used the creative arts to manage her own Social Anxiety Disorder, Maggie considers her greatest accomplishment to be her work back in the late 90s developing and running an extracurricular program for at-risk teen girls that used music, creative writing, and drama to encourage self-exploration and positive emotional coping skills. She holds an MFA in Creative Writing and an undergraduate degree in Digital & Graphic Design, but her greatest education has come from her life surrounded by other amazing artists, creatives, and inspiring survivors.

SOCIAL MEDIA:

https://margaretsesmith.wixsite.com/digitalbard
https://msessmith.wixsite.com/mses
https://twitter.com/MargaretSESmith
https://www.greenappleent.com/project/blood-type/ (TV Series Pilot I wrote.)
https://fineartamerica.com/art/maggie+smith
https://www.stage32.com/margaretsesmith
https://www.imdb.com/name/nm6295659/

***

"Neighborhood Watch" by Lauren Stoker. Copyright © 2020 by Lauren Stoker.

LAUREN STOKER is a native Californian transplanted to New England for the thrill of skiing on ice and owning a snow blower. Lauren enjoys playing loud music, ranting about anti-environmentalists, and collecting beer coasters, while drinking a fine British ale. Since the tender age of 15, she has struggled with the written word (and sometimes won). Aside from some memorable Op-Eds, Lauren's had short stories published by The Hedgehog Poetry Press (U.K.), *The Arcanist (a contest winner), Page & Spine, 50-Word Stories, Quantum Shorts* and Thurston Howl Publications.

www.ingramcontent.com/pod-product-compliance
Lightning Source LLC
Chambersburg PA
CBHW020515080526
44583CB00013B/608